Racialized boundaries

This book is an attempt to develop an overall perspective for analysing the constructs of race and racism. It maintains that the concept of race has to be located within the wider category of 'ethnos'. Ethnicity is understood as a political as well as a cultural phenomenon.

The authors explore the ways in which 'race' and racism serve as a structuring principle for national processes, both in terms of defining the boundaries of the nation and the constituents of national identity. They examine the ways in which 'race' and racism inter-relate with other social divisions, such as class and gender and the ways 'Blackness' can play a part in the racialization process. Finally, the authors consider some of the ideologies that have influenced the 'Race Relations Industry' as well as some of the struggles around it. In particular they look at the ideology of 'the community' which underlies, in different ways, both the 'multi-culturalist' and 'anti-racist' schools of thought, and they link it to a critical examination of 'identity politics'. Systematic and well-informed, the book will be of interest to students of ethnic studies, the sociology of stratification and gender studies.

'*Racialized Boundaries* engages with current conceptual debates over the nature and status of racism, confirming the centrality of ethnicity as the central pivot of race categorization and anti-racist struggles, despite recent attempts to dissolve, or just ignore it. There are cogent and challenging excursions in the notoriously difficult areas where racism crosses paths with class and gender and a probing look at the assumptions underlying multi-culturalism and equal opportunities.'

Ellis Cashmore, *University of Tampa, Florida*

Racialized boundaries

Race, nation, gender, colour and class and the anti-racist struggle

Floya Anthias and Nira Yuval-Davis
(in association with Harriet Cain)

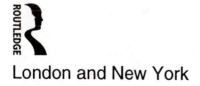

London and New York

First published 1992 in hardback
Paperback edition first published in 1993
by Routledge
11 New Fetter Lane, London EC4P 4EE

Simultaneously published in the USA and Canada
by Routledge
29 West 35th Street, New York, NY 10001

Reprinted 1995, 1996

Routledge is an International Thomson Publishing company

Typeset in Baskerville by LaserScript Limited, Mitcham, Surrey
Printed and bound in Great Britain by
Biddles Ltd, Guildford and King's Lynn

British Library Cataloguing in Publication Data
A catalogue record for this book is available from the British Library

Library of Congress Cataloguing in Publication Data
A catalogue record for this book is available from the Library of Congress

ISBN 0–415–10388–6

Contents

Preface

This book grew out of our engagement, for many years, with both the theoretical and the political projects of anti-racist struggles. The perspectives from which we have been engaged in these struggles have been partly shaped by our own position as members of ethnic minorities. One of us is a Cypriot, one an Israeli Jew and one is of African-Caribbean descent. This book is an attempt to develop an overall framework for analysing the phenomena of ethnicity and racism, and the ways in which they interrelate with nation, state, gender, class and 'community politics'.

In this book we have chosen a number of central themes and questions for special consideration. These are themes that relate to understanding racism neither as a reified and abstracted phenomenon outside other sets of social relations, nor as one that is merely the epiphenomenon of other real phenomena constituted elsewhere. In the selection of the themes we have also taken into account certain contemporary debates which by their continual re-appearance, albeit in different ways in different social and political contexts, relate to some of the essential theoretical and political problems posed by the phenomena of racisms. The book makes a theoretical intervention in a number of central debates relating to the analytical status of the category of race, ways of conceptualizing racism and nationalism, issues of race and class and race and gender, the role of the category of 'Black' within racialization processes, and the roles of the ideologies of multi-culturalism, the community and identity politics in anti-racist strategies.

The perspective developed in this book was partly informed by the work we undertook in a south-east London borough as part of the Gender and Ethnic project at Thames Polytechnic. It is primarily in the final chapter of the book that the field work is used as part of the argument. However it does draw upon the body of knowledge and experience gained to understand central facets of contemporary racism and anti-racist initiatives and struggles. We would like to take the opportunity here to thank the many people – too numerous to mention here – in the borough, the council, the community groups and Thames Polytechnic, who contributed to our understanding of the issues involved. We didn't always agree with them, but we always learned from the dialogue we had. We would also like to thank the School of Social Sciences of Thames Polytechnic for providing us with resources for research for a number of years.

Challenging racism, theoretically as well as politically, often extracts a heavy emotional toll from the people at the forefront. We would like to dedicate this book to the memory of our first research assistant, Sylvia Erike, whose tragic death was partly a result of some of the contradictions of race, class, gender and colour, that are the focus of this book.

The perseverance and challenging spirit of Harriet Cain, our last research assistant, has affected the formulation of many of the ideas in this book. This book is the product of common deliberations, research and study over a number of years with much cross fertilisation of ideas and points if view. This resulted in the development of a broadly common theoretical and political framework for analysing 'race', ethnic, class and gender relations. However, Chapters 1, 3 and 4 were primarily prepared and written by Floya Anthias and Chapters 2, 5 and 6 by Nira Yuval-Davis. Part of Chapter 6 is based on work undertaken with Harriet Cain.

The first chapter provides the theoretical framework within which the book can be located. It examines critically the analytical status of the concepts of race and racism. It argues that 'race' must be located within the wider category of 'ethnos' that provides its analytical axis. Racism, on the other hand, cannot be seen as derivative of race or ethnic phenomena but needs to be understood with reference to the discourses and practices by which ethnic groups are inferiorized, excluded and subordinated. These meet a diverse number of political and economic projects. A major argument is that racisms cannot be understood without considering their interconnections with ethnicity, nationalism, class, gender and the state.

Chapter 2 examines the ways in which 'race' and racism serve as a structuring principle for national processes, by defining both the boundaries of the nation and the constituents of national identity. The chapter explores the ways different elements of nationalist projects – citizenship, culture, religion and origin – can become racialized, and demonstrates this in relation to Britain.

The third chapter looks at the central issue of 'race and class', a theme that has been dominant in much writing on race and racism. Although race and class are linked, it is argued that racisms are forms of discourse that may, but need not, articulate class processes. Race, it is argued, is a component of class formation rather than being merely derivative of it, as much of the literature has suggested. The chapter examines the concrete economic positioning of racialized groups in contemporary Britain, which raises additional problems for many of the theorizations within the terms of reference of the 'race and class' debate.

Chapter 4 examines the relationship between two central social divisions, those of ethnicity/race and gender as they interplay with each other, both in terms of their conceptual similarities and differences, and in terms of the ways they intermesh in concrete social relations. It considers the specific position of ethnic minority and racialized women in contemporary Britain and shows how class, sex and race interact, particularly in the areas of state action around nationality, and in employment.

Chapter 5 examines the ways in which race processes have been theorized and understood through the signifier of skin colour. It considers a number of theories which have specifically linked racism and Black skin and examines the explanatory power given to 'Blackness'. The chapter looks at the emergence of Blackness as a category of resistance and empowerment and at the ways in which the boundaries of the category 'Black' have been constructed in Britain.

Finally Chapter 6 explores some of the ideologies which have constructed the 'Race Relations Industry' as well as some of the radical struggles around it. In particular it looks at the ideology of 'the community' which underlies, in different ways, both the 'multi-culturalist' and 'anti-racist' schools of thought, and links it to a critical examination of identity politics.

Chapter 1

The concept of 'race' and the racialization of social divisions

There has been much written on the issue of race. Most universities and polytechnics now run courses of one kind or another on race relations or racism. There is a mass of empirical writing by both academic researchers and by official bodies and the newest 'Race Relations Industry' has meant the emergence of both the professional ethnic and the ethnic academic as experts in the area. Two recent books, that of Gilroy (1987) on the one hand and that edited by Cohen and Bains (1988) on the other, in different ways, not only reappraise the state of the enterprise, but go some way towards clarifying some of the central theoretical and political issues involved. We want to develop this process further by contextualizing race and racism within the parameters of ethnic processes and in relation to the other prime divisions of class and gender.

In this chapter we want to provide an exploratory framework for the analysis of what have been termed 'race' phenomena. Our basic position is that race categories and their specification require an incorporation into the social ontology of collectivity and belongingness in order to be understood. Whilst agreeing with Miles (1982a) that the race relations problematic is inadequate and that racism has to be located within economic, political and ideological relations rather than relations between 'races', we do not agree that the category of race has to be ruled out of court 'because it is a category of everyday life and should not be employed analytically (Miles 1982a: 42). Certainly race typologies which derive from a scientific racism which purported to specify criteria for designating individuals to phenotypical types has been both a historical product and totally discredited (Guillaumin 1988,

Rose *et al.* 1984, Miles 1989). None the less, from a sociological point of view, 'race' denotes a particular way in which communal differences come to be constructed and therefore it cannot be erased from the analytical map as Miles (1984) suggests.

On the other hand Gilroy (1987) sees it as a valid social construct. His position is that organization on the basis of 'race' as a socially constructed but also real cultural entity can at times have primacy over class in the class struggle which in modern societies entails race structuration. However, he fails to provide the axis upon which phenomena of race depend. In our view such an axis can be found within constructs of collectivity and belongingness (that is, ethnic phenomena) postulated through notions of common origin or destiny, not in terms of cultures of difference but in terms of the specific positing of boundaries. These involve mechanisms of both inclusion and exclusion of individuals on the basis of the categorization of human subjects into those that can belong and those that cannot.

Race is one way by which the boundary is to be constructed between those who can and those who cannot belong to a particular construction of a collectivity or population. In the case of race this is on the basis of an immutable biological or physiognomic difference which may or may not be seen to be expressed mainly in culture or life-style but is always grounded on the separation of human populations by some notion of stock or collective heredity of traits.

Our position also entails distinguishing between the specification and explication of the category of race and the question of understanding and explaining the discourses and practices of racism. As Cohen notes 'the first and largest problem is how to devise a framework, whether analytical or organisational, which both distinguishes clearly between different types of racism and recognises the historical individuality of those subjected to them' (1988: 13). For us this entails understanding racisms as modes of exclusion, inferiorization, subordination and exploitation that present specific and different characters in different social and historical contexts. Extreme examples are those of extermination, segregation and slavery. These are differentially experienced by different class, ethnic and gender categories. There is not a unitary system of signification that can be labelled racist nor is there a unitary perpetrator or victim. This position requires addressing the ways in which the categories of difference and exclusion on the basis of class, gender and ethnicity incorporate processes of racialization and are intertwined in producing racist discourses and outcomes. In our view, the explication of racisms therefore cannot be undertaken purely with reference to ethnic or race phenomena. An adequate analysis has to consider processes of exclusion and subordination in intersection with those of the other major divisions of class and gender as well as processes of state and nation.

This chapter begins by looking at the issue of ethnic groups and their boundaries in order to develop a framework within which the understanding of race phenomena can be undertaken which recognizes on the one hand their specificity and on the other hand incorporates them within an analysis of the ways in which difference and identity are attributed and proclaimed. The axis to racism however is not confined to the arena of race attributions but requires the ethnic category more broadly conceived as a building block or raw material. We shall turn to this issue later on in this chapter.

ETHNOS, ETHNICITY AND NATIONALISM

What are usually lumped together under the category of ethnos or ethnic phenomena are in fact highly heterogeneous. As we argued elsewhere (Anthias and Yuval Davis 1983),

> The only general basis on which we can theorise what can broadly be conceived as ethnic phenomena in all their diversity, is as various forms of ideological construct which divide people into different collectivities and communities.

Historically, ethnic, national or racial categories have been formed in various ways, through conquests, colonization and immigration, and of course the modern variants of these categories under the sway of capitalism and imperialism as well as their most prominent political form, that of the liberal democratic state. While each of the groups and their designation require a historically specific analysis it is not possible to distinguish in an abstract way between ethnic racial or national collectivities but rather one can distinguish their different discourses and projects.

In different social and historical contexts, a process of re-labelling or redesignation may occur. For example, immigrants from South Asia can be defined as ethnic, racial or religious groups, using the terms Pakistani, Black or Muslim; Jews in different contexts can be constructed as a primarily religious, ethnic or national group. Therefore, groups that have been called or have called themselves national at one point, or in one territory, have become ethnic or racial in other contexts (for example Jews have been referred to sequentially in this way in the Soviet Union, the USA and Nazi Germany). The use of one or other of these categorizations has often been determined by the political intentions of those involved (see for example de Lepervanche (1980) for the ethnicization of the Aborigines in Australia).

However, while they are difficult to ground, what is common to them, in all their diversity, is that they involve the social construction of an origin as a basis for community or collectivity. This origin, mythical or real, can be historically, territorially, culturally or physiognomically based. It can be internally constituted by the group or externally imposed, or both. As well as a social construction of an origin as unifying the group, the idea of a common or shared fate can act in the same way. Anderson (1983) refers to ethnic groups as 'imagined communities', since all those who belong assume a sense of commonality with others but not all members can interact concretely to form a real community.

Ethnic groups involve the positing of boundaries in relation to who can and cannot belong according to certain parameters which are extremely heterogeneous, ranging from the credentials of birth to being born in the right place, conforming to cultural or other symbolic practices, language, and very centrally behaving in sexually appropriate ways (Anthias and Yuval-Davis 1989). Although Barth (1969) makes a valid distinction between ethnic boundaries and the cultural stuff of the group, in practice the cultural stuff often provides the credentials for being able to cross the boundary or being excluded.

Although the boundaries are ideological they involve material practices, and therefore material origins and effects. The boundary is a space for struggle and negotiation. Ethnic resources (such as language, culture, religion, gender relations) can be used in interplay with the class and political resources and positionings of the group. Ethnic processes are often implicated therefore in the pursuit of diverse political ends. These may involve exclusionary and inclusionary practices for maintaining the privileges along a number of different dimensions, or for countering those of other groups. Ethnicity can therefore be a medium for class, nation or state formation. In this way, national or nationalist projects will be centred around claims and practices for separate political representation, territory or unification. Class projects may use a variety of means, which may include racist formulations of an immutable essential difference to the group for pursuing exploitation. Racial projects may be a mode for preserving ethnic exclusivity and privileges within the nation state of the dominant ethnic group. This list is by no means exhaustive and indeed racist discourses can be introduced within all the projects mentioned and others such as those that focus on gender (see Chapter 4).

The boundary of ethnic collectivities is most frequently determined by being born or marrying into the group although conversion or assimilation can also provide the right credentials. The boundaries often change over time and in response to concrete economic, political or ideological conditions. Different criteria or signifiers of inclusion may be used by those on the inside and those on the outside. For the Nazis, anyone with a Jewish grandparent was designated as Jewish; for Orthodox Jews only those who have Jewish mothers or converted according to the Halkha are Jewish; and to many secular Jews, whoever defines themselves as a Jew can be one. In South Africa, people of mixed race are defined as a separate racial category of 'Coloured', whilst in Britain they may be defined and/or define themselves as Black. Members of specific ethnic groups may in addition see themselves as part of a more embracing collectivity. For example Jamaicans in Britain may see themselves as part of the African-Caribbean community, and both Asians and African-Caribbeans in Britain may see themselves as part of the Black community. In other words, the notion of where and how the boundary is constructed is not only diverse, but is also contextual and relational (to other groups). What is at stake are processes by which criteria for identification emerge and are transformed.

Ethnic positioning provides individuals with a mode of interpreting the world, based on shared cultural resources and a shared collective positioning *vis-à-vis* other groups, often within a structure of dominance and contestation. Therefore belonging, or indeed being designated as a member of an ethnic group, is often seen to imply that one cannot belong to other groups (that is, that membership is exclusive). However, in practice individuals may belong to a number of ethnic groups. For example, British-born migrants may regard themselves, or be regarded, as both British and Asian, British and African-Caribbean, or British and Cypriot. Such cases, however, may produce conflict between different universes of meaning, and may involve identity shifts in different contexts. Therefore membership in ethnic collectivities provides individuals with a sense of roots, and is often a pivotal element in their understanding of 'who I am'. In the modern era, Bhabha (1990) notes the growth of hybridity and 'counter narratives' pertaining to those who cross boundaries continually.

Having argued for a commonality to ethnic phenomena, there are important differences in the discourses of ethnicity, nationalism and, as we pointed out earlier, racism. Ethnicity is a problematic notion and has been subjected to a number of definitions (Weber 1969, Barth 1969, Cohen 1974, Wallman 1979, Kahn 1981) as well as being found sorely wanting by more radical writers (CCCS 1982, Bourne 1985, Gilroy 1987). Hall (1988), on the other hand, has attempted to retrieve the concept of ethnicity from the conceptual baggage of the ethnic studies approach and deploy it in a more radical way.

ETHNICITY

Ethnicity is a term that is often identified with the ethnic studies approach, just as race is identified with the race relations tradition (Miles 1982a, Anthias 1982 and 1992). The problematic of the ethnic studies approach is that of cultural interaction between ethnic groups and its effects. Race and racism are seen as complicating variables within the central focus on questions of cultural adaptation, maintenance, integration or assimilation of ethnic minorities. Within American sociology, this tendency finds expression in the enormously influential debate about assimilation (Glazer and Moynihan 1965 and 1975). In these discussions, ethnicity is often treated as a voluntaristic normative identification process, or as a form of culture. The notion of 'resurgent' ethnicity reaffirms the view of ethnicity as 'ethnic identity' or cultural differentiation. For Glazer and Moynihan (1975), ethnic identity has become an alternative to national identity whilst at the same time class identity is seen as declining.

As Omi and Winant point out, ethnicity theory in the United States assumes that, the key factor in explaining the success that an ethnic group will have in becoming incorporated into majority society . . . is the values or 'norms' it possesses. (1986: 22)

This means that the role of racism in structuring the position of 'Black' groups is ignored. This racism will limit assimilation even where the norms and values adopted by a group are in keeping with those that have made other ethnic groups successful, according to Omi and Winant. Such an approach also tends to treat all Blacks as belonging to the same ethnic group, ignoring the diversity within the category. They point out, however, that 'many Blacks . . . rejected ethnic identity in favour of a more radical racial identity' (1986: 20). On the other hand, Gans (1979) notes the growth of symbolic ethnicity, as a personal affirmation of belonging in American society. Hall (1988), writing in Britain, sees the revival of ethnicity as an affirmation of identity which is seen as emanating from the postmodern condition.

The English 'ethnic school' (set up in Bristol in 1971) attempted to provide insights into the culture of ethnic minorities, Asians in particular, and its meaning for the actors. Jeffery (1976) is interested in processes by which a group maintains its culture, for example. Often a view is expressed (for example in Dahya 1974 and Wallman 1979) that ethnic groups as distinct cultures will choose certain occupations or forms of social participation.

In her review of the sociology of race relations in Britain, Bourne (1980) argues against this approach in terms of its necessary political effects. But no theorization has necessary political effects, nor can it be countered by saying that its empirical premises are mistaken. The central difficulty with the ethnic school approach is the way it formulated ethnicity merely as identity or shared culture, and the role it assigns to these in understanding the placement of ethnic groups in society. The notion of 'reactive ethnicity' advanced by the school sees it as a cultural affirmation. This is regarded as a response to the individual sense of rejection that the members of ethnic groups face (Ballard and Ballard 1977). This is grounded in a passive and personally instrumental response (for a fuller account of the concept of ethnicity within the ethnic studies approach see Anthias 1982 and forthcoming).

We would question the focus on relations between cultures and identities. This is also one of the reasons why Gilroy (1987) rejects the concept of ethnicity. We would also take issue with Hall's (1988) location of ethnicity as a subjective identification process that forms part of the fragmentation of postmodern society. Ethnicity is regarded as coterminous with culture and identity here also. We will therefore present our alternative formulation, which means retaining, but redefining, the terms of reference within which the term should be located.

Ethnicity at its most general level involves belonging to a particular group and sharing its conditions of existence. This will include not only being regarded as having the right credentials for membership but also being able to muster ethnic resources which can be used for struggle, negotiation and the pursuit of political projects, both at the level of individuals making their way but also for the group as a whole in relation to other groups. Ethnic resources can be economic, territorial, cultural and linguistic, amongst others.

All ethnic groups, majorities and minorities are characterized by a notion of 'community'. However, dominant groups, whether majorities, as in the case of the English in Britain, or minorities, as is the case of the Whites in South Africa, have the potential to naturalize their *Weltanschauung*. This results from their control of the means of communication and cultural production, and their dominant position within the state. This does not mean that dominant groups are always successful in doing this, however, as can be witnessed by the ethnic conflict which has emerged, for example, in the Soviet Union.

It is clear therefore, that although cultural commonality is one of the ingredients that characterizes ethnic groups, ethnic and cultural groups are not coterminous. Ethnicity is not predicated only on common culture and indeed can be focused around other signifiers of an essential or 'natural' community of people. These include religion, language or race. For example, Omi and Winant (1986) refer to Blacks as having a radical 'racial' identity. There is a potential growth in the wake of the 1992 Single European Act of a 'White European' identity despite the existence of diverse languages, cultures and traditions. Ethnicity is the active face of ethnic consciousness and always involves a political dimension, therefore.

At any specific time, there may be a dominant view of what characterizes the essential character, needs or interests of an ethnic group. None the less, this is always subject to shifts and transformations; myths of descent or history may be in a constant state of reinvention and re-evaluation. For example, Cypriots may be divided, on the one hand, between the different categories of Greek or Turkish under the sway of colonialism and right-wing nationalism. But they may be beginning to reinvent themselves as a Cypriot people that can encompass both Greek and Turkish Cypriots in the pursuit of a solution to the Cyprus problem (see Anthias and Ayres 1983 and Anthias 1986). We can also currently witness the changing boundaries of the category of Black British (see our Chapter 5).

Ethnicity is more than merely a question of ethnic identity, either in the personal sense *vis-à-vis* the individual's identification with a group (as the term is used in the 'British ethnic group') or in terms of a collective sentiment (as in Schlesinger 1987). Ethnicity involves partaking of the social conditions of a group, which is positioned in a particular way in terms of the social allocation of resources, within a context of difference to other groups, as well as commonalities and differences within (in relation to the divisions of class and gender, for example, within the group). Ethnicity cross-cuts gender and class divisions, but at the same time involves the positing of a similarity (on the inside) and a difference (from the outside) that seeks to transcend these divisions.

Indeed the existence of a conscious ethnic identity may not even be a necessary condition for the existence of ethnicity. Ethnicity may be constructed outside the group, by the material conditions it faces, and by its social representation by other groups, or by the state. For example, migrant labourers from different ethnic origins may become ethnicized through state legislation, and by the ways they are identified by the indigenous population. However, in practice ethnic identity and often solidarity, will occur either as a prerequisite for the group, or as a result of its material, political or ideological placement.

The conditions of reproduction of ethnic groups, as well as their transformation, are centrally linked to the other prime social divisions of class and gender. For example, class homogeneity within the group will produce a greater cohesion of interests and goals. Access to the state apparatus will often lead to the cultural hegemony of one group over others, and a subsequent natural-ization of its specific cultural symbols and practices. This may lead to the imposition of its world-view in society at large. Women are

often central in ethnic and national reproduction and transformation, not only as biological reproducers of the members of
the group, or central in the transmission of its cultural artefacts,
but also as markers of the boundaries of collectivities (Anthias and
Yuval-Davis 1989).

We will be discussing nationalism in relation to the state more
specifically in the next chapter, but it is useful here to note how
nationalist discourse may differ from ethnicity. Nationalist discourse includes demands or practices for separate political
representation or territory. National identities involve the postulate of a necessary political or territorial separation, and thus are
tied to specific political projects of the ethnic group. Often the
autonomy desired involves further political projects, which in the
modern era have been linked to modernization and industrialization (Gellner 1987), and therefore a break with the traditional
structures and internal forms of control of the group. However,
nationalist projects often articulate the interests of oppressed
classes against colonialism and imperialism (Hechter 1975), and it
is therefore difficult to see them as emanating from an ethnic
essence. The conditions for the development of nationalist
ideologies and national liberation struggles have to be sought in
the interplay of factors the group faces, in relation to ethnicity and
class.

Having explored some of the characteristic features of ethnic
phenomena and ethnicity we shall now turn to the construct of
race and the exploration of racism.

THE CATEGORY OF RACE AND THE PROBLEM OF RACISM

There is an enormous literature on the question of race and
racism and we do not intend to review it here. But as a preliminary
to presenting our own formulation, we have found it necessary to
begin by exploring the ways in which race and racism have been
connected in the literature.

For Banton (1987) racism was linked to a hierarchical racial
typology and since this is now defunct, the concept of racism
should no longer be used. Banton, along with other writers,
associates racism only with the 'scientific' racism, promulgated in
Europe. Supposed scientific evidence was marshalled, to establish
both the existence of different racial types, and their depiction
within a hierarchy of superior and inferior, where the Black was

regarded as inferior (Guillaumin 1988, Rose *et al.* 1984). Treating racism as a doctrine, as Miles (1989) rightly points out, leads to it being seen as a relatively coherent set of assertions. Other writers want also to add that racism occurs when racial categories are imbued with negative meaning (Benedict 1968, Miles 1989).

Most of these positions make an analytical conflation between race and racism (Anthias 1990). Miles criticizes some views (such as that of Benedict 1968) that link race and racism for challenging the dogma of racial inferiority, but none the less retaining the use of the term 'race' as denoting a valid scientific typology. Miles rejects the analytical validity of the notion of race and instead prefers the term racialization. Commenting on the use of the term 'racialization' in the literature he concludes,

> there is minimal agreement that the concept be used to refer to a representational process whereby social significance is attached to certain biological (usually phenotypical) human features, on the basis of which those people possessing those characteristics are designated as a distinct collectivity. (1989: 74)

He himself employs the concept of racialization

> to refer to those instances where social relations between people have been structured by the signification of human biological characteristics in such a way as to define and construct differentiated social collectivities. (1989: 75)

Racialization is also used to refer 'to the historical emergence of the idea of "race" and to its subsequent reproduction and application' (p. 76).

What this view retains is the notion of race as the social construction which is at the heart of the racialization process, and which is converted to racism when it is imbued with negative valuation (1989: 84). Miles therefore restricts the use of the term 'racism' to those ideologies (not practices, institutions, structures or effects) which work on supposed racial hierarchies.

This would exclude culturalist forms of racism, or what has been termed the 'new racism' (Barker 1981, Solomos 1989) which do not depend on racial typologies. It would also exclude the experiences of migrant ethnic groups, refugees and so on, which construct them as inferior, but not on the premise of a supposed racial categorization, but as cultural, political or national outsiders and undesirables.

We believe that the specificity of racism lies in its working on the notion of ethnic groupings. It is a discourse and practice of inferiorizing ethnic groups. Racism need not rely on a process of racialization. We believe that racism can also use the notion of the undesirability of groups, in the form in which they exist. This may lead to attempts to assimilate, exterminate or exclude. These may be justified in terms of the negative attribution given to culture, ethnic identity, personality as well as 'racial' stock. For example, anti-Muslim racism in Britain relies on notions of the 'non-civilized' and supposedly inferior and undesirable character of Islamic religion and way of life, rather than an explicit notion of biological inferiority.

The distinction often made between ethnocentrism, xeno-phobia and racism (Cox 1970, Cohen 1988, Rattansi 1992) needs to be made but not in the commonly perceived ways, where racism is usually confined to racially stigmatized groups. Ethnocentrism occurs when one's own culture is taken for granted as natural, and is characteristic of all ethnicities to a greater or lesser extent. Xenophobia, or the dislike of the stranger or outsider, on the other hand, becomes racism when there are power relations involved. These can then put into practice the sentiments of antipathy and produce racist effects. Indeed the question of power and racist effects is central to our own definition of racism.

There is an insistence in some of the literature that the question of racism should be divorced from the question of practices and structures. Racism may or may not be seen to include practices of racial discrimination. Some writers distinguish between ideology and practice. Sivanandan (1973) for example, defines racism as ideology, and racialism as discrimination, in his early work. More recently, he uses the term racialism to refer to individual prejudice, and racism to structures and institutions (1985). The notion of institutional racism is commonly used, as a structural or objective practice, which is contrasted with individual racial prejudice or racial ideology (Carmichael and Hamilton 1968, Sivanandan 1982).

Miles's view is that racism should be restricted to ideology: 'I use the concept of racism to refer to a particular form of (evaluative) representation which is a specific instance of a wider (descriptive) process of racialisation' (1989: 84).

The two characteristics of racism, in this view, are firstly that racism uses biological characteristics to identify collectivity (which is what Miles means by racialization) and secondly, it negatively evaluates the group's biological or cultural characteristics. Miles opposes the wider definition of racism that includes in its ambit a set of practices, commonly defined as institutional racism. His argument is that structural practices can lead to disadvantages for Black groups without necessarily the causality being racism. Not all practices, such as those found in labour market processes, lead to the subordination of Black groups because they are racist practices but may be the result of class-related factors.

This is an important point to make, for the structural disadvantages of groups in the labour market, or in housing, may be the product of broader class, gender and state processes linked to locality, skills, eligibility for housing, juridical criteria, year of entry to Britain and so on. However, the juridical or formalistic criteria which categorize people as eligible for housing or employment, such as residential qualification or skill and education, may function to produce outcomes that are racist. Therefore, the question of racist practices need not rely on a notion of racism as explicitly underlying the structures and practices involved. Racist practices do not require the racist intentionality of structures which underpins so much of the work on institutional racism. Practices may be racist in terms of their effects. These practices may exacerbate or even produce exclusions and subordinations which are coterminous with supposed 'racially' different populations. This aspect of racism needs to be included in any definition whose object is not only the academic trajectory of a concept, but the formulation of policies and strategies for undermining and correcting it.

Moreover, to define racism as merely ideological produces it as a set of false representations. For Miles, ideology 'represents human beings, and the social relations between human beings, in a distorted and misleading manner' (1984:42). This is a very narrow and in fact old polarization between ideological and true statements. Even as a Marxist notion, it has now been largely supplanted by the development of Marx's other definition, which regards ideology as embedded in the hegemonic *Weltanschauung* or world-view. The contributions by Althusserian (Althusser 1971), and post-structuralist writers as well as the development of Gramsci's approach (Laclau and Mouffe 1985) are now widely disseminated. Miles's retention of the notion of ideology as 'false' is therefore somewhat surprising, as he is a writer who, over the years, has developed a more sophisticated Marxist approach to racism than many. Although Miles is at pains to argue that racism is often used to provide meaning to the real conditions and experience of working-class actors, he is by default restricting it to socially determined attitudes that are false, but seized upon by individuals for functional purposes.

Rattansi (1992) too wants to distinguish racial discrimination from racism. For him, racism is a set of beliefs about groups which is to be distinguished from the causality that may be attributable to racial discrimination. This again is valid but the danger here is that racism can then be denied as present in British society (as it has been in Germany, see Nora Rathzel, 1991). The most common forms of racism are to be found not as explicit ideologies or discourses of biological inferiorization, but as different forms of exclusion, on the basis of a group not belonging to the culture of origin of the dominant ethnic group within the state apparatus (Solomos 1989). The notion of cultural difference has largely displaced the notion of biological difference, as a basis for excluding or inferiorizing, both in discourse and practice.

The positions noted above treat racism as endemically tied to the postulate of 'race'. Some of these views restrict racism to ideology (particularly Miles). We wish to challenge both these positions. A third position is that which regards racism as pertaining to the attitudes or practices exercised by White people over Black people. As Cohen notes, however, 'there are some clear parallels between the experience of the Jewish and Asian, or the Irish and African-Caribbean communities in terms of class trajectories and responses to racism. But there are equally significant differences' (1988: 13).

Some writers wish to go further than linking racism to race and restrict it to 'colour racism', with its connotations of physical visibility. The argument is that colour visibility makes assimilation into the hegemonic culture and structure of a society impossible. Racism is here usually confined to the product of colonialist discourse of 'the other', which is seen to have ongoing effects in the present, often derived from class interests (as in the work of Rex 1973, Sivanandan 1982). In some arguments this prototype is seen to predate the colonial experience and to be a product of the historical signifier of Blackness (for example, Jordan 1974). As Cohen argues, though, racist discourses have never confined themselves just to body images . . . and racist codes behave opportunistically according to an economy of means; they choose those signs which do the most ideological work in linking – and naturalising – difference and domination within a certain set of historical conditions of representation. (1988: 14)

Although this quotation reads too much like a functionalist or causal explanation of racism, none the less it makes the important point that racism is a set of postulates, images (and we would add practices) which serve to differentiate and dominate. These can use all kinds of signifiers or markers. We would add that they serve to deny full participation in economic, social, political and cultural life by the essence that they posit. The supposed essence of difference is given a negative evaluation. This does not mean that racism is always coherent or conscious. As Cohen notes, racism may construct demonic images which are contradictory. In Homi Bhabha's view (1990) they are also embodiments of desire. For Rattansi (1992), the imagery is intricately linked to sexuality. Although anti-Semitism and colour prejudice, to use Cohen's words, have quite distinct patterns of development and use different images, they none the less both construct their objects as demonic and with 'legendary powers of sexuality' (Cohen 1988: 21).

The dichotomous categories of Blacks as victims, and Whites as perpetrators of racism, tend to homogenize the objects of racism, without paying attention to the different experience of men and women, of different social classes and ethnicities. They fail to note racism towards Jews, the Irish, Third-World workers, refugees and so on. They treat all White people as racist without paying attention to the different articulations of racism within social class and gender categories (Anthias 1991). For example the condemnation by radical Black writers of White sociology (Amos, Gilroy and Lawrence 1982) does both of these things. It constructs a Black identity that is present only as victim of White society and in the process reduces racism to what White people do to Black people, because they are Black. (See Chapter 5 for a more detailed discussion of the links between colour and racism.)

Gilroy (1987) regards the formulation of Black identity as a reaction to racism as inadequate. He stresses the existence of a Black culture and organization that is not merely structured in and through the experience of racism. However, he assumes a homogeneous cultural and political entity. Miles (1989) extends racism beyond colour, and indeed points out that racism is not the privileged domain of Whites and that Blacks can be racist. We would want to modify this by saying that racism is not just about beliefs or statements (discourse, in this narrow sense), but about the ability to impose those beliefs or world-views as hegemonic, and as a basis for a denial of rights or equality. Racism is thus embedded in power relations of different types. From this point of view, although Blacks may be racist in terms of believing that some groups are endemically inferior, they do not usually possess the power to effect change. On this basis, it does not seem reasonable to consider their racism as the same type as that exercised by dominant groups over subordinate ones.

Miles himself notes the importance of exclusionary practice, and refers to 'racism and related exclusionary practices which are a component part of a wider structure of class disadvantage and exclusion' (1989: 9). However, for Miles, racism is an ideology and not identifiable with any particular exclusionary practice. It remains an object of investigation, for Miles, to note what the related exclusionary practices are. Our view is that all those exclusionary practices that are formulated on the categorization of individuals into groups whereby ethnic or 'racial' origin are criteria of access or selection are endemically racist. Further, our view is that racist practices are also those whose outcome, if not intention, is to work on different categories of the population in this way.

There is indeed a great repertoire of forms of racism: inter-subjective, ideological and systemic. It is important also to differentiate between racism within the state and racism within civil society. This requires us to recognize that the idea of a racist state conspiracy, or the idea of a racist imagination, are both too restrictive. Racial harassment, for example, takes place not only at the level of the state, through practices deeply entrenched in social regulation such as those of the police force, but also in civil society through class and youth cultures (Cohen 1988).

We have mentioned several times the importance of analytically separating the division of race and ethnicity from other social divisions, whilst at the same time looking at their interplay. We shall now turn to a preliminary formulation of the main differences and commonalities between gender, ethnic and class divisions. The chapters on Class (Chapter 3) and Gender (Chapter 4) will explore the connections in more detail.

ETHNIC, GENDER AND CLASS DIVISIONS

All three divisions involve differential access to resources and processes of exclusion and inclusion, and at times oppression and domination. They all involve systems of representation concerning capacities and needs, both within everyday language and embodied in official documents and state practices and legislation. However, each division relates to different existential locations in society, that is, to different ontological spheres (for a more detailed analysis see Anthias and Yuval-Davis 1983 and Anthias 1991).

Class relates to the sphere of production processes but can't be reduced to the economy. It is important to distinguish the ontological basis of class, which is in the sphere of production, from the formation of concrete classes involved in class struggle. These are not only the product of processes endemic within the sphere of production, but are historically constructed in relation to the divisions of gender and ethnos (including race). Therefore an investigation of concrete class processes finds them enmeshed with those of social relations more broadly defined. However, it is possible to separate out not only the ontological basis of class, but also the forms of discourse and practice that characterize it.

Notions of the hierarchization of human subjects often accompany class discourse, but in the sense of individualized capacities and competencies. There is no given population that these capacities are seen to have their origin in, rather it is the capacities that are seen to construct the category. However these capacities may be seen as genetically transmitted, thus allowing a collective capacity to be attributed to a class group. Individuals will be seen to be able to move into and out of the group in relation to these capacities. Unlike Cohen (1988) we do not think the genealogy of inheritance functions in the same way for the working class as it does for racialized groups. The attributes in the case of class are seen to derive from the unfortunate lower genetic intelligence of the parents, and therefore the lineage via the family. In 'race' it is a different human stock that is posited, which cannot transmit genes which are parallel to other races. 'Race' is therefore deterministic whereas notions of inherent capacities in class are fluid. In class, there is always some universality and humanity which is missing in race. However, social and economic classes can be defined in racial terms, and this is the argument that Cohen (1988) is making, we believe.

Exclusions and subordination characterize class relations, but its prime relation is that of economic exploitation. Exclusions and subordination are legitimated, through seeing the human subjects involved as unable to seize the opportunities available through low intelligence, moral lassitude, incompetence or deprivation, to name a few of the justifications or explanations offered both in everyday life and by sociologists.

Gender relates to the social organization of sexual difference and biological reproduction, and involves social constructions and representations of these, but cannot be reduced to biology. Unlike class, gender works with a notion of a natural relationship between social effects and a biologically constituted sexual difference. With gender, there is an object of discursive reference which posits groups of subjects defined by their sexual difference. But the practices and representations around gender are themselves not the product of this difference, but originate in social relations that include those of class and race/ethnicity. (See Chapter 4 for more discussion.)

Gender and racialized ethnic divisions are both underpinned by a supposedly 'natural' relation. In gender, necessary social effects are posited to sexual difference and biological reproduction. In ethnic or racialized groups there exist assumptions concerning the natural boundaries of collectivities, or the naturalness of culture. This supposedly natural difference in capacities and needs, on the basis of gender or of ethnicity/race, then comes to enter into economic relations as legitimizers of inequalities in class position. At the same time, class processes are involved in the racialization of particular social/ethnic categories, and in the specific contents of ideologies of sexual difference. For example, there has been an increasing racialization of Third World migrant labour in this latest phase of international labour migration. The fluidity of racialization processes is also indicated by the European experience of guest workers and the new forms of migration from Eastern Europe (Sivanandan 1988b, Moroksovic 1991).

The naturalized depictions of ethnicity or race, and gender, are used both for legitimating inequality and for struggle against it. In the first case, it becomes natural that White men should be defined, for example, as the major bread-winners and should have greater access to well paid full-time work. It also becomes natural that non-Whites (or a given population whatever marker is chosen – it need not be colour of skin as long as it relies on some notion of a racial stock) should similarly occupy a lower position in the class structure since their biology or culture (the argument will vary) limit their skills, education interests, etc.

These naturalized depictions can also be used to struggle against racism or sexism. For example, women may call to women to unite by stressing the positive elements of female experience. Here 'femininity' becomes defined as some sort of essence. The 'Black is beautiful' rhetoric as well as that of national liberation 'freedom fighters' for the motherland, are other cases. Such rallying points, although strategically useful, will raise problems of the long-term unity of class groupings, for example.

Class provides the material conditions for different ethnic and gender groups, who often have unequal access to economic and political resources. The state is important here, for it structures all these exclusions by all the three divisions being represented within it, in a relation of unequal participation on lines of dominant ethnicity, gender and class.

CONCLUSION

In this chapter we have set out the theoretical framework within which the book as a whole is located. We are arguing for an analysis of racialization and racism that pays attention to the relationship between race phenomena and ethnic phenomena. This requires attending to the different political projects relating to ethnic and national phenomena, and how race and racism are concretely articulated within these. Such an approach requires an analysis that looks at the question of race structuration within the context of economic, political and ideological relations. Such a position also requires that race phenomena should be addressed with regard not only to processes of ideology, whereby racism is treated as a doctrine or dogma that specifies biological racial types. Racism should also be looked at with regard to practices and discourses within a range of social forces, which include social classes, gender relations, the nation and the state. There is a process of contestation and negotiation amongst these different social forces that also needs considering.

The claim that there are different histories to racisms (for example, Hall 1980, Gilroy 1987) has been an important challenge to the more deterministic and static analyses that have often passed for a history of racism. In relation to anti-Black racism in Britain, the exploitation of the colonies for slave labour as well as the ethnic, political and cultural domination within colonialism and imperialism have been a vital but not a sufficient explanation. A concrete analysis can document the different arguments, representations and structural processes that have been implicated in it. These cannot be seen as static, or as having ever-present effects without being modified and re-articulated continuously. The heterogeneous nature of racism must also be considered in terms of class, ethnicity, gender, life cycle and generation in British society. Racism cannot be limited to the experiences of Black people but has taken different forms in relation to the Irish, the Jews, the Gypsies and Third-World migrant workers, as well as other White minorities who may be migrant workers (Sivanandan 1988b). How and by whom the boundary is constructed between so called Black and White minorities also needs examination (see Chapter 5).

However, the boundaries of the ethnic collective do not remain static. They are continuously being redrawn to serve processes and interests that form part of a diverse number of political projects, including economic ones. These have collective actors as their perpetrators and resistors. Collective actors need not be only those drawn on class lines, for class positioning may itself be an outcome of collective action over, say, citizenship, territory, or even cultural, linguistic or educational resources, which may be pursued along lines of ethnic or race formation rather than class formation.

We believe that an effective analysis requires exploring how exclusions and subordinations are linked to produce diverse outcomes with regard to the placement of collective subjects within the different major divisions that construct them. That is, our approach requires that we look at the intersection between class, ethnicity, race and gender divisions and processes within the state. It is particularly important that we should examine the state from the point of view of the ethnic and nationalist sentiments it articulates. This is the task of the following chapter.

Chapter 2

Whose nation? Whose state?
Racial/ethnic divisions and 'the nation'

INTRODUCTION

In the last chapter we explored the concepts of race and racism. In this chapter we shall examine the concepts of nation and nationalism and the ways in which they can become racialized. In the first part of this chapter we look at issues such as nationalism, ethnicity and the state; producers and reproducers of nationalist ideologies; different kinds of nationalist projects; and the ways in which citizenship, culture, religion and origin relate to nationalism and to racist exclusions. In the second part of the chapter we explore these themes in relation to Britain. We look at the changing boundaries of the British national collectivity and at how legislation and ideology affect them.

The right for national self-determination which has been, in different ways, part of the demands of both the liberal and socialist movements, has assumed an ideal type of a nation-state, in which all citizens will be members of the same national collectivity. Indeed, Gellner (1983: 1, 36) has defined nationalism as a 'theory of political legitimacy which requires that ethnic boundaries should not cut across political ones, and in particular, that ethnic boundaries within a given state . . . should not separate the power holders from the rest . . . and therefore state and culture must now be linked'. Today there is virtually nowhere in the world in which such a pure nation-state exists, if it ever did, and therefore there are always settled residents (and usually citizens as well) who are not members of the dominant national collectivity in the society. The fact that there still exists this automatic assumption about the overlap between the boundaries of the state citizens and 'the nation', is one expression of the naturalizing effect of the hegemony of one collectivity and its access to ideological apparatuses of both state and civil society. This constructs minorities into assumed deviants from the 'normal', and excludes them from important power resources. Deconstructing this is crucial to tackling racism.

Some anti-racist struggles have gained enough power to break, to a certain extent, this 'naturalness' of the hegemony of the dominant national collectivity in various western societies. This relative success (which should be recognized in spite of the general oppressive economic and political climate) has exposed, however, the need for new and adequate tools for constructing an anti-racist strategy which would transcend the conventional solutions of anti-racist strategies (of assimilation/separation) which have failed in the past, and would tackle head-on the racist criteria for membership in the national collectivity itself (Yuval-Davis 1987a, 1991a), or, in Schlesinger's terminology, tackle the problem of 'the internal processes of ideological boundary management' (1987: 245).

Of crucial importance in this endeavour, then, is not only the actual role the state occupies in imposing/resisting racial/ethnic divisions in the society, but the actual way in which we view the state itself. Theorizing the state, as a separate sphere from both the 'nation' and 'civil society' is vital for any adequate analysis of nationalism and racism. Theoretical perspectives that have expanded the domain of the state to include all major ideological apparatuses, or that have dispensed with the category of state as a meaningful analytical category altogether, cannot explain struggles and differential power access of different ethnic collectivities (as well as other groupings in civil society) to it. As we have explained elsewhere (Anthias and Yuval-Davis 1989) we define the state as a body of institutions which are centrally organized around the intentionality of control with a given apparatus of enforcement at its command and basis. This does not mean that the state is unitary either in its practices, projects or its effects. Different forms of the state involve different relationships between the coercion–control twin that is the residing characteristic of the state. Different processes, including ideological, juridical and repressive mechanisms, can be used by the state for this process. Education and the media are the prime institutional forms for ideological production in the modern liberal democratic state but they are not inherently part of the state as such.

Civil society includes those institutions, collectivities, groupings and social agencies which lie outside the formal rubric of state parameters as outlined, but which both inform and are informed by them. These include the family, social strata, ethnic and national groupings, as well as institutions such as education, trade unions, and the means of communication like the media. These produce their own ideological contents as well as being subjected to those of the state. In this way ideology does not reside (in a privileged sense) in either civil society or the state, nor is it monolithic in terms of its contents.

Different states (and the same state in different historical circumstances) differ in the extent to which their powers of control will be concentrated in the central state government or in local state governments, and the tolerance towards different political projects that conflict with those which are hegemonic within central government.

These questions of the correspondence in political projects of the different components and levels of the state also involve the questions of what are the mechanisms by which these projects are *can* being reproduced or changed, of how state control ca be delegated from one level to another and, probably most important, how sections and groupings from the civil society gain access to the state's coercive and controlling powers. It is within this context that the relationship between nations and states, as well as between other forms of ethnic groupings and the state has to be analysed. We shall next turn, therefore, to examine the notion of the 'nation', as a separate ideological and political construct from that of the 'nation-state'.

THE NOTION OF THE 'NATION'

There is great controversy about what constitutes a nation, and the extent to which it is a particularly modern, or even western phenomenon. On the one extreme there are the 'primordialists' (Shils 1957, Geertz 1963, Van den Berghe 1979), who claim that nations are natural and universal, an 'automatic' extension of kinship relationships. Their historical importance might rise or fall, but they are always there, waiting to be discovered, rather than to be historically constructed.

On the other extreme are the 'modernists' who see nationalism and nations as a phenomenon which is particular to capitalism (Althusser 1969, Hobsbawm 1990).

Marxists have developed very different theories of nationalism (for example, Otto Bauer (1940), Tom Nairn (1977), Samir Amin (1978)). But all Marxists share the 'modernist' viewpoint to the extent that they see in nationalism and in nations social rather than 'natural' facts. However, not all of them considr the construction of nations as specific to capitalism. Samir Amin, for instance, links the emergence of nations to the existence of a strong state bureaucracy, and claims that a 'nation' already existed in societies with centralized states, such as ancient Egypt.

Recent popular modernist approaches include those of Anderson (1983) and Gellner (1983), who claim that nations are a direct result of particular historical developments and that their beginnings can be located no earlier than eighteenth-century Europe. Anderson anchors the development of nationalism on the development of printing, which popularized culture. Printing allowed for the establishment of 'imagined communities' which came under capitalism to occupy the place religion used to play. Gellner, on the other hand, traces the development of nationalism to the need by modern societies for cultural homogeneity in order to function. This need, when satisfied, is sponsored by the modern nation state; but when it is unfulfilled, it stimulates the growth of ideological movements among the excluded groupings (those who have not been absorbed into the hegemonic culture), which call for the establishment of alternative nation-states.

All these modernist approaches see the development of nationalism, like capitalism, as originating in Europe. Gellner, and recently Hobsbawm (1990), trace nationalism in Europe, and following Europe, – corresponding with the uneven development of capitalism – in the rest of the world. They observe the nationalist phenomenon as undergoing certain evolutionary stages of development, and, at least according to Hobsbawm, even the beginning of a decline (although, given recent developments in Europe, even he has had to change his mind somewhat, 1991).

NATIONALISM, ETHNICITY AND THE STATE

Another influential approach to the study of nations is that of Anthony Smith (1971, 1986) who looks at the 'ethnic origins of nations'. While agreeing with the modernists that nationalism, both as an ideology and as a movement is a wholly modern phenomenon, Smith argues that the 'modern nation' in practice incorporates several features of pre-modern ethnie and owes much to a general model of ethnicity which has survived in many areas until the dawn of the 'modern era'. (1986: 18)

Smith claims that the specificity of the ethnie has to be found in its 'myth–symbol complex', which is very durable over time (although the specific meaning of the myths and symbols can change over time), rather than in any other social, economic or political features of the collectivity.

Sami Zubaida, in criticizing this approach, has anchored the durability of ethnicities in certain socio-economic and political processes. He claims (by using historical examples from both Europe and the Middle East) that historically ethnic homogeneity is not a cause, but rather a result of a long history of centralized governments which created a 'national unity' in the pre-modern era. It 'was not given – but was achieved precisely by the political processes which facilitated centralization' (1989: 13).

Whether it is the state which homogenizes ethnicity or some other socio-economic and political processes (how can one explain the Kurdish national ethnicity? – they never had a state), it is important to recognize, as both Smith and Zubaida have done, and as we mentioned in the previous chapter, that there is an inherent connection between the ethnic and national projects. While it is important to look at the historical specificity of the construction of collectivities, there is no inherent difference (although sometimes there is a difference of scale) between ethnic and national collectivities: they are both the Andersonian 'imagined communities'.

What is specific to the nationalist project and discourse is the claim for a separate political representation for the collectivity. This often – but not always – takes the form of a claim for a separate state.

The conflation of 'state' and 'nation-state' is problematic in several ways, some of which we shall mention later in the chapter in relation to citizenship and multi-culturalism. Here, however, it is relevant to mention Otto Bauer's position (Bauer 1940, Nimni 1991, Yuval-Davis 1987a); he saw as a possible adequate political solution for nations with no territorial continuity (as was the case in the Austro-Hungarian empire where he wrote) an eventual separation between nationality (and national political representations) and the state. This is somewhat similar to the separation between religion and the state – an unimaginable state of affairs during earlier periods of European history. This, of course, raises the semantic question of the extent to which one can distinguish between the boundaries of a civil society and the boundaries of a nation.

DEFINITIONS OF THE 'NATION'

If nations are not to be identified with nation-states – in reality or in potential – one questions if there are any objective characteristics according to which nations can be recognized. This question is not purely theoretical, given the wide consensus regarding the right of nations to self-determination. While Marx and Engels developed a tautological differentiation between 'historical nations' which are entitled to their own states and 'history-less' nations which are not, Lenin differentiated between nations who fight against their oppression by others and therefore have the right to be supported by socialists, and oppressing nations who do not (Davis 1978, Lenin 1972). Stalin, who, when he came to power, differentiated between 'positive' 'proletarian nations' and 'negative' 'bourgeois nations' (1976), is best known in this respect for the 'formula definition' he developed at an earlier period as 'the expert on the national question' among the Bolsheviks. According to Stalin, 'A nation is a historically evolved, stable community of language, territory, economic life and psychological make-up manifested in a community of culture' (1972: 13).

In contrast, Otto Bauer's definition dispensed with the economy, language and territory (although in objecting to the Bund's adoption of his model for the Jewish collectivity, Bauer claimed that a certain territorial concentration is vital for the development of a nation (Bauer 1940, Yuval-Davis 1987a). He concentrated on a common culture and on what he called 'common destiny'.

This element of common destiny is of crucial importance and is what is lacking from Smith's focus on the ethnic origins of nations. It has future, rather than just past, orientation, and can explain more than individual and communal assimilations within particular nations. On the one hand, it can explain the subjective sense of commitment of people into collectivities and nations, such as in settler societies, or in post-colonial states, in which there is no shared myth of common origin (Stasiulis and Yuval-Davis, forthcoming). At the same time it can also explain the dynamic nature of any national collectivity and the perpetual reconstruction of boundaries which take place in them, via immigration, naturalization, conversion and other similar social and political processes.

A third element in the definition of the 'nation' is either derived from or a precondition to a shared myth of 'common origin' or 'common destiny', or both. This is the element of 'common solidarity', so emphasized by the French historian Ernest Renan, and it presupposes the other two elements:

> A nation is a grand solidarity constituted by the sentiment of sacrifices which one has made and those that one is disposed to make again. It supposes a past, it renews itself especially in the present by a tangible deed: the approval, the desire, clearly expressed, to continue the communal life. (1882: 27)

PRODUCERS AND REPRODUCERS OF NATIONALIST IDEOLOGIES

In an attempt to locate the specific social agents of the production and reproduction of the phenomena of nationalism and nations, materialist analyses, such as those by Amin (1978) and Zubaida (1979) and Wallerstein (1974), give primary importance to state bureaucracy and other state apparatuses in establishing and reproducing national (as well as ethnic) ideologies and boundaries. Although national and ethnic divisions operate also within the civil society, it is the differential access of different collectivities to the state which dictates the nature of the hegemonic national ethos in the society (Anthias and Yuval-Davis 1989).

Other theorists of nationalism and the sociology of knowledge, such as Smith and Gellner, have stressed the particular importance intellectuals have had in the creation and reproduction of nationalist ideologies, especially those of oppressed collectivities. Being excluded from the hegemonic intelligentsia and from open access to the state apparatus, they 'rediscover' 'collective memories', transform popular oral traditions and languages into written ones, and portray a 'national golden age' in the far – mythical or historical – past, whose reconstitution becomes the basis for nationalist aspirations.

Unlike bureaucrats and intellectuals, women are virtually never mentioned in the theoretical literature on nationalism. And yet, as we have elaborated elsewhere (Yuval-Davis, 1980; Anthias and Yuval-Davis 1989), women have been playing crucial roles in the reproduction of national collectivities and states – and not only in the biological sense, by giving birth to the future members of the collectivity. The construction of the individual's subjectivity – in which collective myths, symbols and identifications are embedded in an individual *Weltanschauung* – is founded and formed primarily during the early part of childhood. Here, too, is the acquisition of the mother-tongue (*sic!*), taste in food and other facets of one's way of life. This is, of course, the period when the rearing of the children is usually done by mothers or other women.

But women have additional important roles in the construction and reproduction of nationalist ideologies. By dressing and behaving 'properly', and by giving birth to children within legitimate marriages, they both signify and reproduce the symbolic and legal boundaries of the collectivity. More than that, a female is often used as the actual symbolic figuration of the nation; *la patrie* was a figure of woman giving birth to the nation in the French Revolution – the same revolution that limited its universal message to the *fraternité* – the brotherhood of men! (Pateman 1988, Vogel 1989, Yuval-Davis 1991b). Also, the defence of 'Womenandchildren' (Enloe 1990) is a usual ideological legitimation of men going to war. Last, but not least, women also participate in national projects and struggles themselves – either as members of the national collectivity, or in their specific role as mothers – as has been the case in many recent Third-World struggles, in Argentina, South Africa and Palestine, to mention but a few.

DIFFERENT KINDS OF NATIONALIST PROJECTS

So far we have discussed nations and nationalist ideologies as if they were a single phenomenon. However, as Sami Zubaida pointed out back in 1978, 'The general designation of "nationalism" as a unitary object or phenomenon and the general "theories" of it . . . would not help very much in the task of adequate analysis of particular social formations' (p. 70).

There have been many attempts to classify the different kinds of nationalist movements and nationalist ideologies which have arisen in the world during the last two hundred years. Good summaries of these classifications can be found both in Snyder (1968: chapter 4) and Smith (1971: chapter 8). Two 'classical' typologies relate to the 'moral' nature of various nationalist projects. The typology of Kohn (1967) differentiates between 'western' and 'eastern' nationalisms – between the benevolent Western Europe nationalism and the oppressive nationalism of the rest of the world. Hayes (1948) developed a more universalistic model based on a basic differentiation between what he called 'original' (liberationist) and 'derived' (post-independence oppressive) nationalism. More recent classifications have tried to maintain scientific neutralism. Either they take the form of historical taxonomies (which focus virtually exclusively on Europe), or of sociological taxonomies (which focus on the various social locations and specific goals of the national movements, both of majority or minority, aimed either at secession or pan-national liberation, etc).

Anthony Smith (1971, 1986) has developed a typology which is based on the specific character of the nationalist project, including both the 'ethnic-genealogical' movement and the 'civic-territorial' movement. In this he is continuing a German tradition which tends to differentiate between nation-states and state-nations, or, to use the terminology used by Stolke (1987) – *Kulturnations* and *Staatnations*. This dichotomous division, however, conflates origin and culture. We would differentiate between *Staatnation, Kulturnation* and *Folknation;* in other words, between nationalist ideologies which focus on citizenship of specific states (in specific territories), such as American nationalism in its 'purest form'; those which focus on specific cultures (or religions) – such as classical French nationalism, or Pakistani nationalism; and those which are constructed around the specific origin of the people (or their race) – such as classical German nationalism, or White South Africanism.

However, rather than attempting to classify all different states and societies according to these different types – an ahistorical, impossible and misleading mission as most such classifications of social phenomena are – we shall turn next to a brief discussion of the issues of nationalism in relation to these three dimensions of nationalist ideologies and projects, especially those aspects most affecting the interrelationship between nationalism and racism. As we shall see later in the chapter, British nationalism has elements of all three types of nationalist ideologies.

NATIONALISM AND CITIZENSHIP

It is not only in 'new nations' that citizenship is used, at least in some ways, to indicate membership in a national collectivity. Theodor Shanin once remarked (1986) that in English (and French) – as opposed to East European and other languages – there is what he called 'a missing term' which defines nationality in its ethnic rather than its civic meaning. For one product of the historical circumstances of the rise of the nation-state in Western Europe is an inherent assumption that, in the nation-state, there is an overlap between the boundaries of civil and political society (to use Hegel's and Marx's terminology), the members of the national collectivity and the citizens of the state (Anthias and Yuval-Davis 1989). The most popular definition of citizenship which is used, at least in British social science, is that of T. H. Marshall (1950, 1975, 1981). He defines citizenship as 'membership in a community'. This definition, as we have elaborated elsewhere (Yuval-Davis 1991b), assumes a given collectivity, with pre-defined boundaries.

This is not to say, of course, that Marshall and his followers assume that all those who are included in the community also enjoy citizenship rights. On the contrary, Marshall's work constructs an evolutionary model in which more and more people who are members of the civil society gradually acquire citizenship rights. But the boundaries of the society and of the community are virtually static in this model. The differentiation between civil and political societies is a functional differentiation, relating to the same national collectivity or community and the people within it, rather than marking, as is usually the case, two kinds of groupings whose boundaries partially overlap. Members of the national collectivity can also live in the diaspora and be citizens of other states, while some citizens and permanent residents can be members of other national collectivities. In addition there can be cases in which a national collectivity is divided between several neighbouring countries (such as the Kurds). Moreover, there can be cases of disagreement about the boundaries of the membership in the national collectivity based on conflicting ideologies. (For example, such categories as Arab Jews and Black British can be compatible for some and incompatible for others when relating to the same national collectivities.)

As Stuart Hall and David Held (1989) point out, in real politics, the main, if not the only arena in the west in which questions of citizenship have remained alive until recently, has been the discourse about race and immigration, questions which challenge any notion of fixed boundaries of the 'community'.

Debates concerning the citizenship of ethnic and racial minorities have developed in relation to all levels of citizenship – civil, political and social (to use Marshall's categories). However, the primary concern of many relevant struggles and debates has been an even more basic right: the right to enter, or, once having entered, the right to remain in a specific country. Boundaries are constructed according to various inclusionary and exclusionary criteria, which relate not only to ethnic and racial divisions but also to those of class and gender. This central arena of struggle concerning citizenship remains completely outside the agenda of Marshallian theories of citizenship. The 'freedom of movement within the European community', the Israeli Law of Return and the German nationality law, are all instances of ideological, often racist, constructions of boundaries which allow unrestricted immigration to some and block it completely to others.

Racist boundaries of citizenship and freedom of movement do not always relate to outside immigrants. In settler societies such inhibitions apply also to the indigenous people. For example, the Australian Aborigines received the right of citizenship only in 1967, and Black South Africans are only now in the process of achieving it. The same can apply to stateless minorities, as has been the case for Jews and Gypsies in large parts of Europe.

Even when questions of entry and settlement have been resolved, the concerns of people of ethnic minorities might be different from those of other members of the society. For example, their right to formal citizenship might depend upon the rules and regulations of their country of origin as well as those of the country where they live, as well as the relationship between the two. The USA, for example, allows dual citizenship with certain countries but not with others. Concern over relatives and fear of not being allowed to visit their country of origin prevent others (such as Turkish migrant workers in Germany) from giving up their original citizenship. Thus, although they might spend the rest of their lives in another country, they would have, at best, limited political rights in it. Also, given specific combinations of nationality laws, children can be born stateless in countries such as Israel and Britain. Such countries confer citizenship on those whose parents are citizens rather than on those born in the country.

Immigrants can also be deprived of social rights enjoyed by other members of the society. Often, the right of entry to a country is conditioned on a commitment by the immigrant that neither he nor she nor any other member of their family would claim any welfare benefits from the state. Proof of a sizeable fortune in the bank can be used to override national and racial quotas for the right to settle in a country. Class difference, therefore, can sometimes override ethnic and racial difference.

Gender differences are also important in this context. Women of majority and minority groups are affected differently by sexist limitations to their citizenship rights. This can concern their right to enter the country or bring in their husbands, their right to receive child benefits or their right to confer citizenship on their children, to mention just a few examples (WING 1985). Similarly, men and women of ethnic and racial minorities suffer from gender specific racisms: they can have different legal rights (for instance for getting permits to bring their families into the country); they would often have different rates of participation in political organizations, and similar differences would exist between them on a whole host of civil and social rights (see Southall Black Sisters 1990).

Differential access to the state and its resources can also exist among different ethnic and racial minorities within the same state just as their location within the labour market can be very different. Some minorities would have high access to welfare benefits and low access to employment, while others, in the same state, would be employed as cheap labour and would have almost no access at all to welfare benefits.

Of course, it is not only ethnic and racial minorities which have differential access to the state. Various regions within the boundaries of the same 'national collectivity' can sometimes have such different levels of access to the state, that Hechter (1975) and others developed the model of 'internal colonialism' to analyse the relationship between them. These, together with class, gender, age and other cross-cutting differences within the civil society which affect their access to the state, highlight the fact that the state should not be seen as a neutral universalistic institution. Neither can the 'national projects' of the state (both in times of peace and in times of war) be seen as equally representing the interests of all members of the nation.

NATION AND CULTURE

Political divisions which are so easily and intuitively understood in relation to state politics become much more obscure when in relation to the nation. Patriotism is supposed to affect everyone similarly, whether from upper or lower classes, man or woman. 'Our troops' have to be cheered, whether the 'national project' in hand is the Gulf War or an international cricket game.

This mythical unity, this imagined community which divides the world between 'us' and 'them', is maintained and ideologically reproduced by a whole system of what Armstrong (1982) calls symbolic 'border guards'. These border guards can identify people as members or non-members of a specific collectivity. They are closely linked to specific cultural codes of style of dress and behaviour as well as to more elaborate bodies of customs, literary and artistic modes of production, and, of course, language. These border guards are used as shared cultural resources and, together with shared collective positioning *vis-à-vis* other collectivities, they can provide the collectivity members not only with the Andersonian 'imagined communities', but also with what Deutch (1966) and Schlesinger (1987) call 'communicative communities':

> Membership in a people consists in wide complementarity of social communication. It consists in the ability to communicate more effectively, and over a wider range of subjects, with members of one large group than with outsiders. (Deutch 1966: 97)

It is important, however, not to reify these border guards as the national culture. They are cultural resources which are used in the struggles for hegemony which take place, at any specific moment, not only between collectivities but also within them. Different, sometimes conflicting, cultural border guards can be used simultaneously by different members of the collectivity. One example is the use of different Suras in the Koran to argue for and against abortions in Egypt; another is the promotion of Hebrew versus Yiddish by Zionists and Bundists respectively. Although at certain historical moments there might be a hegemonic construction of the collectivity's culture and history, its dynamic, evolving, historical nature, continuously re-invents, reconstructs, reproduces and develops the cultural inventory of various collectivities. In extreme cases, these processes involve not only the redefinition of boundaries but also the complete dissolution or transformation of the collectivity and its positioning of difference *vis-à-vis* other collectivities. Two such examples are the 'absorption' of East Germany into the 'new' (and old) Germany, and the evolving category of the 'African American'.

The ability to communicate more easily, which is prevalent among members of the same collectivity, derives not only from a common sharing of cultural forms, but also, on a deeper level, from the fact that national cultures can supply answers to some basic human questions regarding one's position in the world, the meaning of history, and what 'proper' behaviour is. This is done through the absorption, on conscious and unconscious levels, of what Smith (1986) calls 'the mythomoteur': that is, the constitutive myth of the ethnic polity which describes how and why the collectivity was created, why it is unique, and what its mission is. Although this constitutive myth would have different versions among different classes and segments within the collectivity, it would be continously narrated.

NATIONALISM AND RELIGION

The questions which are dealt with by the 'mythomoteur' parallel very closely the general questions about the meaning of life and beyond which are answered by religious systems. It is not surprising, therefore, that 'modernist' theorists of nationalism saw nationalism as replacing religion, which was expected eventually to 'wither away' in a secularized world (see Althusser 1969, Anderson 1983).

The reality, of course, is very different. Religion, in the form of liberation theology, and even more so in the form of religious fundamentalism, is rising all over the world. Even in Eastern Europe, where religion was excised from the public domain for more than fifty years, it has had a major come-back, probably more powerful than ever. And some of the most enduring and problematic international and inter-ethnic conflicts in the world today – whether in Northern Ireland, the Middle East or the Indian sub-continent – are waged in the name of religion.

There are two major reasons for this. The negative one concerns the failure of the secularist-enlightenment project within which Eurocentric nationalisms have established themselves. The positive one relates to the centrality of religious codes in existing national cultural codes.

The crushing failure of the civil religion which was attempted in France after the Revolution should have probably alerted social scientists to the limits of rationality and human-centred cosmology. While some of the nationalist 'mythomoteurs' in Europe linked their constitutive moments to pre-Christian times, only very rarely was Christianity fully excluded on that ground. Despite the development of secularist ideologies which completely rejected religion as an anachronism in the age of enlightenment, the prevalence of liberal ideologies in Western Europe meant that on the political level, religion was at most pushed into the voluntary sector rather than banned from the public domain. Moreover, the long struggles for the recognition of religious pluralism did not necessarily secularize the national culture. Even in the USA, which established total separation between church and state, the national slogan is 'In God We Trust'. By God is meant the Christian God, or, at most, the Judeo-Christian God. Thus biblical myths and narrations, Christian holidays as national holidays, musical and other cultural heritage, as well as an ethical code which is broadly based on the Christian code, have continued to survive and be reproduced (although probably minus the literal ideas of post-mortem heaven and hell – people became much more occupied with heaven and hell on earth).

However, this was not unproblematic. With the withdrawal of active state support for religious institutions, and the hegemony of rational discourse in the scientific and political spheres, churches gradually started to lose their hold over people and membership in religious institutions dropped. As Don Cupitt has put it,

> There is a world of difference between a society in which your religious beliefs are supported by reason and confirmed by daily experience, and a society like ours in which the truth of religious beliefs is no longer a matter of common knowledge and, what is worse, the religious consciousness itself has come to be regarded by many people as deviant. (1991: 32)

Given that religious ethics have continued to be the basis for the moral code in the nationalist social order, together with failures in the modernist enlightenment project (Bauman 1991), secularization has brought fears of anomy, nihilism and a general sense of disorientation which, among other factors, has prompted the rise of religious fundamentalism in the west.

At the same time, religious specificity has proved to be more durable and resistant to assimilation than many other parts of nationalist cultures. Moreover, in many countries, especially in the Third World, traditional religions were incorporated into, rather than replaced by, the new national states. (This was usually done, however, in a selective and controlled manner, often by concentrating on personal law and through use of women as cultural symbols of the national collectivity (Yuval-Davis 1980, 1991; Sahgal and Yuval-Davis 1992). With repeated failures by nationalist and socialist movements to bring about successful liberation from oppression, exploitation and poverty, both in the Third World and among Third-World minorities in the west, religion has become both a comfort and a base for new militant mass mobilizations. As the boundaries of the 'new nations' have often been imposed by the ex-colonial powers, religion (unlike secular nationalism, which has been identified as a western project) has been utilized by militants for their nationalist projects as an 'indigenous' ideology with which to confront imperialism and racism. This, of course, has not been confined to the Third World. Catholicism, for instance, in both Ireland and Poland, has played a similar role.

The continuation of the co-opted, non-problematic reproduction of religious codes within nationalist cultures has also been affected by the growing heterogeneity of western societies through the gradual settlement of new Third-World minorities in them. This has been the result of post-Second World War labour migration (Castles 1984), as well as of immigration of refugees and others from their countries of origin. These minorities did not share part or all of the dominant nationalist cultural code and therefore have forced the question of the relationship of the nationalist project to multi-culturalism.

NATIONALISM AND MULTI-CULTURALISM

Different national collectivities are constructed with varying degrees of tolerance to cultural difference. 'New nations' or states which from their inception have included more than one collectivity (as Switzerland or Belgium), have some built-in mechanisms to deal with questions of cultural difference, at least of certain kinds, although their effectiveness depends on the specific political situation. For example, there might be more than one formal language (like in Canada) or they might offer, as an institutional right, interpreters for those who cannot speak the formal language (as in Australia).

Other countries (or the same countries in relation to cultures of minorities outside the constitutive ones) might be much less tolerant of cultural difference. The recent debate in France about the schoolgirls who wore headscarfs is but a symptom of the persistence of the French perspective, so prevalent during French imperialism, that living under French rule must involve becoming culturally French as well.

. Even in countries where there is a formal policy of multi-culturalism, there are problems. In Chapter 6 we shall discuss problems of multi-culturalism as an anti-racist strategy. Here we want to point out some of the more theoretical problems relating to multi-culturalism and the boundaries of difference.

First of all, defining the boundaries of difference between the actual different cultures is problematic. Which cultures, or elements of cultures, would be 'legitimately' included in the multi-culturalist vision and which would not? Outlawing cultural systems such as polygamy or the ritual use of drugs immediately come to mind, as well as, for instance, such issues as the Aborigines' demands to apply their customary laws among themselves rather than the laws of the state. How tolerant the hegemonic culture is about various social practices clearly will determine what can or cannot be allowed.

However, hegemonic legitimacy is not the only deciding factor. There is also what the Australian 'National agenda for a multi-culturalist Australia' calls 'the boundaries of multi-culturalism'. An important issue in allocating resources under multi-culturalist policies to different cultural 'needs', is the determination of what are considered to be 'private needs' and what are 'public collective needs'. The boundaries between public and private are socially determined, within specific cultural, class and gender contexts (Jayasuriya 1990, Yuval-Davis 1991b). Whether or not facilities for specific religious needs, child-care facilities for working mothers or certain leisure activities are provided, depends, among other factors, on who has the power of decision at a specific point of time.

An even more basic problem in the construction of multi-culturalism is the assumption that all members of a specific cultural collectivity are equally committed to that culture. It tends to construct the members of minority collectivities as basically homogeneous, speaking with a unified cultural voice. These cultural voices have to be as distinguishable as possible from the majority culture in order to be seen as 'different'; thus, the more traditional and distanced from the majority culture the voice of the 'community representatives' is, the more 'authentic' it would be perceived to be within such a construction.

Therefore, such a construction would not have space for internal power conflicts and interest difference within the minority collectivity: conflicts along the lines of class and gender as well as of politics and culture, for instance. So the whole notion of multi-culturalism assumes definite, static, ahistorical and essentialist units of 'culture' with fixed boundaries and with no space for growth and change.

An alternative dynamic model of cultural pluralism has been developed by Homi Bhabha (1990). Emphasizing the constantly changing boundaries of the national imagined communities and of the narratives which constitute their collective cultural discourses, Bhabha notes the emerging counter-narratives from the nation's margins, by those cultural hybrids who have lived, because of migration or exile, in more than one culture. Those hybrids both evoke and erase the 'totalizing boundaries' of the nation. Such counter-narratives do not have to come, of course, from immigrant minorities. The growing voice of Indians in Canada, for example, is an instance of a counter-narrative which is heard from within. On a much larger scale, such counter-narratives are disintegrating, such as, at the moment of writing, the 'Soviet nation'. It is important to note in this context, however, that 'counter-narratives', even if radical in their form, do not necessarily have to be progressive in their message.

NATION AND *VOLK*

While Homi Bhabha's analysis emphasizes the constantly changing boundaries of national collectivities, some at least of the nationalist ideologies completely reject such a perspective, and condition membership in the national collectivity on being born into it. (The requirements vary. Sometimes it must be both parents, and sometimes only the father or the mother who have to be members of the collectivity. In the extreme Nazi case, even one great-grandparent from the wrong 'blood' was enough to 'contaminate' the 'purity' of the race.)

Occasionally even birth into the national collectivity would not be enough: marriage to an 'outsider', especially by women, could exclude one from the national collectivity. In Egypt, for instance, there is no legal status for a Muslim woman who married a Copt. In other cases, particularly in *staatnations*, receiving citizenship and being assimilated are sufficient. (However, this might prove impossible in many national cultures for people with different physical appearances, at least before several generations of intermarriage.)

Can there be, then, a general relationship between nationalism and racism? As mentioned above, Hayes and Kohn both divided nationalist projects into liberationist and exclusionary – depending where they developed or what stage of development they reached. More recently Tom Nairn (1977) described nationalism as a Janus, with two opposite facets. Eli Kedourie (1960), on the other hand, sees nationalism as always inherently illiberal and in constant tension with universalism.

Anderson (1983) separates absolutely nationalism and racism. For him nationalism and racism are opposite sentiments. He views nationalism as a positive sentiment, 'which thinks in terms of historical destinies', while racist discourse is negative:

> racism dreams of eternal contaminations, transmitted from the origins of time . . . On the whole, racism and anti-Semitism manifest themselves, not across national boundaries but within them. (1983: 136)

While it is clear that not all nationalist ideologies are equally racist, we do not accept Anderson's dichotomy. Wherever a delineation of boundaries takes place, as is the case with every ethnic and national collectivity, processes of exclusion and inclusion are in operation. These can take place, as we discussed, with varying degrees of intensity, and with a variety of cultural, religious and state mechanisms. But exclusions of 'the other' can become a positive and inherent part of national ethnicities. Nazi Germany and Apartheid South Africa are two examples in which such exclusions have become a major and even an obsessive preoccupation for the national culture. But, in lesser degrees, many, if not most, other ethnicities of hegemonic national collectivities include elements of racist exclusion within their symbolic orders.

In the second part of the chapter we shall look at the situation in Britain. Like Sivanandan (1982), Miles (1982a), Gilroy (1987), Cohen (1988) and other critics of British nationalism, we argue that racism is an inherent part of the hegemonic Anglomorphic ethnicity in Britain. To substantiate this, we shall look at the exclusionary and inclusionary assumptions in the construction of British nationality.

THE BOUNDARIES OF THE BRITISH NATIONAL COLLECTIVITY

Phil Cohen argues,

> Racism is not something 'tacked on' to English history, by virtue of its imperialist phase, one of its abberant moments; it is *constitutive* of what has come to be known as the 'British way of life'. (1988: 3)

Indeed, with the development of capitalism we see at least two types of exclusionary ideologies emerging which use biological determinism (in its pre- and post-Darwinian formations (Downing 1980)) as a justification for the emerging social order. One type relates to the internal class structure of English (and other western) society, and is an attempt to 'explain' the growing social inequalities in the 'home countries' in an era influenced by universal human rights ideologies (Stolke 1981: 37). As Hobsbawm (1975: 247–8) points out,

> Hence the growing importance of the alternative theories of biological class superiority, which pervade so much of the nineteenth century bourgeois *Weltanschauung.* Superiority was the result of natural selection, genetically transmitted. The bourgeois was, if not a different species, then at least the member of a superior race, a higher stage of human evolution, distinct from the lower orders which remained in the historical or cultural equivalent of childhood or at most adolescence.

The second type of exclusionary ideology is specifically racist, and was developed as an explanatory principle of the constitution of the English nation itself. MacDougall claims that by the mid-seventeenth century there was

> the first comprehensive presentation of a theory of national origin based on the belief in the racial superiority of the

Germanic people, a theme repeated a thousand times in succeeding centuries. (1982: 49)

Whether or not one agrees with MacDougall, or one agrees with Banton (1977: 18–25) that the notion of 'race' transformed itself from a mark of lineage to a mark of superiority only in the nineteenth century, it is clear that by then it served, as Miles (1985: 11–12) points out, a dual object: to explain both the hierarchy of interdependence between the English and the colonial races, and the difference in productive relations and material wealth between England and much of the rest of the world at this time.

Exclusionary and racist ideologies were used, then, as the basis for legitimizing the domination and exploitation of other collectivities by the British empire: at 'home' ('the lower orders'); 'close to home' (racism against the Celts – especially the Irish); and then further afield, against what is known today as the Third World, that which constituted most of the British empire. P. Wright (1985) has written on how racism has been fundamental to national identity in Britain, intrinsic to the sense of what he calls 'Deep England' to which those who truly belong are naturally attuned and from which outsiders are forever excluded. War and the summoning up of imperial greatness serve as 'quickening' agents to inform a 'united people' who they really are.

This construction of a united people is based in specific historical circumstances. As Tom Nairn (1977) claims, British nationalism has been patrician in its character because there was never a need to mobilize the English working class in order to carry out a bourgeois revolution. He argues (pp. 368–9) that the Anglo-British nationality is 'strong but synthetic; there have never been "Britons" except in newspaper disaster lists ('Indian air crash, 8 Britons feared lost'), any more than there were "Austro-Hungarians" before 1917'. What unites them all, he claims, referring to the Anglo-British nationality, is that 'the mass political reflexes it rested upon were unbroken by revolution nor tested by defeat and national humiliation'. It 'was uniquely stamped by collusion with imperialism'. This, according to Nairn (p. 43), created 'a particularly powerful inter-class nationalism – a sense of underlying insular identity and common fate, which both recognized and yet easily transcended marked class and regional divisions'.

Nationalism, like racism, is not a homogeneous ideology in Britain. Differences of class, place of birth, ethnic origin, religion, political beliefs, gender and other factors radically affect the specific kinds of collectivity ideologies different segments of the British population hold and the ways they construct their boundaries (see, for example, the discussion of Phil Cohen (1988) on the different codes of breeding carried by different classes in British society). The ideological constructions discussed in the following sections of the chapter are those which have achieved hegemony and have been applied in various state practices. State policies themselves are not unitary and are often contradictory. However, they can represent certain states of contestation among different social forces in relation to different political projects.

Any attempt to generalize on such a complex, diverse, and constantly changing issue as the construction of the British national boundaries is doomed to be over-simplistic. And yet, outlining the main dimensions about which ideological and legal discourse over boundaries is taking place in contemporary Britain might help to clarify some of these complex interrelationships and the ways they relate to different sorts of racialized exclusions in the construction of the national collectivity.

One major dimension includes the struggles which exist over the internal division of Britain into England, Scotland, Wales, and Northern Ireland. The fiercest struggle and the most racialized one relates to Northern Ireland. Another dimension concerns Britain's imperial past and the post-Second World War settlement of minorities from former colonies and then from other Third-World countries in Britain. A third dimension relates to the character of Britain as a Christian society and to its links with Europe.

'THE BREAK-UP OF BRITAIN'

In the 1991 census there is a specific question concerning 'the country of birth' of the British population. However, the categories of the requested answers do not include countries in the different continents from which people come to the UK. The census results would not enable the public to have information concerning how many Americans, East Europeans or Japanese live in Britain. The 'countries of birth' which are mentioned are: England, Scotland, Wales, Northern Ireland – and the Irish Republic.

A unified concept of the boundaries of the British national

collectivity has never existed. Tribal, and later regional collectivities have always existed in varying degrees of power and
saliency, partially overlapping the hegemonic construct created by
the state boundaries. However, the relative positions of the various
sub-collectivities were not equal. Robert Miles (1982b: 287)
describes how 'While in England, "Englishness" and "Britishness"
tend to be overlapping and equally positive political identities, in
Scotland "Scottishness" and "Britishness" are distinct and not
equally positive political identities.' 'For those living in England,
therefore, this has meant that national identity is fluid and
imprecise, floating between "Englishness" and "Britishness" because the centre of economic, political and ideological power in
Britain is in London (and so England).'

The relationship between the English and what Hechter (1975)
has called 'the Celtic fringe' in Britain has largely been that of an
uneven exchange between centre and periphery. This uneven
exchange also exists within England itself. The boundaries of the
division of Britain into 'North' and 'South' which have deepened
under Thatcherism pass within England rather than between
England and Scotland, Wales and Northern Ireland. However, the
separate histories of identifications, domination and resistance of
the different components of the 'United Kingdom' persist.
Paradoxically, the move of Britain into the European Community
is supporting the gradual, if limited, move of these components
into greater autonomy and self-rule. Further, the discovery of oil
off Scotland's shores has been a major issue in the relationship
between England and Scotland. The anti-poll tax movement which
helped to bring down Margaret Thatcher in England, started in
Scotland, where it took the character of a national campaign. Tom
Nairn's vision of the 'break-up of Britain' (1977) is far from being
materialized, but the national boundaries within the UK,
especially in relation to Scotland, are being strengthened.

The fiercest struggle on national boundaries within the UK is
taking place in Northern Ireland, where, during the last twenty-two
years British troops have been occupying the country, ostensibly to
keep the social order. There the Republicans and the Unionists
fight over whether Northern Ireland should join the Republic of
Ireland, stay part of the UK, or – as many believe – have autonomy
from both (Curtis 1984; Rossiter, forthcoming).

While the national divisions which divide Northern Ireland are
constructed primarily in terms of religion and class, there has also

been a certain racialization of this division. All Celts, and especially the Irish Celts, have been considered an inferior, often dangerous 'other' in British history. They were the first to be colonized and to be used as a reserve army of labour. The film *Red-legs in Barbados* (1987, Channel 4) documents the terrible conditions of life and the enslavement of exiled prisoners, mainly Irish, which were sent to the Caribbean islands before a large number of African slaves were brought there and to other British colonies. It also quotes reports and diaries of the day, in which these prisoners are constructed as sub-human animals. Indeed in them the exclusionary discourses of internal class divisions and external race divisions have been enmeshed.

In more recent periods of Britain's imperial past, the Irish and other Celts have joined, at least to a certain extent, the hegemonic colonial ethnicity. In Australia, for instance, despite internal divisions which persisted well into the twentieth century, the hegemonic ethnicity is called Anglo-Celtic (unlike the Anglo-Saxon one in both Britain and the USA, for instance) (de Lepervanche 1991; Yuval-Davis 1991b).

In contemporary Britain, the Irish, both from the Republic of Ireland and from Northern Ireland, constitute the largest ethnic minority. They are a major source of migrant labour. As such, they are constructed with a strange combination of invisibility and exclusion. On the one hand, they have never been included – at least until the late 1980s in a very minimal way – in the British 'Race Relations Industry', in which ethnicity is constituted virtually exclusively in terms of colour (see discussion in Chapter 6). As Whites , they were not considered threatening, nor perceived to be 'swamping' the country. Therefore they have not been subjected to immigration controls in entering the country. This is now the case with all the other members of the European Community, who are allowed to work and settle in Britain, no matter what state of unemployment exists in the country.

On the other hand, unlike other members of the European community, a census question is being asked about the Irish. So they are not just an indistinguishable part of the British proletariat, or of the European Community. Because of the ongoing civil war in Northern Ireland, they are all considered potential 'dangerous IRA terrorists' or at least callous supporters of their actions. The collective criminalization of the Irish, like the collective criminalization of Black youth, does not exist only in the realm of interpersonal prejudice but is also institutionalized by law, via the use of the anti-terrorist laws. Like the notorious SUS laws against Blacks, these laws give the police authority to arrest people without giving any reason. Suspicion based on 'a hunch' is sufficient cause.

'THE EMPIRE STRIKES BACK'

While the Irish have been contradictorily constructed as part of the collectivity of White Europeans on the one hand, and outside it as migrant labour and 'dangerous terrorists' on the other, people from what is known as 'NCWP countries' (New Commonwealth Countries and Pakistan) have been racialized as inferior, or dangerous and foreign, and therefore outside the boundaries of the British national collectivity. Even in counter-ideological constructions which defended the rights of the NCWP settlers in Britain, they have been constructed as outsiders, as essentially different. To use the terminology of the anti-discrimination legislation, they are a 'race' apart. The role of Britain's imperial past in these constructions, however, has been changing.

Paul Gilroy (1987), when rejecting Anderson's separation between racism and nationalism in the British case, points to the patriality clause in the British immigration law in 1968 as their common articulation:

> It is important to recognize that the legal concept of patriality, introduced by the Immigration Act of 1968, codified this cultural biology of 'race' into statute law as part of a strategy for the exclusion of Black settlers. (1987: 45)

The patriality law Gilroy refers to demonstrates the way in which British immigration law reflects Britain's coming to terms with its loss of empire. It constructs a legal boundary between the colonizers and the colonized, something for which there was no need in the earlier period of imperial glory.

The widest boundaries of the British national collectivity existed during the height of the British empire. They were not merely boundaries of state control but came to signify a national symbol of a global superiority 'where the sun never sets'. It was not only a question of territory; both British colonies and the British colonized were seen as an inherent part of the national glory, as inherent as the feeling of racial superiority of the Anglo-Saxons, and later on, in the empire's periphery, (such as Australia) of the Anglo-Celtic, over those they ruled. The 'White Man's Burden', as Rudyard Kipling wrote (1899), included the almost sacred duty to rule and to 'civilize':

> Take up the White Man's burden –
>   Send forth the best ye breed –
> Go, bind your sons to exile
>   To serve your captives' need;
> To wait in heavy harness
>   On fluttered folk and wild –
> Your new-caught, sullen peoples
>   Half-devil and half-child.

After the Second World War, with the beginning of the decline of the empire on the one hand, and the growing need, for a time, for migrant labour in Britain, on the other, the external (colonial) and internal (class) dynamics of exclusion combined in Britain itself. To a great extent this new constellation shaped the struggle over national boundaries and immigration controls in Britain for the next four decades.

Until the 1981 Nationality law, the concept of British nationality was connected not so much to membership in the national collectivity but to loyalty to the British monarch (hence the use of the legal term 'British subject' rather than 'British citizen'). Historically, under common law, loyalty to the monarch was considered an automatic outcome of being born in Britain, no matter who one's parents were. Therefore, for a long time, children of British parents who were born abroad were considered aliens. Only with the expansion of the British empire did things start to change. At first both fathers and mothers could transfer British citizenship to their children (if the mothers travelled abroad with their husbands' permission (WING 1985: 11)) and between 1740 and the 1981 Nationality Law, exclusively via their legal fathers.

Since the concept of British nationality was connected to British sovereignty, the boundaries of the national collectivity expanded as the British empire expanded. And just as the concept of British nationality did not differentiate within Britain between people of different classes, it also did not differentiate in the colonies between the colonized and the colonizers, and included international as well as intranational divisions of labour within the empire.

No legal or other effort was made to limit emigration from the

British Isles and there was a generous readiness to give the title of British subject to the inhabitants of every territory the British had conquered. However, unlike the French empire, for instance, there were no intensive efforts made to convert the 'natives' in the British empire to the English culture (this despite the fact that English culture and England as the 'mother country' became popular ideological constructions particularly among the middle and upper classes of the colonized).

In contrast to this form of inclusiveness in the empire, exclusionary positions started to emerge in relation to settlement and nationality inside Britain itself. These questions were not initially raised concerning the groups of migrant labourers (who often came on a short-term basis, as did the Irish), but concerning immigrants who came as refugees to settle in Britain (mainly East European Jews, who came around the turn of the twentieth century).

As well as being a country of emigration, Britain has always been a country of immigration. Some, especially in Britain's earlier history, arrived as conquerers, such as the Romans, Anglo-Saxons, Vikings and Normans. Others, such as the Jews, French Huguenots and Irish, came to settle peacefully, attracted by prospects of political security and economic prosperity. Yet others, such as Africans and Asians, were brought in as slaves or servants.

Similarly, immigration and settlement in Britain in the twentieth century, including the post-Second World War period, has been far from homogeneous. Like all other metropolitan societies, Britain, and especially London, has attracted tourists, students, professionals, and social activists from all over the world, some of whom have remained in Britain. Along with other metropolitan countries Britain has been (although more and more reluctantly) a shelter for groups escaping or being exiled from their countries, such as the European Jews, the African Asians, the Vietnamese, the Tamils, and the Kurds. Similarly, like all other advanced capitalist societies, postwar Britain needed and recruited, especially during the 1950s and 1960s, cheap migrant labour from wherever it could. These were mainly postwar refugees ('European voluntary workers'), Irish (who have been the major source of cheap labour in Britain for centuries) and people from its colonies and new commonwealth countries – mainly the West Indies and the Indian subcontinent. These different kinds o immigrant groups were not treated homogeneously by the British state. The differential ways in which they were treated have constructed, legally and administratively, the boundaries of the British national collectivity.

In 1905 the Conservative government passed the Aliens Act, to control 'undesirable and destitute aliens'. Despite several specific acts which had ordered the deportation of certain 'undesirable' groups in earlier British history (Jews and Blacks), it was the first time in which residents in Britain were divided formally into those who belonged and those who did not belong to the national collectivity.

Further exclusionary legal mechanisms were introduced in later years. Racist–nationalist ideologies as well as economic needs determined those shifting categories of undesirability which determined the boundaries of the national collectivity. Since the 1960s, in declining Britain, there has been a process of escalation in the blocking of 'undesirable' (especially Black) immigration. First the Commonwealth Immigrants Act of 1962 established a system of employment vouchers for Commonwealth subjects which became more and more difficult to obtain. Then exclusionary measures were applied to actual British citizens who were not 'patrial', under the Commonwealth Immigrants Act of 1968 and the Immigration Act of 1971.

This racist concept of 'patriality' was introduced into the British legislation system when African Asians began to flee to the UK in the 1960s. It was claimed that the act differentiated between those British citizens whose passports had been issued to them (or their forefathers) in Britain itself and those who received them outside Britain, in actuality it mainly served to exclude those Black British citizens who were part of the colonized rather than the colonizers. These changes were part of a gradual process which generally followed the direction set out by Enoch Powell as early as 1964 (Nairn 1977: 258–9) – for the British to 'cut their losses', 'to come home' from the empire and to stick to 'old England'. At the same time Powell also warned of 'rivers of blood' if Blacks continued to enjoy rights as nationals.

The process of excluding the colonized from the British collectivity culminated in the 1981 Nationality Act, which defined British nationality more narrowly. Tory policy under Thatcher closed the growing gap between the nationality boundaries as they were outlined under the previous Nationality Act and those which were created by the later Immigration Control Acts. Now even people who were born in Britain cannot become British citizens or settle permanently in Britain unless they are born to British citizens, or are at least legally settled in it. Non-patrial British subjects have received overseas British citizenship that does not entitle them to come to Britain, as in the case of the people of Hong Kong. (An exception was made for the people of the Falkland Islands after the war, but then they had become a national symbol and are White . . .)

Immigration controls and nationality legislation are what define, both symbolically and actually, the boundaries of the national collectivity. It has always been part of the official ideology of the Conservative Party in Britain (and to a certain extent also that of the Labour Party) that strict immigration controls are a precondition for 'good race relations' in Britain. A central part of this ideology holds that only if 'the people' were not afraid that 'the British way of life' was being threatened, would they be willing to accept immigrants into their collectivity. (Competition for scarce resources in employment, housing, health, education, etc. as such, has *not* been the overriding argument used, for after all there was never an attempt to curb Irish and EEC migration.)

With the growing economic crisis and especially with the introduction of increased immigration controls, the number of immigrants to Britain started to fall in the late 1970s, especially among those from commonwealth countries. What has changed more dramatically has been the composition of the immigration. As a result of the developments in the immigration controls policies in the last two decades more and more NCWP Blacks have been prevented from coming to the country at all. As a result, there has been a shift. Before, the bulk of the immigrants came from commonwealth countries (although many of them, especially from the old commonwealth conuntries, were not included in the immigration statistics because of being patrial); now, more and more immigrants come to Britain as 'aliens'.

One resulting paradox is that relative to other 'foreigners' in Britain, the legal position of many Black people in Britain, especially those whose families originally came from the West Indies, is relatively secure, the result of having settled (or their families having settled) before harsher immigration control legislation came into effect. However, being 'legal' residents or citizens of the state is not a sufficient condition for them to be perceived by other citizens and by the authorities as a legitimate part of the national collectivity and therefore part of the civil society. Strict immigration controls and the new Nationality Law, apart from preventing many people from coming to Britain, have also created categories of people who are deprived of British citizenship even if they were born in the UK, and new categories of illegal immigrants who are criminalized and are in danger of being deported.

This has created a legal situation for migrant workers in Britain which is similar to that in other EEC countries. At the same time EEC countries themselves have become a growing source of migration, although their numbers do not appear in the immigration statistics. At the same time that border controls, at least within Europe, become less strict, other means of controlling Third-World immigrants are being developed – such as the growing number of raids on sweatshops and other places of work where 'illegal immigrants' might be found, and then deported. Such strategies are being devised by the different European states in co-ordination with each other and with exchange of 'black lists', so that if anyone is expelled from one European country, he or she would not be allowed entry into any of the others.

Another significant shift in the composition of immigration, especially among those who continue to come from NCWP countries, has been from workers to family dependants. The 'right to family life' – with all its racist and sexist assumptions about who can constitute a family (not homosexual, no extended family (WING 1985)), has come to be the only claim many people have to enter or remain in Britain.

In the 1981 census 3.4 million people in Britain were found to have been born overseas (out of a total population of 52.7 million). It is very significant that of those, 607,000 came from Ireland, 153,000 from old commonwealth countries, 1.41 million from the new commonwealth countries and Pakistan, but even then, 1.13 million – almost half of the total number of immigrants – came from countries which never had constituted part of the British empire. The proportion now will no doubt be even higher. On the other hand, Blacks are estimated by the Commission for Racial Equality (CRE) to constitute almost half of the 4.5 million people who in 1981 were living in households with a non-UK-born head, a clear obstacle to the pursuers of a racially homogeneous Britain.

When calculating the overall number of minorities living in Britain, we have to add to those who immigrated to Britain those who were born in it. According to the LFS (Labour Force Survey) of 1985, there have been in Britain about a million 'non-Whites ' (1.01 million) born in the UK, and 1.3 million born outside it. Of 'Whites ' living in the UK, 1.8 million were also not born in it. To them must be added the households of those who belong to longer-term 'White' minority communities in the country, such as the Jews (estimated as 336,000 (Waterman and Kosmin 1986)) and the Gypsies (estimated as 909,000 in the Minority Rights Group Report 1986). It is an open question to what extent second- and third-generations of other 'White' minority groups (for example, Italians, Poles) feel a part of the British national collectivity.

As shown by the statistical data which assigned a special place to the old and especially new commonwealth countries, the British imperial past played a specific and important role in the construction of British national boundaries prior to the 1980s. These boundaries extended far beyond the geographical boundaries of the UK.

The introduction of the new Nationality Law, the increasing limitations on new immigration, the growing percentage of Blacks born in the UK and the greater importance of the European Community have all changed the principles of construction of these national boundaries. As before, this has been reflected in the changing categories of official statistics. The category of NCWP has disappeared and instead the statistics become more focused on the division between White and non-Whites , as in the LFS data and the 1991 census (see discussion on official statistics in Chapter 5). Racial boundaries rather than imperial boundaries have come, then, to be the significant markers of national rights in Britain today.

On the one hand, the differentiation between those Third-World immigrants with British and commonwealth nationalities and others, especially from other Third-World and other 'non-White' (to use the LFS term) nationalities, is becoming more and more blurred. According to government statistics (Home Office 1987), 83 per cent of those who are currently holding work permits in Britain, come from 'foreign (i.e. non-Commonwealth) countries', while visas have been introduced for NCWP countries (such as Bangladesh, Ghana and Nigeria). Meanwhile EEC nationals, who are not included in the official statistics on settlement in Britain, have a virtually automatic right to immigrate and settle in Britain. (These are the same statistics which have been used in the past to point to the possibility of being 'swamped' by waves of immigrants and to the heavy burden of extra numbers on the labour market and the Welfare State.) While this state of affairs does not mean that other types of exclusions operate *vis-à-vis* EEC immigrants (this especially applies to the Irish, as we discussed above; see also Hickman 1985), it does construct the official boundaries, and indeed the new official statistics, in terms of race and colour.

This has strengthened racial barriers, and not only in terms of exclusionary external national boundaries. It has also created a situation whereby, in order to have access to health and welfare services, proof of eligibility, based on legal settlement here, may be required. This is practised mainly on people with certain accents and skin colour. In other words, there has been a close relationship between tightening the boundaries of the national collectivity (through immigration controls and nationality laws) and the practices of institutionalized racism.

The British 'Race Relations Industry' (as it is commonly known) has been developed in order to counter exactly those kinds of exclusions; but, as we shall discuss in Chapter 6, in many ways it has also reproduced them in somewhat different forms, by constructing the minorities as separate races, cultures and communities. Part of the explanation for this, as Paul Gilroy (1987: Chapter 2) points out, is the naturalization of racist modes of nationalist thinking even among people on the British Left. Attacking figures such as Raymond Williams, E. P. Thompson, Eric Hobsbawm and Michael Ignatieff, Gilroy challenges notions of patriotism based on 'one nation' which proliferated in the Left around and after the Falklands war, and rightly claims,

> The suggestion that no one lives outside the national community is only plausible if the issue of racism is excluded. What is being described by these writers is a national community, not imagined in the way that Benedict Anderson has suggested, but actual. The construction of that community is overlooked. It is accepted a priori as the structure around which the struggle to gain hegemony must take place. (1987: 54)

A somewhat different kind of racist articulation which can be found in the British Left appears in Fay Weldon's pamphlet *Sacred Cows* (1989). Writing in the midst of the 'Rushdie affair' Fay Weldon defended the right of Salman Rushdie to write, and denounced the call by Muslim fundamentalists (and other Muslims) to ban the book and even kill the author. But she did this on the basis of the cultural supremacy of the Christian European culture over the barbaric Muslim one: 'The Bible is at least food for thought. The Koran is food for non-thought' (p. 6). The 'Rushdie affair', the Gulf war and the Single European Act are all part of the racialization of religion which is gradually becoming hegemonic in British racist discourse.

'REFUSING HOLY ORDERS'

In this section we look at the relationship between religion and the state in Britain and how this might relate to racist exclusions.

There has never been full separation between religion and the state in Britain. This is all too often ignored in the analysis of both the Left and of sociologists of religion, who have assumed that religion has either disappeared in secularized society or has withdrawn into the private arena. So the enquiry into religion in Britain has focused predominantly on attitudes, beliefs and membership in religious organizations.

According to the recent statistics (*Social Trends* 1989), less than 20 per cent of the population are members of religious organizations. (Only 15 per cent are members of 'trinitarian churches', such as the established and the Catholic Churches.) However, 75 per cent of the population has a religious affiliation, and the majority of them associate with the established churches. In a survey carried out by the Independent Television Authority (ITA) in 1970, 8 out of every 10 Britons stated that the Christian identity of Britain is 'very important' or 'important' to them. This is the context in which Enoch Powell's notion of Englishness which was expressed in the 'rivers of blood' speech, and the 'fear for British culture' which was mentioned as the main reason for supporting him (Spearman 1968), has to be perceived (see discussion on p. 56). And indeed, when David Jenkins (1975) wrote *The British, Their Identity and Their Religion*, he remarked,

> The more I considered what it means in specific terms to be distinctively English, Scottish or Welsh, the more important became the place of religious inheritance in the process of definition (1975: vii)

The Christianity of Britain, however, is not just a question of religious affiliation or even just a part of British nationalist ideology. It is anchored in law, and extended beyond the symbolism of the Queen as the symbolic head of the Churches of England and Scotland. Firstly, the Church hierarchy participates in the British legislative process. The two archbishops and twenty-four bishops are members of the British Parliament in the House of Lords ('the Lords Spiritual'). It is the duty of the Prime Minister to appoint the Archbishop of Canterbury, and as debates in the media before the last appointment showed, the religious affiliation and attitudes of the Prime Minister have to be accommodated in an appropriate manner. Moreover, the Jewish Yearbook, in the section on British laws which specifically concern the Jews, claims that it is unclear whether a Jew (or any other non-Christian for that matter) can legally become a British Prime Minister, as it is illegal for a non-Christian to appoint the Head of the Church. The rule on appointing applies to the British royalty, who nominally appoints him, but possibly also includes the Prime Minister, who recommends the candidate. The case has never been tested in British history (d'Israeli converted to Christianity).

Another major way in which the relationship between Church and state in Britain has affected British public life has been the existence of the blasphemy law. It protects the Church of England from those same offensive attacks which are legal against other religions. Attempts in court by Muslim leaders to expand the application of the law to Islam, at the time of the Rushdie affair, have failed. The blasphemy law might not often be invoked, but because it has been used (for instance, by Mary Whitehouse when she brought an action against *Gay News* for printing a poem which implied that Jesus had homosexual fantasies), it is of more than merely symbolic importance.

Another facet of the incomplete separation of religion and the state in Britain, and probably the most important one in contemporary political debates in Britain, is the fact that under the 1988 Education Reform Act all state schools are required to have a daily act of worship. (Not incidentally this amendment in the law originated in the House of Lords.) Christianity, therefore, is given an affirmed legal status as the ideological cement of national culture. As such, it also provides legitimate grounds for eminent Church personalities to express opinions on social and political matters such as poverty and homelessness, which cause great discomfort to the government. Nevertheless, this construction assumes a correspondence of national and religious identity, which means that non-established churches and especially non-Christians, can only be partial members of the British national collectivity. They are defined to a lesser or greater extent as outsiders. In multi-cultural educational programmes in British schools, it is the different religions, especially the different religious celebrations and holidays, which have come to signify cultural differences.

While membership in the established churches has tended to fall continuously, at least until recently (*Social Trends* 1988 mentions the figure of 14 per cent in the previous three years, but since then the figure seems to have stabilized) membership in minority churches (such as Spiritualists and Jehovah's Witnesses) has risen by 26 per cent during the same period. Most non-Christian religions, especially those of Muslims and Sikhs, have almost doubled their membership. Religious affiliation has come, therefore, in different ways, to signify collective identity among ethnic minorities in Britain, as well. Significantly, the broadcasting bill exempts only religious programmes from censorship for expressing partisan opinions; this legislation can only enhance such construction.

Since the 'Rushdie affair', the exclusion of minority religions from the national collectivity has started a process of racialization that especially relates to Muslims. People who used to be known for the place of origin, or even as 'people of colour' have become identified by their assumed religon. The racist stereotype of the 'Paki' has become the racist stereotype of the 'Muslim fundamentalist'. The coming together of Europe, including Eastern Europe, with the demise of the Cold War, has created a space for a new threatening 'other'. While anti-Semitism has started growing again within Europe, collective 'memories' of the Crusades have started to become a focus of a construction of a world dichotomy of the western Christians versus the oriental Muslims.

Both anti-Islamism and anti-Semitism are racist ideologies which can cement a European nationalist ideology, in ways which anti-Black racism cannot. Unlike those in Britain, most of the migrant labourers on the continent are not Black, but – coming from Turkey and North Africa – are Muslims, as are a significant proportion of the British Blacks. Anti-Blackness, like anti-Semitism, has been part of a European and Christian demonological heritage since the Middle Ages (see the discussion in Chapter 5). However, it was around anti-Semitism that the Nazi ideology, which is the ideological model of so many of the far-Right organizations in Europe, crystallized. The defeat of anti-Semitism is connected with the national defeat of Germany at the end of the Second World War and its split into two states up until very recently. Also in France, the period of Nazi occupation, and the co-operation of large elements of the French population (headed by the national hero of the First World War, General Paten), is a 'national trauma' that has tended to be repressed. The denial of the holocaust and the resurrection of anti-Semitic conspiracy theories can be useful, therefore, in more than one European nationalist project.

Given the very different location of Britain in the Second World War, anti-Semitism has been much more marginal. Unlike anti-Blackness, it has been one of the main ideological differences between far-Right organizations, such as the British National Party and the National Front, in which anti-Semitic ideologies play an important part, and the Tory 'New Right', in which it has been, at least until now, much more muted.

THE 'NEW RIGHT'

The Powellian 'English come home' has eventually become a hegemonic ideology in the form of Thatcherism, in which the 'New Right' has used anti-Black racism to weld together the Conservatives (the 'natural' guardians of the national identity) and the petrified White working class (Wright 1985). It is not incidental that out of 1,444 reasons given in a sample taken from the letters of support given to Enoch Powell after his 'rivers of blood' speech in 1968, 1,128 had to do with 'fears for British culture' (Spearman 1968: 14). In the empire 'Englishness' was not threatened but glorified by the proximity of the colonized. It was a different story when the colonized started to 'come home' together with the ex-colonizers.

The post-colonial constellation, then, has determined to a great extent the framework and dynamics of the political and ideological struggles that have taken place in contemporary Britain. Although the discourse concentrated supposedly on culture – 'Englishness', it was actually focused on origin. As Powell so clearly put it,

The West Indian does not by being born in England, become an Englishman. In law, he becomes a United Kingdom citizen by birth; in fact he is a West Indian or an Asian still.

(Eastbourne, 16 November 1968, quoted in Gilroy 1987)

Powell was but a first, to a whole group of right-wing ideologues (like John Casey, Ray Honeford and others connected with the *Salisbury Review*), who articulated what Martin Barker (1981) has called 'the new racism'.

Martin Barker claimed that with the discrediting of Nazism after the Second World War, some of the more vulgar forms of racism became unacceptable. These forms of racism have openly identified the non-European 'races' as biologically inferior. The 'new racism' on the other hand merely identifies them as 'different' (see discussion in Chapter 1) and speaks about 'nations' rather than 'races'. As Paul Gilroy sums it up,

> Its novelty lies in the capacity to link discourses of patriotism, nationalism, xenophobia, Englishness, Britishness, militarism and gender difference into a complex system which gives 'race' its contemporary meaning. (1987: 43)

Bob Miles (1985) challenged the 'newness' of this 'new racism', claiming that it is the same 'old racism' but linked to nationalist discourse. We disagree with this reductive equation, as we see the British 'new racism' as part of the phenomenon which Balibar (1988: 33) calls *racisms différentialiste*, in which 'cultural groups' need to be kept in their countries of origin, in order not to harm or be harmed by the unmixable foreign elements. This is a very different formulation of racism from that of the neo-Nazi organizations like the National Front and the British movements, with their 'old fashioned' racism, which speak unabashed about the biological inferiority and inherent danger emanating from Blacks and Jews. However, both 'types' of racism could unite around demands for repatriation of the Blacks from Britain and resistance to policies of integrated housing and education. However, as we have mentioned above, new ideological and political factors are gradually overshadowing the constructions of 'new' and 'old' racisms as they have crystallized during the 1970s and early 1980s. On the one hand, more and more of the Blacks in Britain (mainly as a result of the British immigration policy discussed above) have been born in the country; debates about limited immigration and even 'repatriation' can no longer be relevant as strategies for their exclusion (in contrast to the case of refugees and migrant workers from other parts of the world who have come to Britain). On the other hand, since Britain's joining the Common Market, and especially during the 1980s, there has been also a shift away from the post-colonial 'commonwealth' construction of boundaries towards a growing incorporation into the European Community (the old rivals during the empire times) and establishing exclusionary boundaries around 'Fortress Europe' as a whole (Sivanandan 1988b, Gordon 1989). Parallel to these developments has been the continuing civil war between the Catholics and the Protestants in Northern Ireland, and the racialization of the British Muslim population around, first, the Rushdie affair, and then the Gulf War (Modood 1990). All these developments are constructing new racialized boundaries within the British society, around new notions of culture which are probably more overtly linked to religion than most analyses of British racism have been allowing.

CONCLUSION

In this chapter we explored the national phenomenon and the ways it relates to racist exclusions. We looked at the construction of nations as specific ideological and political forms and linked them with specific socio-economic conditions and the emergence of strong centralized states. We defined nationalist ideologies as those with a claim for a separate political representation of ethnic collectivities and looked at myths of 'common origins' and perceptions of 'common destiny' as the main building blocks of ideologies of national solidarity and 'common culture'. Rather than attempting to classify different types of national ideologies, we explored notions of citizenship, religion, culture and gene-ological origin as assuming different types of national exclusions which might be racialized.

We then looked at the situation in Britain and at different forms of racialization in the construction of the boundaries of its national collectivity – national, colonial and religious, and their relation to the state.

While this chapter examined the relationship between nationalism and racism, we do not want to imply that there are no other major ideologies in Britain which are inclusionary and at least non-racist, if not anti-racist, in their nature. Two such ideologies are the 'leftist' social democratic one, which has been promoting the Welfare State, and a 'rightist' libertarian one, which has been promoting a *laissez-faire* market. However, just as worries about the 'quality of the British race' have been inherently connected with the rise of the British Welfare State (Beveridge 1942), so have been the 'free-marketeers' part of the Thatcherite 'New Right'.

The analysis of the interrelationships between the various forms of racial exclusions, as well as of the economic and political context in which they are embedded is vital for the understanding of British nationalism. Ethnic, racial and national divisions are not mutually exclusive categories, although the linkages between them can be complex and are indeed historically specific and undergoing continuous, though not arbitrary, change. Our argument is that racism in Britain cannot be fully understood unless it is located as a central dimension of a hegemonic 'Anglomorphic' ethnicity. This ethnicity, or rather cluster of ethnicities, has been constructed primarily around a Christian European cultural heritage, and more specifically, around the rise and fall of the British empire, with its dominant centre in London. It is enmeshed, although not reducible to, international and national class and gender divisions. Ideological and political processes as well as economic ones are therefore central in the construction, reproduction and transformation of these hegemonic Anglomorphic ethnicities. It is important, however, to note the existence of a number of constructions of ethnicity in Britain as well as more than one kind of racism, and the fact that important changes around the '1992 factor' and the strengthening influence of the European Community are taking place.

In fully understanding the relationship between racism and nationalism, class divisions are of central importance. Phil Cohen, for instance, links three main variants of 'internal' racism in Britain to different classes. These three variants, according to him, relate to different 'codes of breeding' as guiding principles of racialized constructions (1987: 9): an 'aristocratic code of breeding', based on social pedigree and ancestral blood linked to a hierarchy of 'human sensibilities'; a bourgeois or democratic code based on a pseudo-scientific reading, emphasizing inherited differences in intelligence and natural aptitude; and a working-class 'code', centred on inheritance of labour power mediated through rules and rituals of territoriality. Similar different codes could be found in peripheral regions and territories of the British state and empire. They have served the double purpose of resisting central hegemonic codes of exclusion as well as enabling identification with the national collectivity's centre against more marginal segments of the empire or other excluded groupings from the national collectivity.

In the next chapter, therefore, we shall turn to examine the relationships between racism and class divisions.

Chapter 3

It's all a question of class . . .

INTRODUCTION

One of the most important debates within theoretical and empirical work on race addresses the connection between race and class. Much of this debate takes as a starting-point the economic position of Black people and explains this with reference to economic processes and their link to racism. However, as Omi and Winant point out (1986: 25), the link between economic processes and class requires an 'analytic leap'. Economic processes and class are different although related concepts. Making the connection between economic positioning and race doesn't actually require the postulate of class. There is also a conflation between concrete class or economic positioning and their explanation. It is easy to show, for example, that Black people are on the whole positioned in the lower echelons of economically defined class groupings (although there are variations both within and between different racialized groups). It is not so easy to show that this is the effect of racism, however. Nor is it easy to show that racism itself is constructed as the medium by which capital benefits from an underclass that can act either as cheap labour or a reserve army of labour (Castles and Kosack 1973, Castells 1975, Nikolinakos 1975). Castles and Kosack epitomize an approach that starts off from an empirical depiction of economic disadvantage, in order to draw out an analytical conception of racial groups as an underclass:

> We may therefore speak of two strata within the working class: the indigenous workers with generally better conditions and the feeling of no longer being at the bottom of society form the higher stratum. The immigrants, who are the most under-

privileged and exploited group of society, form the lower stratum. (1973: 477)

Very few writers on race would dispute the facts of racial disadvantage, particularly in relation to economic disadvantage. The data on employment shows migrants, particularly Black migrants, as well as the Black British population, to be at the bottom of the occupational and income scale. Despite a number of differences between various groups, such as Asians and African-Caribbeans and between men and women, there exists none the less a class distribution effect. Empirically, then, it becomes fairly straightforward to establish the links between race and class, if one is concerned with the distribution of inequality or disadvantage. However, the equation of race and class goes further than the mere empirical correlation pointed out above. As Paul Gilroy (CCCS 1982: 302) notes,

> The class character of black struggles is not a result of the fact that blacks are predominantly proletarian, though this is true. It is established in the fact that their struggles for civil rights, freedom from state harassment, or as waged workers, are instances of the process by which the working class is constituted politically, organised in politics.

Gilroy, in contrast to most writers who make the connection, is asserting that class formation is itself predicated on race structuration. This is a position that essentially develops Hall's views (1980) and we shall be looking at it more specifically later.

The identification of race as some form of class relation is a well-charted and disputed position, which has dominated most of the literature and debate that is tied to Marxism. It also forms an important strand in the more mainstream analysis of race and ethnicity, particularly in its Weberian variant (despite the distinct conceptual categories that are employed). Miles (1984: 218) has suggested in fact that the race relations problematic is shared by Weberians and Marxists because they both 'attribute the ideological notion of "race" with descriptive and explanatory importance'.

Oliver Cox (1970) is often credited as the major forerunner to the contemporary formulation of 'race and class'. However, both Miles (1980) and Gabriel and Ben Tovim (1978) have shown in different ways that there is as much connection with Weber as with Marx. Cox equated race with colour, made a distinction between discrimination on the basis of ethnicity and of race, and saw race discrimination as developing out of class interests, that is, as a mode for justifying economic exploitation. For Cox, racism grew out of capitalism and provided a means for furthering the use of labour as a commodity, pure and simple, resulting in a greater exploitation. This was legitimated through ideas of racial difference and inferiority. It was the use to which physical difference (that is, colour) was put, in the interests of capital, which constituted racism.

In much of the analysis that links race and economic processes, it is racism as an ideology that connects race groups with a specific economic positioning. This involves assumptions about the effects of racism on economic position that treat market mechanisms or capitalist economic processes as secondary. As Miles points out, there are a range of exclusionary practices in society that are not merely coterminous with racism but are 'a component part of a wider structure of class disadvantage' (1989: 9).

Generally however, the role of racism is seen to emanate and have its origins in 'the ideologies and racial typologies that were often invoked to justify the open exploitation of colonial times' (Cashmore 1989: 127). Bhabha (1990) refers to a more generalizable form of colonial discourse of the 'other' which is much less reductionist than other attempts that link colonialism and racism. He maintains that the notion of fixity which underlies colonial discourse has effects which are racist:

> its predominant strategic function is the creation of a space for 'subject peoples' through the production of knowledges of coloniser and colonised which are stereotypical but antithetically evaluated. The objective of colonial discourse is to construe the colonised as a population of degenerate types on the basis of racial origin, in order to justify conquest and to establish systems of administration and instruction. (1990: 23)

Carmichael and Hamilton (1968) refer to the situation of Black people in America as a continuation of colonialism:

> The economic relationship of America's black communities to the larger society also reflects their colonial status. The political power exercised over those communities goes hand in glove with the economic deprivation experienced by the black citizens. (1968: 32)

They link this to slavery: 'perhaps the most vicious result of colonialism – in Africa and this country – was that it purposively, maliciously and with reckless abandon relegated the black man to a subordinated, inferior status in the society. The individual was considered and treated as a lowly animal . . .' (1968: 39).

In these arguments, colonialism as an economic, political and discursive system is seen to be the origin of racist discourse that structures the position of Black people. In other words, the role of colonial discourse and practice is linked to the sphere of 'Black' construction. This functions to limit the referent of racism to those who share the ascriptive characteristic of Black skin. The delimitation of racism to colour racism is another common characteristic of approaches that link race to economic processes or to class. For example, Blauner (1969) refers to Black people in America as making up a form of internal colony.

Sivanandan's work is probably the best exemplar in Britain of the position that racism is functional to capitalism and that it originates in capitalist needs under conditions of capitalist expansion with colonialiam. For Sivanandan such a phase required a philosophy of justification and functions to blur class divisions in the present, ensuring the super exploitation of Black labour (1976). This is very much in accord with Cox's view (1970).

This position is in contrast to a number of other causal explanations of the origins of racism. They include the view that racism is a product of the contact between Europeans, who had defined themselves as a race, and non-Europeans (Banton 1977). Van den Berghe (1979) relates racism partly to Darwinism. He therefore does not believe that racism was directly and causally linked to colonialism. Jordan (1974) finds the origins of racism in the way the English constructed Black Africans in the sixteenth century, from their first contacts with them. Jordan claims that the colour Black was already imbued with negative associations with heathenism, savagery and sexual prowess, during the period of Protestant reformation.

In Miles's later work, it was not simply that colonialism produced racism as a system of economic justification, but that it 'actively structured . . . the transformation of existing modes of production' under conditions characterized by 'forms of unfree labour and hence by specific forms of class relations' (1989: 101). Racialization had an independent effectivity in economic relations of primary accumulation, according to Miles, and therefore was not directly determined by economic relations. On the other hand, racism is linked to 'European representations of the Other' which 'were generated and reproduced in the course of a history of contact between different populations emnmeshed in specific forces and relations of production and expressing distinct cultural values' (1989: 100).

As Omi and Winant state (1986: 40), approaches such as these share 'reliance on elements derived from the dynamics of colonialism to demonstrate the continuity of racial oppression from its origins in the national oppression prevailing in colonialism's heyday'. The first requirement of a colonialist discourse on racism is the separation of the population into discrete peoples, and what Bhabha (1990) calls a subject nation or people.

Omi and Winant, in discussing class-based theories of race, divide the arguments into: the market relations approach, which focuses on factors that destabilize the normal workings of the market, such as discrimination; stratification theory, which is concerned with the distribution of economic resources and sees extra economic factors as reinforcing those of economic inequality; and class conflict theory, which focuses on class exploitation, and explains racist ideology as a product of economic class interests. There are a number of different ways in which class-based theories of race have been classified (for example Miles 1982a, Solomos 1986, Gilroy 1987, Anthias 1990). We want to examine briefly five different positions that link race to class – Rex's underclass thesis, migrant labour theories, racism as an ideology that is relatively autonomous from class, Gilroy's view that class formation is linked to race, and dual labour market approaches. Writers may draw on one or more of these formulations. For example, the work of Castles and Kosack (1973) and Phizacklea and Miles (1980) span a number of these positions.

JOHN REX'S UNDERCLASS THESIS

The view that immigrants or migrant workers are an underclass (Carmichael and Hamilton 1968), sub-proletariat (Sivanandan 1973) or class stratum (Castles and Kosack 1973) is a frequently used one (see Gabriel and Ben Tovim 1978 for a useful review). Rex's contribution (1970, 1981) can be seen, despite its Weberianism, in terms of a tradition established by the Black Marxist writer Oliver Cox (1970). This is a mode of argument, that as we saw earlier, reduces races to false ideological categories constituted through the medium of class relations. Racism is given the role of rationalizing and reinforcing exploitation required by the economic system. A problem that is common to this tradition is that false racial stereotypes are left to the construction of individual consciousness (of capitalists for Cox and workers for Rex), in the absence of a mechanism by which the mode of production actually produces ideological effects. An additional problem is that any postulate of the origins of racism does not in itself adequately explain the structural conditions which account for its contemporary effectivity.

For Rex, the 'under-class' nature of colonial immigrants (note than he does not use the term migrant labour) consists in their inferior position within the working class, and in the fact that they are politically separate from the organized labour movement. The colonial heritage is responsible for the 'stigmatization' of Black workers by the White working class, who consider them as outsiders or competitors. For Rex, the victims of racism are colonial immigrants who are Black, and the perpetrators are White indigenous workers who are White. Rex is positing a political division between 'natives' and 'outsiders' within the working class (Rex and Tomlinson 1979), and assumes a homogeneous indigenous class, not already divided.

The theoretical connection between Rex's depiction of race relations as class relations, and the role of the colonial context in structuring racial stigmatization is, however, unclear. Rex is not suggesting that it is a capitalist class that constructs racism in order to pursue its continuing economic interests. Rather, for Rex, racism is produced by one class, which is White, which is in a state of class conflict with another class, which is Black. The class character of Blacks is not constructed so much by their economic insertion into capitalism at the centre, but by their 'stigmatization' through colonialism and through the greater political power of natives. Rex assumes a homogeneous White working class and also a Black/White divide. The final result is to reduce both race and class to the idealist representations of social actors. The structural location of migrants becomes reduced to the expression and effects of racial ideology. This has become a psycho-social mechanism for the pursuit of principles of economic rational 'interests' by actors.

MIGRANT LABOUR THEORIES

The main notable position that does not focus on the effects of racism in constructing the economic position of Black people, within a Marxist paradigm, is Migrant Labour theory (Castles and Kosack 1973, Castells 1975, Nikolinakos 1975). This focuses on the economic role of migrant labour in capitalist societies and was predicated on the experiences of *gastarbeiters* or guest workers in Western Europe. Phizacklea and Miles (1980) have tried to apply this problematic to Britain by formulating it in relation to settler Black migration. In the process, the problematic has actually shifted to the whole of the Black population, rather than remaining with migrants and migration.

Castles and Kosack regard migrants as a reserve army of labour, seeing migrant workers being brought in to 'keep wages down and profits up' (1973: 5). Nikolinakos (1975), on the other hand, sees migrant workers as a structural requirement of the capitalist economies of Western Europe. Capital reconstruction processes set in from the end of the 1950s and the growth from the beginning of the 1960s involved the internationalization of the labour market. He sees migrants as taking on the role of the reserve army and as a sub-proletariat that splits the working class. Racism is seen to result from competition between fractions of labour, which is structured by fractions of capital in their attempt to lower the cost of variable capital.

Castells sees migration as characteristic of the 'current phase of monopoly capital' (1975: 44), and links it to uneven development. He notes particularly the role of migrant labour for certain marginalized and backward sectors of the economy, and uses the term 'class fraction' to note their role in fragmenting the working class: 'Their legal political position as foreigners and their political ideological isolation leads to a basic point: their limited capacity for organisation and struggle and very great vulnerability to repression' (1975: 52–53).

The postulate of migrants as both a reserve army of labour and cheap labour, found in most of these approaches, is theoretically problematic however, (Anthias 1980, 1982). Also their use as a reserve is jeopardized by the existence of a segmented labour market or dual labour market, and the growth of post-Fordism which separates the workforce into a small permanent core and a larger, peripheral, less skilled sector (Murray 1988).

An interesting attempt to relate colonialism, migrant labour and class is found in Phizacklea and Miles (1980). Their central argument is that Black migrants in Britain form a 'class fraction' of the working class. According to this position, it is the colonialist heritage of migrant labour that structures their specific position as a class fraction and allows them a specific political or legal role in the capitalist social formation. This in addition allows them to be used as cheap labour.

Phizacklea and Miles are very clear about rejecting the notion of a homogeneous working class. According to them, the notion of an underclass and Castles and Kosack's notion of migrant labour as a class stratum, assume a unity of the working class before immigrant penetration. The concept of class fraction recognizes divisions within classes of which racial or ethnic divisions are only two forms.

Phizacklea and Miles focus on the category of 'migrant labour' rather than 'racial group' and particularly on colonial migrant labour, but this for them means Black migrant labour:

> the colonisation process has had as one of its features the direct politico-ideological domination of the colonised social formation such that there was direct or indirect political rule and the development of an ideology alleging the inferiority of the dominated. (1980: 10)

Migrant Labour theory differs from many Marxist approaches to race, in as much as the problematic is that of migration – as providing a supply of labour power through geographical and economic displacement which becomes inserted into the capitalist mode – rather than on the question of racist ideology and its effects. However, depicting Black migrant labour as a class fraction is problematic, and the incorporation into the analysis of the effects of colonialism does not specify the articulation of the 'racial' with migrant labour (as opposed to migrant labour without racialization).

The depiction of Black migrant labour as a class fraction under-emphasizes the heterogeneity of labour categories it presents. The distinct employment characteristics of Asians, African-Caribbeans and other colonial migrants (such as Cypriots) is not raised. This heterogeneity problematizes the unitary application of 'class fraction' and therefore it needs to be addressed specifically. The migrant labour problematic fails to consider the 40 per cent of

Britain's Black population who are not 'migrant'. The concern to show the class bases of Black migrant labour allows divisions within the Black population to be under-explored. There is in fact a conflation in the problematic and categories used. Migrant labour is the focus, but this is equated with racialized groups.

In relation to Britain, we would have to show that they have a particular political and legal position as migrants, that is, because they are migrants, not because a section (for colonial or economic reasons) have become racialized. In Britain, migrants have different political and ideological positions linked to country of origin, year of entry, extent of racial discrimination, employment and so on. Their political, ideological position cannot be extrapolated merely from their migrant status. Phizacklea and Miles have argued that *de facto* discrimination can be theoretically equivalent to *de jure* discrimination. But this latter occurs not only in relation to migrants who are Black, but to their British-born descendants, who are not migrant (as well as migrants from southern Europe who are not 'Black' and other Third-World migrants (for example, see Sivanandan 1988a).

The real social ensemble referred to then is not 'migrant labour' but the Black population. To argue that the whole of this population then constitutes a class fraction would necessitate that they had a particular class position, and that they can be identified in class terms. Although it is true that Black people have a tendency to be clustered within the manual class categories, there is great variation both between different ethnic minorities, and within them. To further argue that they are a distinct fraction – as opposed to stratum, which merely requires that they be identified in the lower reaches – it has to be demonstrated that they have a distinct political organizational position. The ways in which African-Caribbeans and Asians are organizing have therefore to be addressed, particularly where they may have become increasingly differentiated (see Chapter 6).

In fact, when we attend closely to the argument, it is clear that in the final analysis, for Phizacklea and Miles it is racist ideology, rather than, say, the requirements of capital, or the economic categories of migrant labour, that structure the economic position of Black people and the political legal relations they are inserted into. This echoes some of the problems found in Rex's analysis. It structures conflict between groups defined by their colour, as opposed to groups defined by their class position. (Class position becomes an effect of colour and its signifying role within racist discourse.)

RACE AS AN IDEOLOGICAL CATEGORY THAT ENTERS ECONOMIC RELATIONS

Gabriel and Ben Tovim (1978) share the view with both Rex and Phizacklea and Miles that race is ideological, but for them it is an autonomous ideological category that then becomes inserted into economic relation:

if we are to achieve a satisfactory resolution to the concepts of race and racism, then clearly they must be seen as concepts whose objects are ideological . . . the product . . . of determinate ideo- logical practices, with their own theoretical/ideological condi- tions of existence and their own irreducible contradictions. Only subsequent to this process of ideological production do specific racial ideologies intervene at the level of political practice and the economy. (1978: 139)

For this view racism is to be combated by democratic populist ideology rather than economic changes, and it becomes essentially a policy rather than a class issue. What has occurred in this formulation is an opposite effect to the earlier ones, where race has been defined as a product essentially of class, which is the privileged domain of effectivity in capitalist social relations.

Here, following broadly an Althusserian conception of social relations (Althusser 1971), we have race merely present in ideology and thus fractured from class or other forms of social relation, which are then non-ideological. This reification of race as inalienable and unsubjected to considerations other than its own, appears to have become an almost inevitable outcome of remaining within the terms of the earlier debates, but disagreeing with the epistemological primacy given to economic or class relations.

For Miles (1982a, 1989) too, racism is an ideology and he distinguishes between processes of generation and reproduction of ideologies (and their transformation) and therefore, like Gabriel and Ben Tovim, for him it is a question of developing a specific analysis of ideologies in particular historical contexts.

RACE AND CLASS FORMATION

Paul Gilroy (1987) offers a challenging reformulation of the links between race and class. The position he takes can essentially be seen as a development of Stuart Hall's view (1980) that race is as important in class formation and structuration, as class is in race structuration. Using the concept of articulation, he remains within the framework of the debate in seeing race and class as separate but connected sets of relations, but with an agnosticism concerning which is primary. Hall's famous and powerful phrase that 'race is the modality in which class is lived' (Hall *et al.* 1978) also assumes that class consciousness, presumably unlike race consciousness, is never at the point of being, but always in the process of becoming, and therefore requires something else (that is, race) as its representational or phenomenal form.

Gilroy too argues that race is an essential ingredient in the history of class formation and structuration in British society. Unlike Benedict Anderson (1983), he shares with the present authors (also see Anthias and Yuval-Davis 1983, Anthias 1990) the view that racism is linked to nationalism. He sees the new racism as essentially a form of right-wing nationalism. Race discourse is linked to ethnic and nationalist ideologies and is not, as Miles suggests, merely another ideology. The problem with the way Gilroy theorizes this is that he cannot then draw the link between race phenomena and those of ethnos, having rejected the ethnic category.

For Gilroy, race must problematize our thinking about class. A difference with the position argued by us is that he is antagonistic to the notion of ethnicity, although he is keen to argue that Black communities are not only organized through their common experience of racism, but are also cultural communities. Gilroy wants to introduce a 'more sophisticated theory of culture into the political analysis of race and "racism" by claiming the term back from "ethnicity"' (1987: 17). He is clearly arguing with the way ethnicity has often been used in an essentialist way, and with the fact that it is identified with the ethnic school tradition (see Chapter 1). For Gilroy, racial meanings are not part of ideology but part of culture. Although Gilroy fails to clarify the ways in which he is differentiating these terms, he is clear in rejecting the view that 'race' is ideological. He is asserting the reality of racially organized communities and believes that any analysis must take this reality seriously. Gilroy argues that class, and other differentiations such as sex and race, have different histories of subordination, and as we also pointed out, cannot be empirically disentangled. For Gilroy, the antagonisms around race are not limited to those concerned with production. Race is a process which is historically constructed and he is concerned with the 'manner in which racial meanings, solidarity and identities provide the basis for action'. These are both an 'alternative to class consciousness at the political level and a factor in the very formation of classes' (1987: 27).

It is clear that Gilroy's problematic is very much at the level of the concrete, despite the fact that he claims that we have to rethink the concept of class, in the light of race. Essentially, he is suggesting that class and race involve forms of subordination that inform each other at the level of consciousness, organization and meaning, but he has not been able to posit the axis for race. This is largely because he fails to treat race in terms of ideas and practices relating to ethnic collectivities, and how they are under-stood and used, under particular social, political and economic conditions. It is significant to note however, that Gilroy is able none the less to make the connection between racism and nationalism.

DUAL LABOUR MARKET THEORIES AND POST-FORDISM

The development of dual labour market theories is linked to the failure of orthodox theories to acccount for the degree of political and racial dissension during the 1960s, especially in American society. A dualistic framework attempted to understand the phenomenon through seeing male White workers as belonging to the 'primary' sector of the labour market, which was characterized by stable employment, strong trade union organization and representation, relatively high pay and good conditions of work. The 'secondary sector', on the other hand, was characterized by predominantly female or Black labour with instability of employment, low trade union organization and poor conditions of work. Doeringer and Piore (1971) have argued that a dual labour market is partly the result of internal differentiation within particular industrial sectors. In highly capital-intensive industries, skills are acquired through intensive on-the-job training. This requires labour stability and in turn leads to the creation of a differential reward structure, which gives higher rewards to these skills. Women and migrants are regarded as unstable and less reliable in certain sectors. R. C. Edwards (1975), working from within a Marxist perspective, sees the development of a dual labour market as a response to the needs to control a highly organized workforce, which is also highly skilled: 'Employers quite consciously exploited race, ethnic and sex antagonism in order to undercut unionism and break strikes' (Edwards, Reich and Gordon 1975: 5). Two different forms of control thus emerge: control through differential reward and control through fear of job loss, which is legitimized through sexist and racist ideology.

As Blackburn and Mann (1979) note, it is difficult to apply a model formulated on the basis of American industrial structure to the British context. A major criticism is that it is not clear to what extent the focus is on a differentiated labour force finding expression within the market-place, through a 'real' difference in 'skills', 'aptitudes', etc (and ignoring therefore the question of the social evaluation of 'skills' (Phillips and Taylor 1980)) and to what extent a differentiated industrial structure exists which draws on different labour categories and indeed structures them.

One particular attraction of the dual labour market model is that it emphasizes that Black migrants or women are indeed employed more often in unskilled and semi-skilled jobs, in particular occupations and industries, many involving low pay and minimal job security. As Beechey (1978: 177) notes, 'the approach counters the view derived from neo-classical economics that individuals are allocated to occupational positions purely by the play of market forces'.

However, this model is descriptive rather than explanatory, since it fails to account for the growth of a segmented labour market, and concentrates on the question of employer strategies (Anthias 1982). Lever-Tracey and Quinlan (1988) also believe that it is important to examine the various strategies pursued by employers and workers (both native and immigrant) in their conflict with each other. Also as Omi and Winant argue (1986: 36), 'whether understood as dual, segmented or split, the labor market exhibits a great variety of forms and axes of differentiation . . . These overlap and cut across racial lines of division.'

Post-Fordist explanations point to the role of capital restructuration in a period of crisis in the monopoly capital phase, and in line with broader postmodernist developments (Hall 1988). Post-Fordism stresses a dual or segmented labour market, made up of core and periphery also. As Martin Spence points out (1990: 22).

> Post-Fordism's . . . central concept is fragmentation. In produc-
> tion this takes the form of 'flexible specialisation', based on new
> technology and a division of labour separating skilled core
> workers from the dispensable and insecure peripheral workers.

Robin Murray (1988: 11–12) states that under these conditions,

> Workers are no longer interchangeable. They gather experi-
> ence . . . It hastens the divisions between the core and the
> peripheral workforce. The costs of employing lifetime workers
> means an incentive to subcontract all jobs not essential to the
> core. The other side of the Japanese jobs for life is a majority of
> low paid, fragmented peripheral workers facing an under-
> funded and inadequate welfare state . . . rooted in changes in
> production.

Murray goes on to argue that post-Fordism is being introduced in
accordance with the requirements of capital accumulation; it cuts
the labour force in two, leaving large numbers without any work at
all. Stuart Hall, noting that there is still a raging debate as to
whether in fact post-Fordism exists, points to 'a decline in the
proportion of the skilled, male manual working class . . . the
feminisation of the workforce . . . and [the weakening of] older
collective solidarities'. (1988: 24)

It is not clear however, what the long-term effects in terms of
race and class can be apart from both a growth in alternatives to
class identity – what Hall calls a return to subjectivity but in new
forms – and the increasing polarization of the workforce into those
who are employed and the unemployed. Black, ethnic minorities
and women have all been seen to inhabit the latter space (see
Mitter 1986).

CENTRAL PROBLEMS – AN OVERVIEW

There is a series of problems that are shared by most of these
positions. Firstly, theoretical shifts will often occur concerning the
object of analysis. For example, where the object is migrant labour,
a shift may occur to migrant groups, ethnic or racial groups, or
Black (often meaning African-Caribbean) groups. A conflation
takes place between migrant labour as a particular category of
labour, and certain ascriptive characteristics defining 'group
formation' (for example, Black, ethnic). Where a racial or ethnic

group is identified as a class, class stratum or class fraction, this assumes that it is homogeneously constituted in relation to production, that classes themselves are ethnically homogeneous and ignores intra-class and intra-ethnic divisions. Where migrant groups, racial groups or migrant labour are defined as a reserve army of labour, conceptual and empirical problems occur in relation to the use of Marxist economic categories to an inappropriate object (Anthias 1980).

A second problem is that there often occurs a conflation between different levels of abstraction. This leads to the conflation of different kinds of questions. At one level, we can try to conceptualize the role of racial or ethnic categories within the capitalist mode of production. But since such a mode does not require ethnic differences, we must resort to explaining their role within the concrete mode of production, which always exists within a determinate social formation. Here, a tendency has been to see race as reducible to the ideological representation of class – as a kind of false consciousness.

A third difficulty lies in the failure to specify the precise effects of racial categorization on labour categories. If it is racism that determines the incorporation (and exclusions) at the economic level, then economic requirements must be seen as secondary. What generally happens is that racism is seen as constituted in colonialist social relations, and then is seen to have its effects in the present.

In terms of general theoretical issues, we believe that although race and class are analytically distinct concepts, they cannot be treated as two distinct sets of relations, which interconnect in some essential way. Indeed what appears in the guise of 'race and class' is a number of heterogeneous questions about class formation, race formation, racism, exclusion and economic and social position and disadvantage. These questions cannot be collapsed together under the issue of the links between race and class. They involve looking at wider social processes, in terms of economic, representational, political and discursive conditions and of course also relate to other divisions, such as gender.

In addition, to pose the issue in terms of the links between race and class often conflates different levels of analysis, the conceptual and the empirical. This is a problem largely although not only because these groupings cannot be understood as given, outside the question of their structuration which involves the consideration of wider social relations. The terms of 'race and class' often assume an answer which posits some sort of effectivity or determination of one by the other or alternatively the positing of a non-determination and autonomy. Both these positions appear as inevitable outcomes of the way in which the question is posed (Anthias 1990).

 In addition to the general theoretical problems shared by the race and class debate, there is an empirical problem. This is to account for 'class differences' within a racialized population. For if racism is the structuring principle for class, or alternatively is structured by class, then we cannot account for variations in class and political position within racialized groups.

We shall now examine the economic position of Black or racialized groups in Britain, paying attention to employment characteristics, unemployment, variations between different racialized groups, housing and education. We shall then return to assessing the question of the usefulness of depicting racialized groups in class terms.

We have said that the issue of race and class actually raises a set of heterogeneous questions relating to racism, exclusion, economic placement and economic and social disadvantages. Explanations of the empirical reality that faces the bulk of migrants and their British-born children and indeed grandchildren (an increasingly large number are now third generation), have tended to focus on either the deficiencies in skill levels or education of migrants or both. The 1987–9 Labour Force Surveys, however, show that even taking into account equal educational qualifications Black men (their term) fare worse than White men (*Employment Gazette* 1991). Cultural preferences or propensities are also often used to explain economic participation. Although this may account for some of the differences between ethnic minorities it cannot account for their overall lower class placement, however.

Other explanations concern the effects of racism or discrimination. It is important where the latter is concerned not only to regard this as a question of a set of discriminatory practices by individuals, but also as embedded within structures (what used to be known in the literature as institutional racism). Processes of economic restructuring have to be taken into account also. Disadvantage may not merely be a question of racial discrimination in the job market, though there is indisputable evidence that this exists. The overall effects of capital restructuring may have affected Black people more greatly, given their sectoral and subordinate position, through uneven growth, labour market segmentation, and industrial relocation which have actually affected all lower socio-economic groups. In the following section we shall further explore the question of race and class, with particular reference to the economic and social placement of ethnic and migrant groups in contemporary British society.

MIGRANT AND RACIALIZED WORKERS IN BRITAIN

There is much evidence that migration to Britain from the ex-colonies in the postwar period was linked to labour demand in Britain during a period of economic growth (Peach 1968, Sivanandan 1973, 1976, Rex 1973, Miles 1982a) and it is not necessary here to discuss this issue. It is also true that most of the migrant workforce was replacement labour for indigenous workers (who had moved into more skilled and remunerative employment) and entered the labour market on disadvantageous terms. It is also true that these workers not only experienced poor conditions of work, but poor housing (Rex and Moore 1967), and racism and discrimination.

Generally speaking migrants (except for some categories of refugees) have tended to be from the poorest and most under-privileged groups of their countries of origin. In the case of Britain, the last wave of new commonwealth migrants of the post-Second World War period have had their class composition structured through colonial relations. The ways in which they have been inserted into the economic relations of the countries of migration have not only reproduced the class disadvantages present at the point of migration, but have restructured them within relations of racism and other political and economic exclusions.

However, it is also the case that different migrant groups are concentrated in different areas of employment and that they experienced different forms of exclusion and discrimination, depending on their skill and conditions of entry into Britain. This raises the issue of how useful it is to characterize racialized groups as a homogeneous economic and indeed social category and it is our contention that such a depiction is unsatisfactory. This is not because we wish to deny the economic and social disadvantages that the majority of ethnic minority, migrant or racialized people face, but because we think it is important to be clear about the processes by which economic and social positioning is achieved. Like Miles, we have the view that this cannot be accounted for exclusively through the workings of racism or racist exclusions, but that it requires a more sensitive approach, taking into account labour market processes, and the ways in which groups themselves call upon cultural and gender resources in order to manage the structural disadvantages they face.

There appears little disagreement that the key to the concrete economic position of a group lies in employment, although factors such as housing, education and political and legal status are also relevant. It is important to differentiate in the British context between migrant workers who enter on specific work permits and more permanently settled ethnic minorities, by which we mean for the purposes of this chapter new commonwealth migrants and their descendants, although these are clearly overlapping categories.

It has been estimated that the ethnic minority population in Britain constitutes 4.7 per cent of the working population (*Employment Gazette*, February 1991). In addition there are half a million migrant workers and their families in the UK (Ardill and Cross 1987). Around 220,000 are Italian and therefore EC nationals, although the majority came before the freedom of movement provisions came into force. Another 50,000 are Spanish, 30,000 are Portuguese, 20,000 are Filipino and 8,000 are Colombian, and all the groups live mainly in London. The more established groups, like the Portuguese, face similar disadvantages to new commonwealth migrants, such as poor housing, lower paid jobs, particularly in the service industries, and difficulties in relation to welfare provision. Later arrivals, such as Filipinos, Colombians and Turks have greater insecurity under the present immigration law and practice as some are still on work permits which restrict rights to welfare benefits (Ardill and Cross 1987).

It is important to note some of the problems with official statistics. They cannot include non-registered workers, either illegal migrants or those who are working in the hidden economy. The categories used shift and change over time with notions of Black, Asian and non-White used, as well as country of origin. They often only pick up those who were born outside England but say very little about the British-born Black population. The category Black is confused and confusing. It is important to note that Asian and African-Caribbean are the dominant categories defined as problems by both racist and anti-racist discourse, and within official statistics. The terms Black and White are often used in a contradictory way however, and it is sometimes not clear whether all new commonwealth migrants are being referred to or whether only African-Caribbeans and Asians, or even only African-Caribbeans. The Cypriots, who actually share many of the employment and other class characteristics, particularly with Asians, as well as a history of colonialism and migration, are not specifically mentioned in these discussions (see Anthias 1992).

EMPLOYMENT AND UNEMPLOYMENT

Ethnic minorities are unevenly distributed in terms of employment. The initial employment for migrants of all types tends to be in manual work primarily (even though different groups of migrants are in different sectors and occupations) and this tends to be reproduced in the British-born population.

Migrants and their children tend to be overrepresented at the lower end of the class structure. A higher proportion of White men are in non-manual work (53 per cent) compared with ethnic minority men (47 per cent) and more of the latter are in unskilled and semi-skilled work (*Employment Gazette*, February 1991). The PSI survey (Brown 1984) found that 83 per cent of West Indians and 73 per cent of Asians were in manual work compared with 58 per cent for Whites. Over a third (35 per cent) of West Indians and two-fifths (40 per cent) of Asian men were in unskilled and semi-skilled work compared with about one-sixth (16 per cent) of Whites. Between 1974 and 1982, the proportion of White men in semi- and unskilled jobs fell by a quarter; amongst Asian men it fell by an eighth whilst among African-Caribbean men it actually rose.

On the other hand over two-fifths (42 per cent) of Whites were in the professional, employers or management category compared with one-sixth (15 per cent) of West Indians and a quarter (26 per cent) of Asians. It has been estimated (Field 1987) that around 10 per cent of male ethnic minority workers are in professional and managerial work. When we later on look at the differences between different groups we will see that this is not generally the case for all minorities. African-Caribbeans, Pakistanis and Bangladeshis in particular have a far lower rate than this.

As well as ethnic minority men being concentrated in manual

work, we find that they are distributed in different sectors of the labour market compared with White men. Labour Force Surveys (OPCS) in the 1980s have consistently found around one-quarter of West Indian and Indian men were in metal goods engineering and vehicles, compared with less than one-fifth of all workers. The 1987–8 Labour Force Surveys show that distribution, hotels, catering and repairs were the most common sectors of employment for ethnic minority men, with a 29 per cent representation compared with 16 per cent for Whites. The largest single occupational group for ethnic minority men was metal and electrical engineering with 19 per cent, and for women it was clerical and related work with 23 per cent.

Although ethnic minority women are in a particularly disadvantaged sphere with regard to home-working, domestic work, unskilled service work and as unpaid family workers, it is wrong to conclude that all ethnic minority women constitute one economic or labour market category. In terms of economic activity rates, for example, there is a great diversity between different groups, with West Indian women having very high rates and Muslim women very low rates (see Chapter 4). West Indian women are also more likely to work full time than any other category, including White women. But there is a marked lack of choice as to when, how and where the women enter employment (see next chapter for a discussion of home-working). The sexual division of labour both inside and outside the home as well as racism will determine where women enter the labour market. (See Chapter 4 for more discussion of migrant and racialized women.)

It is instructive to take the case of a council's employment of ethnic minorities in one London borough (Ethnic and Gender Project) in order to explore their positioning. We have calculated from the information available that the ethnic minority population in the area is four times less likely to be employed by the council than is the general population. In March 1984, 2.35 per cent of the council's work-force were Black. In fact 60.7 per cent of Black employees were women. The Social Services directorate is the largest employer of Black workers, and in it 35.7 per cent of Black non-manuals (who constitute only 3.55 per cent of all non-manual workers employed by the council) are employed. Of these 70 per cent were women and the majority were part-time workers. Clearly the race relations brief which assumed importance in the community affairs section has had an important role to play. Black employees were only 1.27 per cent of the manual workforce, indicating the greater working of institutionalized racism in this sphere.

Labour networks in employment are extremely important and recruitment to many firms is through such networks, given the time and expense involved in hiring labour in the formal way, and with so many people applying (Ethnic and Gender Project). In this sense discrimination against Black people need not be intentional, although there is evidence of some racial stereotyping by employers. It can be a result of Black workers not being able to have a foot in the door in the first place. Many firms take on workers who are friends or relatives of those who already work there, preferentially treating these candidates and also to avoid advertising jobs publicly. In cases where there have been ethnic minorities already employed entry to others is made much easier.

The PSI survey of 1984 (Brown 1984) found that there were pay differentials between Whites and non-Whites with, in 1983, an average full-time weekly wage for White men standing at £129. For West Indians this was £109 and for Asians it was only slightly better at £111.

For women the figures show much lower wages overall. Although West Indian women have a higher on-average weekly wage (£81) than both White women (£77) and Asian women (£75) when ages between 25 and 54 are considered only (given that ethnic minority age profiles are lower) there is an overall wage difference in favour of White women. Other serious problems with this account will be given in the following chapter but it is sufficient to note here that these figures are severely distorted by not taking account of the distinction between shift and non-shift work (which Black women, like Black men, are more likely to do) nor the number of hours worked. One significant factor is that Black women are far more likely to work full time than White women even when they have dependent children (for a discussion of the implications of this on feminist analysis of women's work see our next chapter).

Despite the facts of lower pay amongst ethnic minorities, more of them are unionized; the PSI study (Brown 1984) found that 56 per cent of Black workers belonged to a union compared with 47 per cent of Whites, although the explanation offered is that this is due to the type of work that Black workers do.

UNEMPLOYMENT

Ethnic minorities have suffered most from the growth of unemployment. One specific explanation that has been offered for the greater unemployment amongst Black people is the 'industry in decline' argument. There are indications that this is not sufficient (see Smith 1981 and Fevre 1984 and Brown 1984, all of which stress the role of discrimination).

The unemployed tend to be in the lower strata of manual work where ethnic minorities are overrepresented. The ethnic minority unemployed are no longer counted (the Department of Employment stopped giving a breakdown by ethnic group in 1982) so modern figures are uninformative, out of date and cannot represent the fact that Black people, like women, are less likely to be registered and more young Blacks are on YTS and other government schemes (see Lee and Wrench 1988).

Whereas two-thirds of young White adults were working in 1984, only two-fifths of African-Caribbeans and Asians were. Also this is an underestimate for another reason than the one offered earlier. The national figures are made to appear lower since ethnic minorities are concentrated in the south where overall unemployment rates are low. The 1986 Labour Force Survey (OPCS) shows that Black people in the West Midlands are three times more likely to be unemployed than White people.

The 1984 Labour Force Survey (OPCS) showed a 20.4 per cent rate of registered unemployment amongst Black people, nearly twice the White rate of 11.1 per cent. The Labour Force Survey of 1985 (OPCS) showed that 18 per cent of White males between 16 and 24 were unemployed, whereas for ethnic minorities this was 32 per cent. For women the equivalent figures were 16 per cent and 33 per cent. Black people are 7.3 per cent of the unemployed although only 4.5 per cent of the population as a whole and 9 per cent of the long-term unemployed. This differential is even greater when we consider Black women who are twice as likely to be unemployed as White women, being 6.7 per cent of all unemployed women while only 3.7 per cent of the female labour force. Also the speed of the increase in unemployment has tended to affect Black people more, and most important, they are more likely to be long-term unemployed. Preliminary results from the 1990 Labour Force Survey show a figure of 11 per cent for ethnic minorities compared with 7 per cent for all persons; Pakistanis and

Bangladeshis have the highest unemployment rate with 17 per cent overall and 24 per cent for women in this category (*Employment Gazette*, April 1991: 191).

Again in order to explore the issue of unemployment further we can use data from a south-east London borough (Ethnic and Gender Project). The Department of Employment has not collected data on unemployment amongst ethnic minorities since August 1982 and the London research centre figures presented here are based on the 1981 census. Unemployment rates in the borough by ethnic origin in 1981 show the rate for ethnic minorities as 16.1 per cent compared with 9.2 per cent for Whites and others, with men having a higher rate than women, although the difference between ethnic minority men and women is not as great as amongst the White population. This compares with the inner London average of 16.9 per cent for ethnic minorities. The unemployment rate for ethnic minority women was more than double the borough average for women, with South Asian women being the worst affected. For men the worst affected were Africans and West Indians.

The discussion on employment and unemployment above shows that if we take the category of ethnic minorities, we find that they are overrepresented in the lower echelons of the labour market, and are more likely to be unemployed than Whites. However, in order to argue that they have a particular class position because of racism, discrimination or because they are an economic category, we need to explore the differences within this population on the one hand, and the issue of self-employment on the other. This discussion serves to problematize the unitary application of racialized groups as a particular class or migrant labour category. Our view is that racism or discrimination on its own cannot account for the positioning of any one racialized group. Ethnic disadvantage in the labour market is also linked to the class and gender resources that the group possesses, both at the point of entry into the labour market and as a result of the ways in which racialized groups are inserted into wider social relations in the society of migration. In addition, they can draw on familial, gender and ethnicity in the attempt to manage the disparate structural disadvantages they face on the basis of class, ethnicity, gender and racialization. The issue of the cross-cutting of gender is important but we shall explore this in greater depth in the following chapter.

CLASS DIFFERENCES WITHIN THE ETHNIC MINORITY POPULATION

One of the greatest difficulties faced by the argument that race is really a question of class is accounting for the heterogeneous nature of the different ethnic groups in relation to the British class structure as well as in relation to political and ideological processes. There has been a greater tendency in recent years for official bodies to define race through colour rather than ethnicity. At the same time there has occurred an increasing ethnicization of groups where traditional cultural divisions are often displaced by the growth of more unifying identities. The Asian category is a case in point, which actually is extremely heterogeneous and yet has been constructed as a unitary category. In the case of African-Caribbeans there have developed distinct forms of cultural and political resistance that present new forms of identity.

We have argued elsewhere the importance of paying attention to the different ways in which different classes and different ethnicities, as well as men and women from different groups, are affected by and experience social relations (Anthias and Yuval-Davis 1983). Classes are heterogeneous in terms of race and ethnicity as well as gender, and it is not possible to refer to class as a unitary category. This also applies to gender, ethnicity, race, migrant labour or whatever the term of reference we wish to use for the object of study of racialized categories.

Labour Force Surveys (OPCS) in the 1980s have shown that different groups have different economic activity rates. Pakistanis and Bangladeshis have the lowest with just over one-half, Indians have a rate of just over three-quarters and West Indians have the highest with four-fifths, similar to Whites (*Employment Gazette*, February 1991). The low rates for Pakistanis and Bangladeshis are however, largely the result of the low economic participation of women, with around one fifth being economically active compared with around four-fifths for West Indian women.

Although as we said earlier one quarter of both West Indian and Indian men are in metal goods, engineering and vehicles we find a number of differences in the employment of different ethnic minority groups. For example, 18 per cent of West Indian men are employed in transport and communications compared with 9 per cent of all men. Of Indian men 21 per cent are in distribution, hotels and catering and repairs industries compared with 15 per cent of all men (Newnham 1986). The distributive trades accounted for 30 per cent of jobs done by Pakistani and Bangladeshi men in 1984. In fact the 1984 Labour Force Survey shows this latter to be the largest sector for all ethnic minority men (26 per cent).

Surveys have found greater differences within ethnic minorities than between them and White workers. Regarding non-manual work for example, the 1981 Labour Force Survey (OPCS) found that if we break down the non-White group we find that 13 per cent of West Indians, 36 per cent of Indians, 46 per cent of Chinese, Africans and Arabic, and 28 per cent of Pakistanis and Bangladeshis were in this category of work. In relation to semi-skilled and unskilled work, when the Asian category is broken down, we find that nearly 70 per cent of Bangladeshi employees are semi-skilled or unskilled compared with 40 per cent of Indians and Pakistanis and 55 per cent of African Asians.

Regarding unemployment, as we showed earlier in the chapter, the Black rate is twice the White rate for both men and women but there are differences between different groups, with Pakistanis and Bangladeshis having the highest rates (36.4 per cent) followed by West Indians (23 per cent) (Newnham 1986).

Regarding self-employment, men and women of Asian origin are more likely to be self-employed than either African-Caribbean or White men and women. About 20 per cent of Asian men are self-employed compared with 7.5 per cent for African-Caribbean and 13 per cent for White men. Far fewer Pakistani men are self-employed than Bangladeshi and other Asian men, however. Self-employment can be regarded partly as a response to lack of opportunities. Also Asians, like Cypriots, can use the family and women as a source of unpaid labour (see Anthias 1982, 1983, 1991 and 1992). Arguments about a dual labour market are dependent on showing a unitary position structured through migration, racism or labour market segmentation for ethnic minorities.

THE ISSUE OF SELF-EMPLOYMENT AND DIVISIONS WITHIN RACIALIZED GROUPS

Approximately the same proportion of White men and African-Caribbean and Asian men taken together are self-employed (13 per cent) but Asians have a greater representation here, with 20 per cent if counted on their own. Given this incidence of self-employment it is worth briefly turning to the issue of Black business.

First, it has to be borne in mind that self-employment is largely structured by lack of opportunities in paid employment, either as the result of racism or the result of limited educational or other skills in relation to the requirements of the labour market. However, there are a number of additional factors. One of these relates to the kinds of networks and familial relations that make small business at least an option when other opportunities are limited. A second issue relates to the economic aims of migration and the symbolic role of the myth of return. Thirdly, it is important to consider the prevalent cultural norms within a specific migrant community regarding the appropriate ways for individuals to further their aspirations. When these factors are taken into account, it becomes easier to see why Asian groups are more likely to turn to self-employment compared with African-Caribbeans.

In relation to the first aspect, concerning networks and familial relationships, Asians, like Cypriots (Anthias 1982, 1983 and 1992) can use the unpaid labour of women and children, because of close ties within the family and between kin. Other strong networks are those of the village and of the ethnic group as a whole. With the African-Caribbeans, on the other hand, their family structure and their lack of the traditional kinship ties found in Asian and Mediterranean societies do not allow family and kinship labour to be utilized to further the economistic aims of migration or act as a buffer to other exclusions in the labour market.

A recent survey of Asian retailers (Luthra and Bajwa 1988) in one London borough shows the growth of Asian businesses to be a relatively new phenomenon (beginning in the mid-1980s) and that they tend to be concentrated in the run-down commercial areas. The 1981 census for the borough (Ethnic and Gender Project) (sample) shows the self-employed category both with and without employees to be 7.6 per cent compared with 6.2 per cent for Whites (compare this with the Labour Force Survey figure of 1984 which shows that nationally 14 per cent of Asians and 9 per cent of Whites are self-employed). Of those who are self-employed, 30 per cent employ others, compared with 24 per cent for Whites. However, most of the ethnic minority self-employed were found to be in distributive trades and catering (41 per cent of NCW men, compared with 23 per cent for Whites) thus confirming that ethnic minority business tends to be concentrated in labour intensive sectors. Only 1 per cent were large employers in manufacturing compared with 7.8 per cent among White self-employed.

Asian small businesses in this particular borough are concentrated in areas where there is a high proportion of ethnic residence and which are those in most decline. The setting up of a small business appeared linked to the increase of unemployment in the area and the Gujerati group were overrepresented in the retail business, followed by Punjabis. Almost all the businesses in the sample were dependent on 'family labour'; therefore women as well as children were an important labour resource. Women entrepreneurs were few (only 3 per cent). The condition of the premises tended to be poor and the hours worked long. Thus there was considerable personal cost involved in setting up a business.

Some further case-studies in relation to employment are provided by the 100 or so intensive interviews we have conducted (Ethnic and Gender Project). These further show that Asians and Cypriots have turned to self-employment as a viable alternative to limited job opportunities; factory work is low paid and vulnerable to redundancies. For example, after deciding to settle in Britain and leaving his job in the Indian High Commission, the husband of one Asian woman interviewed had set up business, since there were few options open to him apart from factory work. She worked in an Asian clothing factory until her husband's business was established. Another Asian woman's husband had set up a market stall in addition to claiming social security benefits. An Asian male interviewee had an engineering job at a factory although he also did a little import and export and car maintenance on the side. He planned to set up a family business in the near future as a response to worsening redundancies and in the hope of a higher income.

In response to this there have been various initiatives to promote Black business and enterprise (for example, CRE 1986a). These initiatives have been given a boost by the depressing prospect of permanent unemployment for large sections of the Black community, particularly the young. However, as the CRE report says, 'There is also a growing recognition that for full equal opportunities to be a reality, Black people must share in the ownership of the economic base' (CRE 1986a: 1). In fact the Scarman report on the 1981 Brixton riots states, 'I do urge the necessity for speedy action if we are to avoid the perpetuation in

this country of an economically dispossessed Black population.'
Indeed the CRE report sees the encouragement of ethnic minority
small business as a means of regenerating the whole economy
(Scarman 1981: 2). Lack of start-up capital has been regarded as a
major obstacle along with lack of business experience, and
discrimination by banks and more widely. The report argues for
the provision of loan finance through a special fund. The setting
up of a government contracts policy and of minority investment
companies are amongst its recommendations.

One issue relating to this is how to conceptualize the role of
business enterprise, firstly in defining the class position of ethnic
minority self-employed or small scale employers, and secondly to
consider some of the effects of a greater representation of ethnic
minorities in this sphere.

Of course in strict Marxist terms the category above would
become a constituency within the petty bourgeoisie and would
merely further add to the class differentiations that already
characterize ethnic minorities. The effects this would have on
dissipating ethnic communality and consciousness is a contentious
issue (see Anthias 1982, 1983 and 1992) and depends on the
primacy in specific contexts of class versus ethnic solidarity. In the
currency of a racist society, ethnic solidarity is likely to be retained
at the expense of class consciousness in differentiating within
racialized populations (see Anthias 1982).

Attacks on Asian businesses are an everyday feature of British
society and this is one of the forms of racist attacks that are on the
increase in this period of mass unemployment and disaffection
(Ethnic and Gender Project). Asian businesses are also ready
targets for organizations such as the National Front and the British
Movement. On the other hand the removal from the competitive
sphere of the employment lottery may make less visible the supposed threat of ethnic minorities in the sphere of paid
employment. However, ethnic minorities are already suffering
from greater unemployment and thus have already been removed
from this sphere to some extent.

A number of additional factors require mentioning in the
context of the complex articulations of race and class. First, is the
issue of the 'hidden economy'. This is not only a sector for people
who are illegal entrants but also characterizes ethnic minority
employment in the pre-industrial sectors, particularly the clothing

industry (Anthias 1983, Phizacklea 1990). This is a special area for women migrants who are very often home-workers, with all that implies (Allen and Wolkowitz 1987). In addition, at the other end of the scale are the Black middle classes, comprising amongst others the 'professional Blacks' of the 'Race Relations Industry' (Sivanandan 1982). The middle-class category therefore includes those groups whose class position was already more favourable at the point of entry, such as certain groups of Asians, as well as those who have been sponsored by the state.

Employment has been emphasized in this chapter as a main indicator of class positioning but the areas of housing and education are also important and we shall turn to these very briefly before coming back to the implications that all these factors raise for the analysis of race and class.

HOUSING, THE INNER CITY AND EDUCATION: SOME BRIEF COMMENTS

There is no doubt that increasingly the position of groups *vis-à-vis* the ownership of housing and its condition and location are significant factors in assessing class position. This was a prime argument in Rex and Moore's study of race and the inner city that used the controversial notion of housing classes (Rex and Moore 1967). Although it is inadequate to refer to class as constituted in any way by the distribution of housing resources, none the less, housing, like occupation is one of its main indicators and a significant effect of economic positioning.

Although data show Asians are more likely to own their own homes than African-Caribbeans or Whites (72 per cent, 41 per cent and 59 per cent respectively) they are also more likely to be in run-down inner-city areas and living in overcrowded conditions. In official data 60 per cent of Bangladeshis and 47 per cent of Pakistanis are classified as overcrowded compared with just over 3 per cent of Whites. On the other hand African-Caribbeans are more likely to be council tenants than Asians (46 per cent and 19 per cent respectively). Discrimination by estate agents and in reports exposed by the press is commonplace. Housing allocation staff also use racial stereotyping and are likely to allocate Black people less desirable property (Gordon and Newnham 1986: 21). Homelessness affects ethnic minorities disproportionately. In a study of Gloucester 4 per cent of young Black people between the ages of 16 and 21 were homeless while 40 per cent were living in temporary accommodation. The routine demand to see passports and work permits in some areas illustrates the wealth of discriminatory practices that exist (Gordon and Newnham 1986).

In relation to the issue of economic but not direct employment processes, it has been increasingly popular to refer to the problems of the inner city, to urban deprivation and issues of urban renewal when discussing the positioning of ethnic minorities. Although it has been generally felt that urban deprivation became a political issue in the 1960s the concern with race specifically in terms of inner-city problems probably owes as much to the more recent outbreaks of riots. However, there is concern about other social problems of inner-city life: civil unrest, crime and violence, as well as the particular 'problem' categories of Black families, or more recently, Black youth. On the other hand the notion of inner-city problems focuses on the specific effects that the physical and organizational aspects of inner-city life bring, such as inadequate housing, crowding, multi-occupation, alienation and disaffection. In addition, the areas cited as having inner-city problems are often those with a concentration of ethnic minority populations and therefore where the racism of the wider society is thrown into sharp relief and needs special management. Policies and practices relating to the needs of the area or the needs of the community in terms of policing, social service provision and the management of social disadvantage are contradictorily presented.

Educational qualifications can be described as a form of cultural capital, along with skills, and in the Weberian tradition of analysis assume great importance (Parkin 1979). However, contemporary Marxist analyses of class also pay attention to education as a structuring principle of concrete class formation (see Poulantzas 1973). Regarding ethnic minorities, the Swann Report (1985) and Eggleston (1983) argue that class and racism are important factors in explaining the under-achievement of Black children (also see James and Jeffcoate 1981). Studies of the links between class and education have been the mainstay of much sociological writing on class and given the uneven distribution of Black people in the class structure we can expect to find class disadvantages compounded by institutional racism. There is also the question of racism within the teaching profession, which may be linked with the failure of Black children to be entered for exams and the identification of behavioural problems.

There has been a great deal of attention to recent developments both in relation to so-called multi-culturalism and to anti-racism in the school system and the debate rages on. In Chapter 6 we discuss some of the ideological underpinnings of these policies. Here, however, we note a number of facets that are important in this context.

Firstly, there is the enormously sensitive issue of language and provision within the school system for multi-lingual teaching and learning and of access to ethnic minority languages and mother-tongue teaching. This is related also to the provision of multi-cultural education in the broader sense, facilitating the maintenance of culture and identity for ethnic minorities and a positive evaluation of these.

Secondly, there is the issue of facilitating the educational attainment of children from ethnic minority backgrounds which is regarded in some ways as linked to our first point, although some consider multi-culturalism would be encouraged at the expense of attainment in the mainstream curriculum.

Thirdly, there is the whole issue of developing an anti-racist educational practice that is more than multi-culturalism or the discussion of racism in the classroom, and of achieving an anti-racist ethos that will carry over into practices outside the school gate.

CONCLUSION

There are a number of central issues that we must now turn to in order to relate the data we have presented to some of the conceptual issues that we spent so much time discussing in the first part of this chapter.

Firstly, the data indicate a heterogeneity within the ethnic minority population and that this cannot be accounted for by seeing racialized groups as one class. Nevertheless, migrant and ethnic minorities, whether we use the term 'Black' as a shorthand to describe them or we want to maintain the distinction between White and Black minority groups with the latter only being our frame of reference, all share certain disadvantages. These are linked partly to the class origin of the majority of migrants but are restructured within an exclusionary and racist society. However, the differences in the structural position of different groups defined also by ethnicity, gender and legal status prevents us from talking about them as a distinct class stratum or fraction of the working class. The growth of self-employment amongst Asians particularly, and the greater unemployment of young African-Caribbeans and Asians and of women, means that different groups are positioned differently in the class structure.

In addition, racism cannot on its own be an adequate explanation for economic position. Sectoral employment must also be considered and a labour market analysis is necessary that looks at developments in those sectors where ethnic minorities are over-represented. These are predominantly the labour intensive sectors that require little skill or education. This is where a segmented labour market approach, which considers the concrete processes in different sectors is a necessary adjunct to those approaches that focus primarily on employer strategies and discrimination.

This chapter explored some of the central issues at stake in searching for the links between race and class. It provided a critical appraisal of some of the most influential approaches to this question and looked at the connections empirically between economic position and ethnic and racial position.

The Marxist concept of class has undergone considerable re-working in the light of contemporary developments within advanced western societies. Marx's view was that capitalism was predicated on two major classes, capitalists and workers, in an essential relationship of antagonism. Intermediate strata existed but they were transitory, because the tendency of capital accumulation was to swallow up the small employer or self-employed and other groups. Marxists have had to rethink this, partly in the light of the growth of the new middle classes (as sociologists call them) or the new petty bourgeoisie, the term that neo-Marxists prefer (for example, Poulantzas 1973). Problems relating to the links between the economic and political spheres found within Marxist analysis and difficulties relating to the concept of class consciousness and class interests have led to attempts to formulate less deterministic forms of analysis. Examples are found in the work of Poulantzas (1973), E. O. Wright (1976) and Stuart Hall (1980).

It is increasingly seen as inadequate to understand other social divisions, like sex or race, as epiphenomena of class, as incipient classes or as functional for capital. This is reflected in the race literature and feminist work as well as within more mainstream

Marxist political analysis. Social classes can thus be seen as the product of struggle within concrete historical processes which will include relations of gender and ethnicity and race, as well as economic, political and ideological relations (see Anthias and Yuval-Davis 1983).

The ramification of local struggles outside the work-place has led to the increasing recognition that there exist different constituencies for struggle: in the streets as in the case of riots or resistance to police harassment; within social movements such as the anti-nuclear campaign; over claimants' rights and the rights of parents; on housing estates; and through feminism in what were, in pre-feminist days, defined as private relations in the home and in personal relations. The possibility that solidarity may be forged in all these different ways has opened up the way to treating traditional class divisions as not necessarily forming the most immediate basis for struggle, at least in terms of concrete manifestations. Also, the growth of mass unemployment has affected the understanding of class and some arguments have posited the development of two classes, of unemployed and employed. Like sociological theory more broadly, Marxists have had to take a position in relation to the central problem of structure and human agency. For example, both the more concrete analyses of class, political action and the state in the work of Stuart Hall (1980) and what has been called 'analytical' or 'rational' choice Marxism (Elster 1985) represent distinct approaches to this question. Both, however, claim to be following a Marxist tradition of analysis.

Most importantly, these different approaches ask us to look beyond the economy in order to understand the position of ethnic minorities. In addition, they both, in different ways, reject the view that the social structure is composed of 'places' that are merely to be filled by individuals in a mechanical way. The individuals who fill the places are essential formative subjects in the reproduction or transformation of the positions they fill, for there are no empty structures at the level of the determinate social formation.

Economic and class processes are constituted through struggle, negotiation and cultural responses which in part relate to the essentially ethnic exclusionary nature of British society. This cannot be merely read from the direct workings of racist ideology and practice, whether it be in an institutional sense or as mediating interpersonal relations. The essentially exclusionary nature of British society relates to the very construction of the British ethnos, which formulates essential and natural political rights to only those who are 'really' part of the national collectivity. British ethnicity is thus to be taken into account. Rather than merely referring to ethnicity as a component of ethnic minority status, as for example in discussions relating to reactive ethnicity, we need to recognize its primary condition as a differentiating mode within the very heart of a social system. This ethnicity seems natural and therefore unaware of itself. Yet it appears continuously around notions of a generically British way of life. This can accommodate outsiders as long as they remain exotically ethnic or if they can lose their concern with their separate cultural interests. In neither case they must not impinge on the inalienable rights of the ethnic collective.

A particular issue is whether, even where we cannot refer to race as some variant of class relations, struggles about racism or ethnicity can construct a unity (a commonality of interests, consciousness and action) that cuts across the class, gender or cultural divisions within racialized groups. Certainly ethnic commonality can function in the interests of capital (as in the use of ethnic labour, or the formation of an 'English' national unity, which we considered in Chapter 2). But can ethnic commonality unite worker and small capitalist in class action, forged through common experience and struggle over culture, ethnicity or racism? Gilroy's (1987) view is that the experience of the structures and culture of racism is only one of the factors in racial solidarity, and that Black people in Britain have a distinct mode of culture and organization. None the less it seems a question of political priorities at specific conjunctural moments that decide whether race or class solidarity wins the day. They cannot in any case be disaggregated easily, as race structuration takes place in the context of class, is one of its conditions of existence, and class structuration in Britain has been within the context of race.

In relation to racism it has become increasingly inadequate to locate it as the product of class interests at the level of production because racism is not a necessary prerequisite of class exploitation although it may, like gender, facilitate it. Also, class is increasingly no longer understood only with reference to the relations of production, but is also understood with reference to struggles located elsewhere (as noted above). Racism cross-cuts class, as, for example, in racism towards middle-class Blacks (and other minority groups). Racism, however, can be used for class purposes and often representational, political and institutional processes relating to racial differences are developed with particular reference to class political interests. Racist premises can be built upon in particular ways to further the interests of specific classes within dominant and aspiring dominant ethnic groups, where ethnic supremacy will involve the privileged exploitation of, or access to, economic or political resources (Anthias 1990). Similarly race discourse can be used to articulate struggle for economic and political power and resources, as a medium of class action.

What ethnic minorities share is not so much a class positioning, although it is true that they are concentrated in the lower echelons of the class structure. Most of all they share a positioning on the outer reaches of the British nation, as its sore spots and as its liberal conscience.

The attention to ethnic divisions that is current in British society has a number of outcomes, which have class effects. One of these is that it serves to mask the essentially divided nature of Britain's indigenous population, the haves and the have-nots, the employed and the unemployed, capital and labour. The constituency of class inequality has been pushed to the back of the agenda and Blacks have become the new proletariat of both the liberal conscience and its more and less progressive allies.

Miles (1984) in this sense is right to see the focus on race at all sorts of levels as a way out of facing the issue of the processes by which social divisions and ideologies are structured and restructured under particular socio-economic and political conditions. However, we believe that collective actors, pursuing political projects which contain the discourse of ethnicity, are themselves instrumental within these very sets of social relations rather than merely being constituted by them.

Chapter 4

Connecting race and gender

INTRODUCTION

The last two decades have seen a decline in the marginalization of ethnicity and race on the one hand and of gender on the other hand within sociology. There is no doubt that

> The impetus in both cases came largely from happenings outside sociology. The civil rights and Black power movements in the USA, the extensive use of migrant labour, including that of the Third World, in Europe and the growth of the contemporary women's movements were all part of the pressure felt by sociologists to reconceptualise some of the central theoretical ground of their discipline. (Allen, Anthias and Yuval-Davis 1991: 1)

The placing of gender as a primary focus of attention within the theory and practice of the human sciences was the result of feminism as a political movement. Sociology had merely added gender to its project without transforming the androcentric nature of the perspectives taken. For feminism a major task was the complete reappraisal of social theory through a thoroughgoing critique of the androcentric character of western society and western theory and science. The whole of social analyses, it was argued, had to be rewritten in the light of feminism, and feminist theory was born (Harding 1986). Much of feminist theory, however, was predicated on the 'sisterhood' of women, endowing the category woman with an essential and static property always in a dichotomous relation to the dominant 'other', man.

Although there are about 6 million women migrants in Europe most of the literature on migration and on race has failed to address their specific position and the way gender processes relate to those of race. Feminist literature also has only recently and then very sporadically become even conscious that it has ignored the ways in which gender and class processes differentially affect women from different ethnic and racialized social groups and has generally assumed a unitary category of women. Where the concept of ethnicity has been given consideration within feminist writing (for example, Barrett and Mackintosh 1985) it merely points to the cultural or ethnic difference between groups rather than rethinking the project of feminism.

Distinct bodies of theory and research have generally been developed around gender, race and ethnicity and where any connections were made they were to class divisions. Indeed, competing theories tended to prioritize one or other division and failed to interrelate them adequately, either analytically or concretely. In addition, the different social divisions were generally conceptualized as internally homogeneous, thus failing to attend to modes of differentiation and exclusionary power relations within each of them. This involved the danger of essentializing the divisions and differences that existed. With regard to women there was a tendency within mainstream sociology to talk of 'the position of women' as though women were undifferentiated in terms of class, culture and ethnicity.

The analysis of the links between class and gender, so characteristic of Marxist feminist work has found an echo within mainstream sociological analysis, although the terms of reference have been different (see Crompton 1988). This has added to the purchase given to critiques of an essential unitary 'sisterhood' and countered the view that gender relations are expressions of the biological category of sexual difference. In any case the most important role for 'sisterhood' was political and the idea of a community of women could hardly be maintained in the face of the competing voices of class, and later, race. Such theorizations have recognized that as a social relation gender is constructed partly through class and economic relations and that at the empirical level the experience of subordination and oppression varies in form within different class and economic contexts. However most of this work has not been able to integrate into its analysis differentiation structured either by racism or by ethnicity.

Partly as a result of the impact of the Black and other minority women's movements and women in the Third World, and the contribution of a number of Black feminist and other feminist writers, this situation is changing. During the 1980s, the yawning gap that existed in the literature with regard to connecting ethnic, race, gender and class processes has been slowly closing (Hooks 1981, Carby 1982, Anthias and Yuval-Davis 1983, Phizacklea 1983, Amos and Parmar 1984, Yuval-Davis and Anthias 1989, Spelman 1988). An increasing sensitivity to issues of ethnicity and racism is also apparent (Cavendish 1982, Westwood 1984, WING 1985). A growing interest in issues of gender and race is testified by the significant although somewhat ghettoized debate within feminist journals in particular (for example, *Feminist Studies*) and the fact that a few books have appeared fairly recently on the issue of gender, race and class (for example, Brittan and Maynard 1984, Cashmore 1989) aimed at an undergraduate sociology market. For the first time, in 1990, the International Sociological Association conference included a sub-stream on gender, race and class. White feminists have begun to pay attention to their own ethnocentrism (Barrett and Mackintosh 1985, Phillips 1987), to explore the links between feminism and racism (Knowles and Mercer 1991), and to begin incorporating into their analysis of patriarchy the issues of ethnicity and gender (Walby 1990). Volumes are being published in Australia, America and Canada that explore the different articulations of gender, race, ethnicity and class within their own societal contexts (Bottomley and de Lepervanche 1984, Stasiulis and Yuval-Davis forthcoming).

As we had already pointed out in 1983, 'Sisterhood is powerful but sisterhood can also be misleading unless contextualised' (Anthias and Yuval-Davis 1983). Elizabeth Spelman argues that the assumption of a 'generic woman' . . . obscures the heterogeneity of women and cuts off the examination of the significance of such heterogeneity for feminist theory and political activity (1988: ix). We believe that the deconstruction of the category woman opens up the way for an analysis that can attend to the diversities and commonalities amongst women from a range of societal, ethnic and class contexts. However, it is not enough merely to celebrate the existence of difference, as some post-modernist analysis has done. As Brah points out:

> Difference, diversity, pluralism, hybridity – these are some of the catch-phrases of our time. Questions of difference are at the heart of many discussions within contemporary feminisms.

Diversity is probably the only reliable persistent theme across the variety of postmodernisms that currently proliferate. (1991: 26)

As she notes, however, there is a danger that 'the specificity of a particular experience' may itself become an expression of essentialism. To posit diversity therefore does not necessarily imply the abandonment of static and ahistorical categories of difference but may merely proliferate them. This is why we believe that a historically contingent articulation of gender, ethnicity, race and class must draw on the analytical distinctions between the categories and their social effectivity and begin to theorize particular ways in which they interrelate in different contexts. This does not require that their interrelationship is always the same nor that one division or category is always prioritized. But it does require that we specify the mechanisms by which different forms of exclusion and subordination operate. From this point of view a position that merely recognizes that difference and diversity exist and that divisions are multiform provides little facility for theorizing:

> If the diversities and commonalities of individual experience are to give rise to more than catalogues of description, however intrinsically interesting or productive of pertinent insights, then the development of theorising incorporating race/ethnicity, gender and class requires serious attention. (Allen, Anthias and Yuval-Davis 1991)

Despite the welcome and timely developments noted above, we feel that there has been an impasse regarding conceptual and theoretical analysis, although the history and political economy of Black and migrant women is being carefully attended to. Among the factors responsible for this impasse must be the conceptual heritage left by radical feminist and Marxist feminist analyses. These have significant theoretical difficulty in accounting for difference and diversity within the essentialist categories on the one hand and the functionalist and class reductionist ones that they construct on the other. A shift is required in the ways we understand gendered identities which can attend to ethnic and racial attributions and identifications.

The earliest attempts to posit a specificity to women's position saw women enduring a double burden and in the case of Black or ethnic minority women a notion of a triple burden was used (for example, Amos and Parmar 1982, Phizacklea 1983, Westwood 1984). However, this depiction is unsatisfactory because it treats forms of subordination and oppression through race, sex, and class as cumulative rather than as articulating or intersecting together to produce specific effects. These cannot be mechanistically understood. It is the intersection of subordinations that is important and they cannot be treated as different layers of oppression (Anthias and Yuval-Davis 1983, Parmar 1988, Spelman 1988). In addition the links are not only to gender or sexual difference but to sexuality (Hooks 1991, Westwood 1990). Indeed the enterprise of connecting social divisions is laden with difficulties and therefore the well-meaning and often rhetorical interpolations regarding their links require a careful assessment in order to avoid the theoretical pitfalls that await.

The Black feminist critique of White feminism has been central in the thinking about the intricate links between gender, race, ethnicity and class and we will begin by critically examining some of the main features of this critique. In order to clarify some of the major conceptual problems involved we will examine the difficulties faced by the variety of feminisms and in particular by radical feminist and Marxist feminist theories. We will then present a framework for beginning to theorize the connections. Through a consideration of the areas of gender, ethnicity and race in the labour market on the one hand, and gender, ethnic and national processes and nationality on the other, we will explore the issue of the interconnections more concretely.

GENDER AND RACISM: THE BLACK FEMINIST CRITIQUE

In the last chapter we sought to contextualize race and racism within class and economic relations. We argued that the relationships between them are complex, reciprocal and require understanding both in terms of their conceptual and discursive distinctions as well as the examination of their interconnections within real social relations. Gender divisions also serve as a central organizing principle of social relations and therefore need to be considered in terms of their connections with race. However, just as we saw in the last chapter that race has often been reduced at a number of different levels to a particular representation of underlying economic or class relations, so gender has often met with the same fate, if not a worse one, of reduction to a biological 'essence' (Engels 1968, Firestone 1971).

Gender relates to the way in which sexual difference is represented and organized and is thus a product of social relations including those of class (and ethnicity). As we noted earlier, the placing of gender as a primary focus of attention within the theory and practice of the human sciences was the result of feminism as a political movement. Similarly it has been mainly the rise of the Black women's movement that has been responsible for bringing the links between race and gender (as opposed to gender and class that the White feminist movement concerned itself with) under examination. However, the Black women's movement has tended towards a number of positions which appear to us as theoretically as well as politically problematic. It is, therefore, worth giving what we regard as the main synthesizing features of the contribution of Black feminism.

THE BLACK FEMINIST CRITIQUE OF WESTERN FEMINISM

Firstly, Black feminists have rightly pointed to the ethnocentric nature of western feminism in positing certain priorities for struggle, such as abortion and the critique of the family, that do not take into account the experiences of Black or Third-World women; this can be termed imperial feminism (Amos and Parmar 1984), that is, the assumption of a unity of women's interests on the basis of White experience.

Secondly, White feminism is regarded as racist since it fails to take as central the anti-racist struggle, which ought to be within the parameters of a social movement concerned with the ways women have been oppressed. Black women are not only oppressed by men and institutionalized forms of sexism in the state but also by Whites (both men and women) and by institutionalized racism. The blindness to race (and the consequent invisibility of Black women) and the failure to take a strong stance against racism are seen as the products of the endemic racism of White feminism.

Thirdly, the pathologizing of the sexuality of Black people, and of the relations within the family and parenthood is regarded as racist. Examples of this are White feminist critiques of the Black family (with African-Caribbean men seen as abandoning their women and babies) and the construction of Asian women as passive and submissive (the arranged marriage, the dowry, clitoridectomy and so on) is regarded as racist. Western feminism also fails to acknowledge that Black women themselves may want to organize around racism using the category of gender.

We fully acknowledge the validity of these claims. However there are a number of conceptual problems hidden in the above formulations. It is clear that 'Black' is itself seen as a unifying category, mainly because it posits the experience of racism as defining the difference with White women. But as we show in the following chapter the construction of Blacks as the exclusive victims of racism, is problematic, especially if we include the racist effects of structures and not only intersubjective forms, like prejudice and discrimination. Generational divisions, the distinction between settlers, refugees and the Black British, the distinct nature of racisms experienced by different groups like African-Caribbeans and Asians, all need us to think more carefully about our analysis and practice. Similarly racism as experienced by migrants, Jews and other ethnic minorities is unaccounted for. However, as Brah states,

> 'white' feminism or 'black' feminism in Britain are not essentialist categories but rather they are fields of contestation inscribed within discursive and material processes in a post-colonial terrain. They represent struggles over political priorities and modes of mobilisation but they should not, in my view, be understood as locating 'white' and 'black' women as essentially fixed oppositional categories. (1991: 39)

Bell Hooks also critiques static notions of Black identity, urging for more 'fluid notions of black identity, or to marginal perspectives' and for 'assertions of identity that bring complexity and variety to constructions of black subjectivity' (1991: 20).

It appears absolutely valid that Black women (laying aside the problem of definition) should organize autonomously in terms of deciding priorities of struggle. However, there has been a tendency at times to fragment issues of sexism in such a way that only those who experience forms of oppression like the dowry or clitoridectomy are seen to be able to postulate whether they are sexist and to evaluate their role in subordinating women. We have some sympathy with the argument that struggles against culturally specific forms of sexism need to be undertaken in the full context of a racist society. None the less we do not believe that dominant cultural forms that subordinate women, from whichever context, should be immune from critique. This has been an important premise of organizations and movements such as the Southall Black Sisters. They have campaigned, for example, against Asian women's refuges that are dominated by a male traditional hierarchy within the community. Women Against Fundamentalism has taken on board a wide range of issues, often coming under attack by a Socialist Left, and has come to accept the sanctity of culture as well as traditional leaders within Muslim communities (Southall Black Sisters 1990, Saghal and Yuval-Davis 1991 and 1992). Moreover, Saghal (1992) claims that it is the definition of racism only in terms of Blackness which delegitimizes other dimensions of experience and forms of oppression (as well as empowerment), such as those experiences that relate to gender.

Hooks argues passionately for the confronting of sexism within 'Black communities, as well as within Black individuals who live in predominantly White settings. Masculinity as it is conceived within patriarchy is life threatening to Black men.' She argues for the 'careful interrogation of the way in which sexist notions of masculinity legitimise the use of violence' (1991: 77). However, unlike Southall Black Sisters, and Women Against Fundamentalism she does not prioritize a political project in common with feminists who are not Black.

A particular problem has been the conflation of racism and sexism. Although it is clear to us that the oppressions of sex and race cannot be mechanistically understood we none the less need to make a distinction between racist and sexist discourse and practice, although at the empirical level as they affect groups of human subjects they may be difficult to unpack. For example, the issue of the dowry is not part of the discourse and practice of racism but that of sexist social relations. We shall return to this issue at the end of this chapter when we look at the relation between feminism and anti-racism.

Knowles and Mercer (1991) accuse Black feminism of equating the struggles of Third-World women and Black women who experience racism. In an article that is essentially a diatribe against *The Empire Strikes Back* (CCCS 1982), they find that such an equation 'leaves the anti racist without a mode of political intervention' (1991: 21) because the concrete positionings of Third-World women cannot be analysed in the same way as those of Black migrant women since they stem from different societal contexts. They also believe that such an approach collapses all oppressions together. Although much of this argument is well founded Knowles and Mercer fail to examine the links in the experience of racialized women between sexism and racism. Separating oppressions at the analytical level does not entail the possibility that we can do so easily at the concrete level. Nor can racism and sexism be treated only as a set of 'effects' or outcomes, for this leaves out the ways in which collective actors are implicated in the exercise of sexist and racist practice and effects. At the end of the day Knowles and Mercer want to dispense with the category of sexist and racist practice, merely looking at the effects of practices in promoting sexual or racial exclusion. We agree that it is not necessary to limit racism to the sphere of ideology (as Miles 1989, for example, does) and that the existence of systemic racism (Anthias 1990) does not require explicit racist intentionality, but on the other hand neither can we dispense with the notion of racist ideology and practice.

Having discussed some of the difficulties with the Black feminist critique it is important to reiterate that this raises the whole issue of identity politics (Yuval-Davis 1992b) around the construction of a gendered identity, on the one hand, and a Black gendered identity on the other. However, this does not require that a Black gendered identity is itself homogeneous – as Hooks eloquently states in showing the existence of competition and distrust of Black women to one another in the context of a racist society (1991). An important development is the recognition of the mutiple layers of identity and oppression which may make the whole pursuit of political struggle over the constituency of identity and community problematic. On the other hand struggles predicated on one major identity (such as that of race), may be instrumental in opening the way for just such a reappraisal of the workings of identities around say class. Ousley sees struggles about race as being able to produce a clearer picture of the workings of class and other oppressions through a type of 'barium meal' effect, which alerts us to the nature of oppressions in general (1991). Similarly we regard the Black women's movement as having a central role in the development of a postmodernist critique of the unitary self. However, identity politics is also full of pitfalls and the complexities are discussed more fully in Chapter 6.

THE FAILURES OF FEMINIST THEORIZATIONS

We now turn to some of the failures of a feminist theory of social divisions, particularly exploring the usefulness of the notion of patriarchy.

Feminism has not dealt with the issue of racism partly because of the following assumptions:

1   Racism was not a concern of the feminist movement since it was defined as emanating from a patriarchal society; White women were not responsible nor did they practise racism towards other groups of women. This was because White women were themselves constructed as socially subordinate to men within social relations – of which racism was part. This failure of feminism is justifiably criticized by Black feminists.

2   The issues that were important for western feminism and reflected the concerns of women from the colonizing nations were those that would always be important for all women. Western feminism has therefore assumed not only a universality to women's interests but these were defined with reference to an ethnocentric notion of womanhood. The notion of essential feminist interests fails to place women's interests concretely in historical social relations, assumes an essential opposition of interests between men and women and hegemonizes the concerns of White, often middle-class, women.

3   Racialized and ethnic minority women were not recognized as a category because of the assumption concerning a unitary category of women and a universal and inalienable sisterhood. They were thus rendered invisible and denied a voice.

4   In the case of Marxist feminism, the priority given to class and economic relations failed to incorporate the specific role of racialized social relations into the account of women's oppression.

Radical feminism faces specific problems in dealing with the way racism interrelates with sexism and patriarchy. Where radical feminism denies that women's oppression emanates merely from class relations it locates it alternatively in essentialist and unchanging antagonisms of interest between men and women and reduces it therefore to a biologically based set of interests. This is not to deny the varying theoretical formulations that have been offered, some of them claiming to be dialectical or materialist (Firestone 1971, Delphy 1977). Alternative radical feminist positions do not explicitly denote the role of biology but locate patriarchy as 'universal' and as a system of power (Millet 1971). But since no other theorization appears for this universality, what is being posited is an essentialist division between men and women. If this is the case then the interests of all men and all women stand opposed and the essential sisterhood of all women is pre-given (for a critique see Anthias and Yuval-Davis 1983, Murphy and Livingstone 1985). However, racism divides certain categories of women and unites them with men. It is these cross-cuttings of forms of subordination that radical feminism cannot theorize adequately. This failure of feminism to deal with the experiences of racialized women ties in with the tendency also to identify racism as having a homogeneous object which is usually seen as Black and male; racialized and ethnic minority women are rendered invisible yet again.

THE CONCEPT OF PATRIARCHY

The development of feminist theory has usually employed the concept of patriarchy as an analytical and explanatory tool. Its basic premise is the universal existence of male domination over women and it attempts to provide an analysis of this in terms of the specificity of the relations between men and women, at times analogous to the ways in which sociology and Marxism refer to systems of relations around normative structures or around economic class relations. Some of the approaches have been ahistorical, particularly those which derive from a radical feminist perspective with its biologistic assumptions of the inevitable conflict of interests between men and women (for example, Firestone 1971). Other approaches have tried to historicize the concept, looking at the ways in which patriarchal relations are, for example, linked to different modes of production, or relating it to economic and other social processes within a more historically specifiable social formation. Marxist feminism, for example, has deployed the term in a number of ways, although the major tendency has been to talk about the articulation of two systems of oppression (Hartmann 1981) or to two modes of production (for example, Harrison 1973), or to the development of dual systems models, inventing the term 'capitalist patriarchy' (Eisenstein 1979). Other writers within Marxist feminism are uncertain and critical of the concept (for example, Beechey 1978). Cockburn (1983), on the other hand, regards the concept as central in the formulation of a distinct feminist theory with its own analytical tools, being averse to the attempts in some Marxist feminist work to subordinate or reduce the concept to the more hierarchically important one of mode of production. She believes that it is an independent mode of subordination.

Our view is that whether patriarchy is used merely as a catch-all phrase for women's oppression or used more specifically to denote particular configurations of male domination (Kuhn and Wolpe 1978) it has limited the possibility of taking account of the historical and contextually related ways in which gender divisions manifest themselves. The historicization and contextualization that some approaches are dedicated to none the less always need to posit it as an independent system in some way or another. For example, there is always the assumption that the sexual attribute of a social actor has a role in producing both a definite social place and a definite social interest with regard to the other sex. Gender relations of inequality and subordination inevitably must then be treated as outcomes of the very relations of gender rather than as outcomes of the interplay of social processes and social divisions more broadly conceived. For example, the equation in Hartmann between class based (capitalism) and gender based (patriarchy) modes of inequality is uneasy as she herself recognizes. This is precisely because the notion of class and its pivotal and defining role in capitalism is theoretically premised on the notion of mode of production found within Marxist theory. An equivalent theoretical location cannot be maintained for gender within a system of patriarchal social relations, for the theoretically contingent terms that would allow this have never been specified systematically. This is because the category of gender used is always dependent on the necessary effects of sexual difference (Anthias 1991). This means that there is always some retention of static and biologistic categories as explanations of the development of admittedly historically contingent gender relations. The form of gender is always regarded as the outcome of a binary and dichotomous sexual difference.

Moreover the term patriarchy has generally assumed a relation where women are passive receivers of an oppression that is exercised upon them. The notion of women's femininity as a product of patriarchy (or of capitalism, as in Foreman) marginalizes the active and passive forms of resistance within which women have been historically engaged (see Foreman 1977, Bruegel 1978 and Anthias's critique 1978).

Kandiyoti (1988) puts forward the notion of the 'patriarchal bargain', that is, that gender divisions and their practice are fluid and negotiable and are the product of both imposition and struggle; different societal forms present different formulations of this bargain. This is a useful intervention although she does not develop the analysis of the processes that produce resistance and bargaining. This is particularly important as men control the means of violence and public legitimation. Also, Kandiyoti sees the patriarchal bargain as emanating from individual women's strategies without discussing modes by which these become either embedded in collective action or institutionalized. But the recognition that women can be both individually and collectively active agents in their own subordination as well as in struggle against it is a necessary step in understanding the widely heterogeneous nature of the degrees of this subordination and its specificities. Femininity may indeed be seen as a coping mechanism (Anthias 1978). We can apply this notion to understanding the different strategies that women from different groups in a racist context use to defend their position when it is under threat. For example, in the case where women are forcefully separated from their families because of racist immigration controls women may staunchly support the nuclear family; where their reproductive rights are being threatened through enforced sterilization the issue will be reproductive rights, rather than, say, abortion (Anthias and Yuval-Davis 1983).

Can the notion of patriarchy allow us to understand the existence of racialized genders? Whilst acknowledging that 'many of the existing grand theories of patriarchy do have problems in dealing with historical and cultural variation', Walby (1990) argues that we can develop a theory of patriarchy that uses more than one causal base. According to her, the main structures that make up patriarchy are paid work, housework, sexuality, culture, violence, and the state and the interrelationships of these create different forms.

But in order to pursue such an approach the distinctive nature of patriarchy within each one has to be retained. This focuses on the relationships between men and women in a situation of female subordination. Patriarchy is defined as a 'System of social structures and practices in which men dominate, oppress and exploit women' (Walby 1990: 20). However, this definition merely describes a set of practices in terms of their outcomes. Moreover, she sees such practices as articulating with capitalism and racism, and thus endows them with a distinctive modality. This position requires treating patriarchy as a distinctive set of social relations that lie outside capitalism. This implies a three systems approach. It is echoed in Caroline Ramazanoglu's view (1989) that racism is an independent form of domination. We believe that although the discourses of racism and sexism are distinct, both patriarchal or sexist gender relations and racism are not independent but are products or outcomes of social relations of power and subordination along different constructions of difference and identity.

Gender relates to the binary social ontology of biological sexual difference and racism relates to the social ontology of collectivity and belongingness. But this does not produce patriarchy or racism as separate systems or structures of domination. We would like to retain the use of the term patriarchal as a descriptive term which denotes relations between men and women that subordinate women. But we do not believe such patriarchal relations are explicable by deploying the term patriarchy as a distinct social system, which then articulates with capitalism. Indeed we would argue that such a dual system approach always requires us to prioritize the relations between men and women within the patriarchal system and the relations between social classes in the capitalist sytem. We would argue, alternatively, that the social system cannot be divided into these different autonomous but interrelated structures and that patriarchal social relations (in the descriptive sense) are endemic and integral to social formations with regard to the distribution of material resources and power (see Gilroy 1987, for a depiction of class formation that treats race structuration as equally central). From this point of view class, gender and race may be dependent on different existential locations, but they are not manifestations of different types of social relations with distinct causal bases (see Walby 1990), within distinct systems of domination.

MARXIST FEMINISM AND THE POLITICAL ECONOMY APPROACH

A Marxist analysis of race and gender has been constrained by the fact that the major conceptual categories used, like class and mode of production, are sex and race blind, to quote Heidi Hartmann's (1979) well-used phrase. As we saw in the last chapter with reference to race, and we can say the same for gender, it had usually tried to understand non-class divisions in terms of class relations or tied them more functionally to the needs of capital. The domestic labour debate of the 1970s is a prime example of trying to rethink Marxism to account for women's position in the sexual division of labour in the home (Molyneaux 1979). It is instructive to summarize some of the inadequacies of this debate and discuss briefly the implications for understanding differences amongst women, whether in terms of class or race but particularly in relation to the latter. To understand domestic labour *vis-à-vis* the production of surplus value directly or indirectly does not explain why and how it is women who perform it. The domestic labour approach did not differentiate between domestic labour in terms of household tasks which are essential and those that are non-essential for the reproduction of the labour force, for example, cleaning toilets and feeding babies. It did not differentiate between household tasks and childbirth and the mothering role. It not only failed to integrate domestic labour with waged labour but also with ideological practices and state policies.

The domestic labour debate failed to relate to migrant women's participation in the labour market as primarily either full-time workers (West Indian women especially (Brown 1984)) or family labourers (Asian and Cypriot women (Anthias 1982)). They were not constituted as outside the parameters of capitalism either in a distinct domestic mode of production (Harrison 1973) or as merely servicing the male workforce. More than any other category, migrant women indicate the problems of focusing on women primarily as housewives (see Molyneaux 1979 for a useful review of the domestic labour debate). For migrant women domestic labour is not at the root of their exploitation or oppression.

The consideration of women as a reserve army of labour (Beechey 1977, Bruegel 1979), on the other hand, failed for other reasons to provide a satisfactory explanation of women's position in the labour market. The reserve army concept could not explain the expansion of women's employment or the existence of a dual labour market (women's jobs) and how women were recruited to this. The view that it was dependent on a male wage that allowed women to be paid less than the cost of the reproduction of their labour (Beechey 1977) did not account, presumably, for the existence of a family wage, in which men would be paid proportionally more (for more detailed conceptual problems see Anthias 1980).

In relation to migrants and particularly migrant women, it is clear that women could not form a reserve army in an undifferentiated way because of the sectoral nature of their employment. They were recruited for jobs and not as a reserve or a pool of unemployed and the jobs were those on the whole that the indigenous population did not want. For example, Filipino women were recruited as single women for specific jobs in Britain (see WING 1985). In addition African-Caribbean women in particular often were not dependent on the male wage and the ability of capital to pay them lower wages could not be explained through the notion either of a real or an ideological dependence on men.

Feminists' theorizations of the position of women in the labour market, particularly the tendency to part-time work for married women, have relied on the way in which gender divisions within the family have necessary implications for labour market participation and positioning (Beechey 1986). This is very much problematized by the work experiences of migrant women and ethnic minority women, who, in spite of patriarchal social relations, have a greater tendency to full-time work. Moreover, such economic participation, even where women have been in a better position than many racialized men in the labour market, has not unproblematically led to changes in their gender subordination (Hoel 1982, Anthias 1983).

GENDER AND ETHNIC DIVISIONS AND THEIR LINKS

We now turn to the analytic separation of the categories of gender and race and a consideration of the issue of their links.

In relation to the conceptualization of gender and ethnic divisions, we argue, unlike Carby (1982) and Barrett (1982), that there is some common basis to these divisions despite certain crucial distinctions also. Both divisions utilize implicit assumptions about the naturalness not only of difference but of inequalities. Both divisions involve practices of exclusion and the structuring of disadvantage in favour of the dominant ethnic and gender group. At the empirical level it is important to explore the different experiences of men as against women; racially dominant as against racialized women; working-class as against middle-class women, in terms of their articulation and intersection and not only mechanistically, since each division is practised in the context of the others.

Gender and race, unlike class, relate to a particular representation of a 'biological', 'physiognomic', or 'natural' difference. The
importance of the material reality of economic relations and other
political and ideological relations will produce however, different
primary organizing principles at different times. Class formation,
though, is the product not only of processes endemic within the
sphere of production, for it is historically constructed in relation
to the history of race and of gender. Therefore an investigation of
concrete class processes finds them intermeshed with those of
social relations more broadly defined.

Gender relates to the social construction, representation and
organization of sexual difference and biological reproduction but
cannot be reduced to biology. The contents of these practices and
representations, however, are not confined merely to the arenas of
sexuality and biology; they posit necessary social effects ranging
from notions about the female capacity to undertake certain forms
of labour and wage labour to notions of the essential mothering
capacities and needs of women. The representations and practices
around gender are themselves not the product of this difference
but originate in social relations that include those of class and race
and ethnicity.

Ethnic or race categories are more difficult to ground; they
relate to community or collectivity in terms of some point of origin
that can be historically, geographically, culturally or physiognomically based and is either internally identified or externally imposed or both. Racism or racial categorization involves discourses
relating to subordination as well as exclusion (in gender the
subordination is often denied, when women are reified as mothers
or as wives, although the practices of subordination are generally
present). Ethnic categorization, on the other hand, need not
involve either subordination or exploitation but is the positing of
an immutable communal difference. This has to be distinguished
from racist forms of discourse that serve to establish subordinating
representations upon ethnic or communal difference or may
indeed construct ethnic difference (that is, what can be called
ethnicization through racism or reactive ethnicity, as it was
erstwhile called). Racism is particularly dependent in the final
analysis on an immutable biological origin although the contents
of specific racisms may focus explicitly on cultural difference,
seeing particular ethnic categories as culturally undesirable or as
having politically disastrous effects for society.

As we noted earlier gender and ethnicity or race are under-pinned particularly by a supposedly 'natural' relation. In gender, necessary social effects are posited to sexual difference and bio-logical reproduction. For ethnicity or race, assumptions con-cerning the natural boundaries of collectivities or the naturalness of culture are used. These supposedly natural differences in capacities and needs on the basis of gender or of ethnicity or race then come to enter into economic relations as legitimizers of inequalities in class position. It then becomes natural that men should be defined as the major breadwinners and hence should have greater access to high status and well paid full-time work. It also becomes natural that Blacks (or a given population whatever marker is chosen – it need not be colour of skin as long as it relies on some notion of a racial stock) should similarly occupy a lower position in the class structure since their biology or culture (at different times there exist different central arguments within racist discourse) limits their skills, education, interests, etc.

These 'naturalized' depictions can also be used to struggle against racism or sexism, as for example when women call to women to unite by stressing the unifying and positive elements of female experience and femininity as some sort of 'essence', and in the 'Black is beautiful' rhetoric (to quote one instance; another might be found in the rhetoric often used in national liberation struggles). Such rallying points, although strategically useful, raise general problems of long-term class unity.

Gender relations differ according to ethnicity. There exist culturally specific practices relating to mothering and sex roles and thus ethnic divisions are particularly important in the household. The gender divisions of the dominant ethnic group will also affect ethnic minority women, that is, there are two sets of relations around gender that affect them (which is not the case for women of the dominant ethnic-majority).

WOMEN, THE STATE AND ETHNIC PROCESSES

The boundary of the ethnic is often dependent on gender and there is a reliance on gender attributes for specifying ethnic identity; much of ethnic culture is organized around rules relating to sexuality, marriage and the family, and a true member will perform these roles properly. Communal boundaries often use differences in the way women are socially constructed as markers.

Such markers (for example, expectations about honour, purity, the mothering of patriots, reproducers of the nation, transmitters of ethnic culture) often symbolize the use of women as an ethnic resource (Anthias and Yuval-Davis 1989). Women therefore reproduce not only class but ethnic groups.

Although the state is unitary neither in terms of its intentions nor its effects, we believe that it is important to retain the concept of the state (for a fuller discussion see Anthias and Yuval-Davis 1989). Women's link to the state is complex. They are acted upon as members of collectivities, institutions or classes and as participants in the social forces that give the state its given political projects in any specific historical context. In this sense they are participants in the relationship between the state and civil society as an integral albeit often subordinate category within wider social forces. However, as a subordinate category, usually relegated to the private sphere (see Pateman 1988), they are often a special focus of state concerns, both with regard to their role in human reproduction but also in a number of other ways, with regard to ideology and the economy also.

A number of attempts (for example, Pateman 1988) to conceptualize the links between women and the state have focused on the central dimension of citizenship and how, far from being gender-neutral, it constructs men and women differently. The state subject is gendered although essentially male in its capacities and needs. Such critiques have failed to see that citizenship is also an ethnicized and racialized concept. Women are not all constructed by the state in the same way. Racialized and ethnic minority women are often deprived of the rights to reproduce the citizens of the state through notions of patriality, for example in Britain (Klug 1989), or through apartheid (Gaitskell and Unterhalter 1989). Thus the state is related to women in a heterogeneous way. This was recognized a long time ago by socialist feminists in the discussion of class as a central differentiating feature. We now need to recognize the importance of ethnicity, nationality and racialization.

The relationship between the state, women, and ethnic and national processes does not take a necessary form. However, it is possible to locate (as we did in Anthias and Yuval-Davis 1989) five major (although not exclusive) ways in which women have tended to participate in ethnic and national processes, in relation to state practices. These are:

1   as biological reproducers of members of ethnic collectivities;
2   as reproducers of the boundaries of ethnic or national groups;
3   as participating centrally in the ideological reproduction of the
    collectivity and as transmitters of its culture;
4   as signifiers of ethnic or national differences, as a focus and
    symbol in ideological discourses used in the construction, re-
    production and transformation of ethnic or national categories;
5   as participants in national, economic, political and military
    struggles (1989: 7).

We would like to add to this, that women are acted on with
regard to the labour market. Ethnic minority women, through
their construction as having limited rights to citizenship and as
being outside the proper boundaries of the nation, and through
racialization, can be positioned in a particularly disadvantageous
position in the labour market.

We can summarize some of the arguments by focusing on the
role of women, symbolically, practically, and in terms of agency in
the following way. At the symbolic level, the characteristics
ascribed to women are also used to foster national or ethnic
interests, for example, in links between the concepts of mother
and nation, symbolism around the nation as a woman nurturing
and caring for her sons. In many societies special honour is due to
the 'mother of the patriot'.

At the practical or policy level, many concerns of the nation or
ethnic group have woman as central subject, for example, all those
policies that are concerned with structuring or restructuring the
form of the family. These include policies directed to the
ideological or socialization role of the family and the centrality of
women within it; population control to maintain or change
existing demographic patterns in favour of the dominant ethnic
group; all policies and laws under which a legitimate national
subject is reproduced, such as marriage rules and the role of the
mother in giving birth to national subjects.

At the level of agency, women act as participants in national
struggles and as members of dominant ethnic groups or classes, as
exploiters and oppressors particularly of subordinate-position
women (Yuval-Davis and Anthias 1989).

GENDER, RACE AND CLASS: THE PROBLEM OF A
GENDERED AND RACIALIZED LABOUR MARKET

We explore some of these facets in a more concrete way in this section, which concentrates on ethnic minority women in Britain.

We have already shown some of the pitfalls of a patriarchy model which treats men and women as distinct and opposing categories to be understood with reference to the dynamics of gender relations. We have also shown some of the difficulties faced by the Marxist feminist political economy approach with regard to accounting for gendered ethnicities and racialized gender. What these two positions hold in common is the primacy given to the separation between men and women in social relations and neither is able to account for the way in which ethnic difference and racialization intersect with gender and class to produce particular effects. For example most of the work done on women and work has taken the view that recruitment to work and the labour market is determined by a person's sex. Dex states that,

> Women are clearly concentrated into a small number of oc-
> cupations and they constitute a very large proportion of certain
> occupational categories. Researchers are agreed that the
> majority of jobs can be categorised either as stereotypically
> female or stereotypically male. (1987: 9)

Explanations of this segregation that is as high as 63 per cent for women and 80 per cent for men range from employer strategies (Beechey 1978) to sexist attitudes held by men and women (Vogel 1990), to exclusion practices by male-dominated trade unions (Rubery 1978).

In addition segmented labour market theory, which we discussed in the last chapter, has been used to account for racial and sexual segregation in the labour market (Piore 1975, Loveridge and Mok 1979). With regard to women, Barron and Norris (1976) suggested that a primary male labour market was a result of the need for firms to retain their skilled workforce to keep wages and conditions undisrupted and to reduce staff turnover. They saw women as an appropriate secondary labour force as they were primarily unskilled and easily dispensable. Beechey (1978) has argued that one of the problems with segmented labour market theory is that it tended to treat women as homogeneous in class terms. We would add that these theories either concentrate on racially or sexually segregated labour markets and do not attend to the intersection of the two with regard to migrant and racialized women.

Women migrants constitute about one-quarter of the foreign labour force and over 40 per cent of all migrants (Phizacklea 1983) but this is an underestimate because of the high levels of unregistered work done by ethnic minority women. Racialized and ethnic minority women are concentrated in the most arduous and poorly paid work as well as being subject to the highest levels of unemployment, the exigencies of unregistered work and the deprivations associated with home-working (Allen and Wolkowitz 1987).

The commonly held view that women migrants come in only as dependants on their husbands is far from accurate. Like men, they came to Britain in their thousands in the postwar period at a time of rapid economic growth. Many both before and after the 'closing of the gates' in the early 1970s have only been recruited on work permits, that is, as short-term migrants rather than settlers. Between 1963 and 1972 nearly 20 per cent of all commonwealth workers and almost half of all non-commonwealth workers, who came to Britain on employment vouchers or work permits, were women. In the next ten years nearly 30 per cent of those recruited were women who were brought in primarily for sectors of the economy where women predominated (WING 1985). Work permits are issued only for jobs that the indigenous workforce won't do. Filipino women, for example, were issued work permits for domestic work, although many additionally have come in as illegal immigrants with all that implies (Ardill and Cross 1987). Black and other ethnic minority women also face racial and gender discrimination which intersects in different ways for different groups of women and in different contexts.

For migrant women the Anglomorphic ideology of the family and female economic dependency is important despite the fact that for many African-Caribbean women at least this is alien to their own reality. For example 31 per cent of West Indian households with children are single parent units (the corresponding figure for White households is 10 per cent and for Asian women it is 5 per cent (Brown 1984: 51). This ideology acts to legitimize paying women less than men, which in turn has been itself partly structured by men's demand for a 'family wage' (Barrett and Mackintosh 1980) and through the notion of the male breadwinner embodied in social security and other welfare legislation and practice (Wilson 1977, Land 1978). Ethnic minority women are also confined to low skill (for a feminist critique of the notion of skill see Phillips and Taylor 1980) and low pay, to home-working or shift work because of child-care and at times cultural rules, but interestingly not to part-time work, unlike White women.

ETHNIC MINORITY WOMEN AND WORK

We shall now turn to a more detailed discussion of ethnic minority women in the labour market for this provides us with a central arena for examining the links between gender, ethnicity or race, and class.

The intersection of sex and race in employment has to be understood empirically in the context of the internationalization of the labour market and the tendencies of firms to move to the periphery to draw on the cheap labour of women both in the Third World and in the advanced societies. This has occurred side by side with the creation of two labour markets, one for permanent White men (a core) and an impermanent casual, predominantly female one which includes part-time work (Mitter 1986). Here segmentation of the labour market is seen as more dramatic, with White males differentiated from racialized or Black males as we saw in the last chapter, but not to such an extent as to warrant treating them in the same category as either White or Black females. It appears that although there is sexual segregation, as we noted earlier, race segregation intersects with this to produce specific effects. Here we want to explore some of the ways in which race cuts across the sexual division of labour for women.

The ethnic minority population on the whole has filled jobs that the indigenous population did not want and it is these jobs, labour intensive, and in what can be called the underdeveloped sectors, that have been most at risk in the recession. In this light ethnic minority women particularly have faced long-term unemployment and unlike the men have not moved more into self-employment or the hidden economy. Where they have it is to assist their men as unpaid family workers.

National data on employment suffers from the handicap of using highly heterogeneous categories. For example, as we pointed out in the last chapter, the term 'Black workers' may be used and at times it is not clear which groups are included in this category. There is also the danger of treating the categories as homogeneous for, as we argued, the groups within the 'Black' category have diverse employment characteristics. But an additional difficulty is found in the way in which the collection of data often hides rather than illuminates both the real differences between men and women (Oakley and Oakley 1979) and the differences between White women and ethnic minority women (Phizacklea 1983, Bruegel 1989).

Empirical studies of racial disadvantage (Smith 1977, Brown 1984) have often pointed out that differences in occupational levels, pay and employment are not as great between Black and White women as they are between White and Black men. The disparities are lower because sexism already disadvantages women in the labour market to such an extent that the effects of race are not so apparent. This is a gross oversimplification for a number of reasons, which primarily result from the problems with collected data on ethnic minority women (Bruegel 1989).

Various studies, particularly of home-working (Hoel 1982, Anthias 1983, Mitter 1986, Allen and Wolkowitz 1987) show that many ethnic minority women are not part of the registered working population. This implies that the economic activity rates in published sources underestimate the extent of women's participation in the labour force and may not give a full picture of its nature. For example, women from ethnic minorities have a greater tendency to work in small-scale factories, retail shops and restaurants (apart from African-Caribbean women) and as unpaid family labourers (for example, alongside their husbands and other members of the family), than indigenous or White women. This indicates that the real average wage levels may be much lower than official statistics show. This puts into question the conclusion that West Indian women have average weekly earnings that are about £4 higher than White women and £8 higher than Asian women (Brown 1984: 212).

Similarly, if we take shift work and number of hours worked into account then the actual wage rates are lower than they would appear otherwise. This is because the number of hours worked and whether they are done in unsocial hours (shift hours) is not represented in the data on wage levels, and we know that ethnic minority women work longer and more unsocial hours than other women (Phizacklea 1983, Westwood 1984).

Also, because ethnic minority women (like men) tend to be concentrated in the south-east, where wage levels tend to be higher anyway, then the picture of average national wages and employment levels gives a distorted comparison. Ethnic minority women are more likely to work full time than White women and their younger age distribution compared with Whites also has to be taken into account in interpreting the data available.

There is also the problem of job classification. Women are bunched in non-manual work in official statistics but this conceals the nature of these non-manual jobs and the overrepresentation of women in the lower echelons of technical and clerical work in the tertiary sector of the economy (see Oakley and Oakley 1979). Ethnic minority women may fall into the same broad categories as White women but this may hide the fact that they are more likely to be in lower status and lower paid work within these categories (as is the case also for ethnic minority men) (Bruegel 1989).

Although ethnic minority women are in a particularly dis-advantaged sphere with regard to home-working, domestic work, unskilled service work and as unpaid family workers it is wrong to conclude that all ethnic minority women constitute one economic or labour market category. In terms of economic activity rates, for example, there is a great diversity between different groups of migrant and ethnic minority women. Brown's survey (1984) shows White women have a rate of 46 per cent, West Indian women 74 per cent, Asian women 39 per cent (Muslim women 18 per cent, Hindu women 59 per cent, Sikh women 54 per cent). Almost as many Asian women were in professional or managerial sectors as White women (6 per cent compared with 7 per cent) and nearly as many West Indian women in 'other non-manual' as White women (52 per cent compared with 55 per cent). More White women were found to be unskilled, which was due largely to more White women working part time than Black women. In fact West Indian women are more likely to work full time. Labour Force Surveys show that about one-quarter of all women are in full-time work compared with two-fifths of West Indian women. We also find that whilst Asian women are overrepresented in the textile and clothing industries, in repetitive assembly line work and as home-workers, West Indian women are more likely to be in low grade professional work and in the service industries (Brown 1984: 203).

In relation to unemployment, in 1984 19 per cent of Black

women were unemployed compared with 10 per cent of White women workers, with Pakistani and Bangladeshi women having the highest rate (40 per cent) followed by Indian women (18 per cent) and West Indian women (17 per cent). In 1990 figures for unemployment show a drop to 6 per cent for White women and 11 per cent for ethnic minority women (*Employment Gazette*, February 1991). This is likely to be an underestimate as it refers to registered unemployment (for problems relating to the collection of data see Chapter 3).

Full-time and high activity rates for Black women may be accounted for in a number of ways. One is the generally lower employment status and pay of Black men (Cook and Watts 1987). Another reason is the different assessment of women's roles in the sexual division of work at home and paid work, different familial structures and expectations, and for first generation migrants, the economic aims of migration including for some groups, dependants in the country of origin and the 'myth of return' (see Dahya 1974, Anthias 1982 and forthcoming).

The intersection between racial and ethnic exclusion and sexism can be found in a particularly complex and illustrative form in the case of both ethnic employment and family labour. It is important to note that this does not tend to be reproduced in the second or third generations, however (see Anthias 1983, Parmar 1988). Later generations are indeed much more like their White counterparts than like their female relatives and men from ethnic minorities.

In the case of the clothing industry, ethnic entrepreneurs, Asian annd Cypriot, play an important role although they are in a subordinate position in relation to the clothing industry as a whole, being in a master–servant relationship with the large contractors (Anthias 1983, Mitter 1986). Although there are cases of ethnic minority women becoming entrepreneurs (Westwood and Bhachu 1988) it is usually men who play this role often because they can draw on the cheap or unpaid labour of women from their own families or their own village or ethnic networks (Anthias 1983). Groups that do not present a familialist orientation, like African-Caribbeans, have failed to enter small-scale business in any significant numbers. As Mitter points out (1986: 129) 'the ethnic economy throughout the UK is marked by a clear division of labour along gender lines. Unskilled, repetitive, machining work gets done by women from small units or from home whereas entrepreneurial skill is practised and monopolised by men.'

One of the most under-explored areas has been the way in which gender divisions through the use of the family and the position of women can help us to understand the differential position of different ethnic groups in the economy and society (Anthias 1983). It is not incidental that those groups that have gone into the labour intensive sectors of clothing, catering and retail distribution, particularly as self-employed or small-scale employers, have been those that have used the unpaid labour of women within the family. Cypriot women, for example, have been the cornerstone of the Cypriot ethnic economy in North London (Anthias 1983). Asians too have entered small-scale business in fairly large numbers. The centrality of gender for the understanding of the patterns of settlement of migrant groups has hardly been touched upon in the available literature.

However, it is important to note that women home-workers are also found in the 'low tech' manufacturing industries. The Greenwich Homeworkers Project has pointed to the 'invisible workforce' who make such things as lampshades and toys, who lick envelopes or fill them, are involved in marketing and selling goods (for example, tupperware, catalogues, diets) and increasingly with word-processing, clerical work and on computer terminals. As Mitter shows, new technology has created a new type of home-worker, whom she calls 'tele worker' or remote-worker, although it is mainly White women that have been involved or second generation ethnic minority women.

There are a number of issues involved in the case of ethnic entrepreneurs using female labour from their own families and ethnic groups. One is that they have often entered small-scale business as a way of avoiding the exclusions and disadvantages they face as migrants and through racism. But in the process ethnic and family bonds are used to gain class advantages over their own groups and over women in particular. This is not to say that ethnic minority women do not feel that it is advantageous to work for a member of their own group so avoiding racism, language and other cultural problems, and as a result feeling less alienated. This is well recognized by both workers and employers. For example, Hoel (1982) quotes one Asian employer: 'I see the majority of women working for me as benefiting from my job offer. They are all illiterate and have no skills, hence no British factory will make use of them.' This of course misrepresents the real incorporation of Asian and other women in the manufacturing and service sectors of the economy, which we have already referred to.

Ethnic commonality between employer and employee can act to curb participation in trade union activity although small firms in any case are under-unionized. It can however act to undermine class action, thus vitiating the development of a class consciousness. For example, it is much more difficult to see your employer in class terms when he is a co-villager or a member of your own family. Where there is geographical concentration, as in the case of the Cypriot North London community, the face to face interaction between worker and employer extends far beyond the mere work-place (see Anthias 1983).

At times ethnic entrepreneurs may use women from other ethnic groups; for example, Asian, African-Caribbean and Turkish women may be used by Cypriots. In this case ethnic bonding does not emerge, but a hierarchy in the work-force occurs, with outside women being at times on different piece rates from ethnic women. This further strengthens ethnic solidarity at the expense of class solidarity amongst women workers.

We have considered ethnic employers and workers and their link not because this is the primary relation that needs analysis in understanding the disadvantages and exclusions that ethnic minority women face – far from it. It is large-scale capital and the needs of capital restructuring that benefits (Mitter 1986). However, the case of ethnic employment casts an interesting and suggestive light on the intricacy of the link between ethnic class and gender divisions. Class disadvantage can be countered by ethnic or gender strategies, by the use of ethnic resources and commonalities and already established familial ideologies and networks. Ethnic disadvantage (for both men and women) can be countered by increasing or utilizing patriarchal gender relations. As we shall see later there is a different link in the case of immigration and nationality law – sexism may be reduced by increasing racism. In all cases, ethnic minority women tend to be the losers, for they are the meeting point of the intersection of class, ethnic, and gender disadvantage and exclusion.

Clearly all these experiences of ethnic minority women have implications for some of the dominant analyses of women's economic position in feminist theory; the latter has focused on women's role in the family and patriarchal social relations as limiting women's economic participation to part-time work (see Bruegel 1979, Beechey 1986). The family and patriarchal relations for ethnic minority women do not have the same effect and therefore the nature of causality involved has to be rethought. Moreover the notion of patriarchy assumes that it is relations between men and women that primarily structure women's position (for an analysis of capitalist patriarchy see Eisenstein 1979), but since many West Indian women in particular do not exist in such relations of economic dependence *vis-à-vis* men this needs reformulation. Similarly the relation of oppression for racialized groups may be one where White or dominant majority women have power over minority men and in such cases too the notion of patriarchy is problematized. The idea of the family as the site of women's oppression has also to be rethought, as it can be a source of resistance to racism (Carby 1982).

UNDERSTANDING GENDERED ETHNICITIES AND THE RACIALIZATION OF GENDER

The disadvantages and exclusions that racialized, migrant and ethnic minority women face can be linked to:

1 Their position as migrants, through the legal political and economic position of migrants but overlaid through the way in which men and women are treated differently. Here we can point particularly to the position of women in immigration and nationality law.
2 Their position in racialized social relations and the specific forms these take for men and women and different groups. Here we can point to racism and its effects.
3 Their position as women, and the wide currency of sexism in contemporary societies, but this is overlaid by the internal sexist relations of the different cultural practices of the groups. Here we can turn to patriarchal relations and the different forms they take but also to sexist social policy. Ethnic cultural and familial differences will prescribe a distinct set of norms and practices relating to the sexual division of labour (what Kandiyoti (1988) refers to as the patriarchal bargain) and to distinct notions about the different needs and capacities of ethnic minority women as opposed to White women.
4 Their position as members of particular classes but ghettoized into particular areas of employment which are overlaid by exclusions and discriminations on the basis of racism and sexism. This is particularly related to their economic positioning.

The dominant stereotypes that exist about ethnic minority women see them as passive and subordinate and ignore differences of culture, generation and class (Parmar 1982). For Asian and African-Caribbean women they have a particular resonance, however, ranging from the victimization stereotype of the Asian woman (a victim of arranged marriages, strict control, etc) to the Black female castrator (the strong Black woman who none the less cannot keep her man). Such stereotyping not only occurs in the racist discourse of the media but is also articulated within academic work on ethnicity.

It is impossible to understand the intersection of sexism and racism without considering the conditions of entry of migrant and Black women to Britain and their relations to immigration and nationality law. We shall therefore turn to this now before exploring the problem of understanding the link between anti-sexist and anti-racist strategy.

MIGRANT WOMEN AND THE BOUNDARIES OF THE NATION

Nationalist discourse includes a particularly telling example of the allocating of different roles to men and women.

The forms of control that migrant women face include the ways in which immigration and nationality law differentiates between men and women and casts them as dependants on men. Under British immigration law women have tended to be seen only as mothers and wives (WING 1985). Successive immigration acts have failed to give women the right to confer citizenship on their children or pass on patriality to their husbands. Also, under the separate immigration rules relating to the 1971 Act (WING 1985: 36), husbands were not allowed to enter Britain to join their wives at all. Despite state discourse about the importance of the family many migrant families remain apart.

The 1981 Nationality Act created three different categories of citizenship out of the old 'citizenship of the UK and Colonies'. These were British citizenship, British Dependent Territories citizenship and British Overseas citizenship. In the first group are mainly White people and in the latter there are mainly Black, who have few or no rights attached to citizenship. The position of women was badly affected, for the 1981 Act has taken away the automatic right of women to British citizenship on marriage and they are subjected to a number of conditions which problematize their eventual status. The Act no longer gives automatic right of citizenship to children born in Britain, but does allow women who are British to pass on their citizenship to their children born abroad (Klug 1989). The principle of sexual equality has been promoted but in the interests of 'equal misery' so that racism has increased. The pursuit of sexual equality has therefore been used to intensify racism.

The 'primary purpose rule' whereby a man must satisfy the immigration authorities that the primary purpose of his marriage is not entry to the UK also takes an ethnocentric form and is now also being applied to women who seek to enter. The vast majority of refusals under this rule however are experienced by Asian men, for one of the conditions is that 'the parties to the marriage need to have met'. But as this is not part of Sikh tradition, for example, it postulates the naturalness of western cultural practices and in the process makes it very difficult for Sikhs to pursue their own.

The 1988 Immigration Act takes away the protection given to the prospective wives of commonwealth citizens who have settled here on or after 1 January 1973. Now they are required to fulfil the requirements laid down in current immigration rules, including subjecting themselves to the primary purpose rule as noted earlier. There are indications that the immigration rules actively discourage marriage with partners from India and that women with some kind of physical or social 'disability' suffer most, since they are least likely to find a husband who is already in Britain. One study also shows that many parents fear arranging marriages with partners in India just in case they are refused entry (Grewal 1989). The primary purpose rule violates the normal process of evidence since it relies on the immigration official subjectively judging the 'motive' for entry and opens the way to large-scale ethnocentrism and racism.

Earlier in the chapter we argued for the centrality of women in defining the boundaries of the nation. Francesca Klug persuasively argues that

> the question of the reproduction of the nation had a profound effect on the development of social policy with regard to women and reproduction. Whilst at various stages the state has encouraged white women to reproduce it has often set to curb

the black population by discouraging the fertility of black and ethnic minority women. (1989: 22)

In Britain Asian women have been subjected to the degradation and humiliation of virginity tests, and having their bones X-rayed or blood samples taken to check parentage at entry. There is some evidence that Black women are more likely to be encouraged to accept sterilization and the birth control drug Depo-provera (Klug 1989, Bryan *et al.* 1985). This may be part of a population strategy of discouraging the reproduction of citizens of the 'wrong' type (Anthias and Yuval-Davis 1989).

In this context it is important to recognize that citizenship is both a gendered (Pateman 1988) and a racialized concept (Anthias 1991, Baucock 1991, Yuval-Davis 1991b). This relates to some extent to the fact that most of the assumptions concerning the community to which being a citizen is dependent, structure it as both ungendered and unracialized. As Walby (1991) points out the term is linked to democracy which in the classical Greek sense was limited to men who were not slaves. The restructuring of democracy in revolutionary France did not allow women the vote until after the Second World War (Walby 1991: 1). One can only be a citizen of a nation-state and this itself draws on the notion of ethnic identity in as much as full rights of citizenship have often been restricted, in an informal if not a formal way, to those who are seen to belong to the nation, that is, have the dominant ethnicity. This is illustrated by the informal controls that often function to limit inclusion within the nation-state (WING 1985).

Marshall's (1950) classic conception of citizenship includes not only formal political rights but also civil and social rights. Developing out of a British model of democracy (Mann 1987, Turner 1990), it was also blind to the ways in which women were excluded as well as the ways in which ethnicity and racialization functioned to exclude access to full citizenship in the sense of political, civil and social rights. This is a point made by Turner (1990: 197) when he says that it has neglected 'the questions of aboriginality, ethnicity and nationalism'. According to Pateman (1988), the separation of society into the public male and private female sphere has been a predicate of the exclusion of women from full citizenship and made it difficult for women to be fully involved at the political level. The ways in which the public and private spheres are constructed, and the relationship of women to them, is in fact not only diverse in relation to ethnicity, but itself is dependent on the exercise of racist exclusions which intersect with those of gender. Women have a different relationship to the state from men, inasmuch as gender divisions are used by the state and the dominant ethnic group in order to pursue their class and national interests (Anthias and Yuval-Davis 1989).

ANTI-SEXIST AND ANTI-RACIST STRATEGY

Having explored some of the connections between gender and ethnic processes, we want to turn to the connection between feminist and anti-racist struggle. This is important, particularly since equal opportunities programmes and policies have tended to separate the issues of sexism and racism. The position taken here is that sexism and racism have to be analytically separated, but that the issue of equal opportunities has to connect together the different ways in which gender, race and class are intertwined in the concrete experience and practice of disadvantage and exclusion.

As we show in the following chapter, some of the effects of these policies have been to forge divisions amongst the very constituencies themselves. They have heralded a process of ethnicization on the one hand and the development of the professional ethnic on the other who serves as the representative of his or her community. In terms of race, there has been a conflation between developing anti-racist policies and practices and ensuring their effective implementation on the one hand, and the funding of local community groups in a broad range of concerns, in terms of ethnic cultural pursuits. A detailed account of these processes is to be found in our last chapter, so we will concentrate here on the issues relating to the links between anti-sexist and anti-racist practice.

There are a number of issues at stake. First is the analytical separation between anti-racist and anti-sexist struggle. There can be no doubt that some issues, like the dowry, exclusions and stereotyping on the basis of sex, arranged marriages, the control of women's sexuality, are all issues to be tackled by anti-sexist struggle; they are not issues that derive from racist social relations. However, where the dowry or arranged marriages, for example, are condemned by White feminists without acknowledging their ethnocentrism and without locating the struggle in terms that are appropriate within a racist milieu, then the issues can become racialized. This partly relates to the accusations that some Black feminists have made against western feminism for its failure to tackle issues of racism within its own formulation of what constitutes feminist issues.

However, if anti-racist and anti-sexist struggle have different objects of reference, as we believe to be the case, then it is necessary to specify ways in which anti-sexist struggle, the domain of feminism, can engage with issues of race. An additional issue is whether being a White woman means necessarily being racist, in which case by definition a White women's movement must be racist. This position however, homogenizes the categories of White and Black in an extremely problematic way (see Anthias and Yuval-Davis 1983). Does every feminist issue have a racist dimension or are there feminist issues that can be separated from issues of racism; do these then constitute universal feminist issues?

The involvement of feminists in anti-racist struggle has been minimal and where it has existed, as in Women Against Racism and Fascism has been linked to the anti-fascist struggle (see Bourne 1985). Third-World and Black women find it difficult to locate themselves within the White feminist movement, a point that has been poignantly made by many Black feminists. Thus there may be a need for separate organization, although Women Against Fundamentalism has successfully acted against separatism. Similarly, in the anti-racist struggle, Black women have been rendered invisible by many of the terms of the agenda. For these reasons Black women, when organizing together as women (that is, via the category of feminism), have placed themselves within the struggle against racism. Thus there is no clear-cut separation in these two struggles as far as many Black and Third-World women are concerned. The category of feminism in any case must include issues relating to the factors that subordinate women, and where issues of racism complicate and intermesh with the subordinations of gender, they must also be included.

The Black women's movements have been engaged in struggle on a variety of fronts, most of which are essentially interlinked to the racialization of gender disadvantage and exclusion. For example, they struggle against the sexism and racism that they experience through the state in such things as immigration law (see WING 1985) and *vis-à-vis* White men, as well as against the racism they experience as women through the use of the

Depo-provera drug and sterilization and from White women who fail to tackle their own ethnocentrism and racism. In the process Black women have organized to pursue anti-sexist struggle within the framework of a racist society. More recent developments have seen Black women divided however, over issues like clitoridectomy, Asian women's sanctuaries, separate schools for Muslim girls, and the rise of fundamentalism (see Southall Black Sisters (1990) and the publications of Women against Fundamentalism). Such issues raise the whole question of the gender divisions within the Black community and often question dominant cultural norms that are patriarchal. They also open the door for co-operation with anti-racist White feminists on common issues such as domestic violence and religious fundamentalism.

Issues that relate to sexism within racialized groups have given rise to much dissension, however. This is understandable in terms of priorities in the context of racialized social relations. However, where Black women have at times been reluctant to criticize sexist relations within their own communities, this means, we believe, a failure to see that the issue of sexism is not confined to the area of White dominant society only. Culture, including the culture of oppressed groups, is highly patriarchal and requires challenging from a feminist point of view.

CONCLUSION

In this chapter, we have explored some of the theoretical and empirical parameters within which race and racism have to be located in relation to gender. We have attempted to demonstrate the need to examine the connections between race and gender and racism and sexism. We believe that the discourses of sexism and racism can be separated even though the practices as experienced by groups of subjects are intermeshed. Where cultural practices serve to deprive women of control over their own sexuality and subordinate them *qua* women this is a feminist issue and concerns all those who are engaged in anti-sexist struggle.

Where the sexist practice derives from a set of social relations that are outside the immediate experience and understanding of western feminism then the struggle against it can only be forged on terms that are determined primarily by women of that group. It is not a question, however, of denying a voice on sexist practices from whatever cultural or social location to anyone who is engaged in feminist struggle. It is a question rather of seeing those sexist practices contextually both in terms of the total culture they are derivative of and in relation to the racialization of gender relations in the western world. Similarly where western feminists are unable to see the feminist issues in their own cultures, say in the ideology of romance and courtship, then it is important that they are asked to abandon their ethnocentric spectacles. The dowry and arranged marriages are merely particular manifestations of the control of women and in that sense can sit alongside courtship, dating and romance.

In the following chapter we shall turn to the theme of colour racism and consider ways in which the category of 'Black' has been used in theorizations of racism and within racist and anti-racist discourse.

Chapter 5

Racism and the colour 'Black'

INTRODUCTION

This chapter is about 'unpacking' and 'decoding' racism against
Black people, so as to be able to evaluate more effectively colour
categories in developing anti-racist strategies. This question
should preoccupy not only Black or other minority people but
everyone who is concerned with questions of social justice.

The chapter first looks at several theoretical approaches to
racism which have focused on Blacks, and questions the extent to
which colour is indeed the explanatory principle in their models.
Next, it examines the category of 'Black' and its development as a
political category in post-Second World War Britain, including the
influence the American Black Power movement has had over it.
The latter part of the chapter explores some of the contradictions
which have emerged in the last few years around the interrelationships between racisms, anti-racist struggles and the category of
Blackness. This is done mainly in relation to British official
statistics.

THEORIZING RACISM AND THE QUESTION OF BLACKNESS

There is sometimes a confusion in the various theories developed
to explain racism. This confusion hinges upon the extent to which
Blackness and racism are necessarily linked in their line of argument. This section reviews several theoretical approaches which
have linked racism specifically with Blacks as its victims. Our
argument is that when examined closely we find that in these
various approaches Blackness is used as the signifier of the target

groups for racist discrimination, but other factors have been used as the explanatory principles for the actual racism.

The first approach to be examined in this context is the Black Marxist approach. Oliver Cox was the first Marxist sociologist who theorized about racism. A Black American himself, Cox concentrated on American Blacks as the subject matter of racism (for a more comprehensive review of his work see Chapter 3). Cox argues for the specificity of the phenomenon of racism and differentiated it from other forms of prejudice, such as intolerance, which he characterizes as the reason for persecution of groups such as the Jews. For Cox, 'The dominant group is intolerant of those whom it can define as anti-social, while it holds race prejudice against those whom it can define as subsocial (1970 [1948]: 400).

The dominant group dislikes the 'anti-social' as long as they refuse to assimilate, and likes the sub-social as long as they do not attempt to assimilate and stay in 'their place'. Therefore, argues Cox, one cannot make a comparison between a pogrom against Jews and the lynching of Blacks. The first one is ultimately aimed at exterminating the Jews, but the second one is aimed at 'teaching the Blacks a lesson'.

This dichotomous approach of Cox is not valid, not necessarily in his analysis of the concrete situation, but in the conclusions he projects from this on a general understanding of racism. Cox defines the principle of ultimate exploitation as *the* racist logic. However, the perspective of this book is that the principle of ultimate extermination has to be included as well as the principle of ultimate exploitation as racist exclusionary logics (see discussion in Chapter 1). Certain minority groups under specific historical conditions can be a target of both racist dynamics (for example, the Jews in the East End of London in the early twentieth century and Asians in contemporary Britain). Moreover, there are other racial minorities, such as the North American Indians and the Aborigines, against whom the primary racist dynamic has been of extermination, even though they were seen as sub-social rather than anti-social. However, even when Cox's analysis is viewed as specifically concerned with racism against the American Blacks, this racism is grounded not in the colour of the skin of the American Blacks, but in their specific history as slaves. As a Marxist, Cox looked for the material conditions of the rise of racism and found them in capitalism and the need for commoditization of the

Blacks, who have occupied a very specific class position in the early part of capitalist history. Similarly Cox sees the superiority of Whites as a specific historical development, a result of the 'dynamism and efficiency of capitalist culture' (1970 [1948]: 345), rather than in any inherent cultural characteristic of colour itself. Cox quotes from J. W. Hall (1927: 4), who summed up the development of White supremacy:

> The White man's conception of himself as the aristocrat of the earth came gradually through the discovery, as surprising to himself as to anyone else, that he had weapons and organization which made opposition to his ambition futile.

It is this historical domination which permeated the whole world.

> Since the belief in White superiority – that is to say, White nationalism – began to move all over the world, no people of colour has been able to develop race prejudice independent of Whites. It may be, however that the Japanese have now reached that stage of industrial development, national ambition and military power sufficient to question their assignment to inferior racial rank. (Cox 1948: 346)

Other Black Marxists have continued to develop this theoretical approach and have expanded it, with a growing specific 'Black perspective'. Cedric J. Robinson, in his book *Black Marxism* sets out to 'map the historical and intellectual contours of the encounter of Marxism and black radicalism, two programmes for revolutionary change' (1983: 1).

Robinson points out that Marxism does not supply any theoretical explanation for the recurrent idea of racialism in the history of western civilization. He locates its origins with the emergence of racial order in feudal Europe and traces it up to the emergence of 'racial capitalism' during the industrialization era, in which 'the phenomenology of the relations of production bred no objective basis for the extrication of the universality of class from the particularisms of race' (p. 3).

Robinson attempts to 'correct' the Eurocentric perspective which distorts Marxist analysis. Since the three hundred years of slave labour are central and integral to the development of capitalism, the Marxist interpretation of history in terms of the dialectic of capitalist class struggles is inadequate. 'From its very foundations capitalism has never been – any more than Europe – a "closed system"' (Robinson 1983: 3). Furthermore, Africans brought with them to the New World their own cultural modes of resistance, which form a radical tradition different and autonomous from that of class politics.

Robinson's work, like Cox's, although important, suffers from some of the more general problems of Marxist analysis (see discussion in Chapter 3). It also suffers from a certain ethnocentric overemphasis of the contribution of Africans in comparison with other people and cultures of the Third World, both to the development of capitalism and to the resistance to it. What is important to our investigation here, however, is the possible theoretical link in Robinson's work between racism and colour. Robinson, quite consciously, does not make this causal link. He locates the ideology of racism in the 'internal' relations of European people, and racialism against Blacks – the 'creation of the Negro' – as an 'obligatory' exercise, given the importance of Black labour power to world economy.

Similar causal relationships can be found in other Marxist and sociological analyses, such as those of Sivanandan (1982) and Rex (1970, 1981) who have analysed racism against Blacks in contemporary Britain. The crucial common analytical factor in their differing approaches is the view of Britain as a post-colonial society where the Blackness of the ex-colonials is not the cause of their institutional and social racist exclusion and exploitation but rather their signifier.

Other theoretical approaches which have likewise linked racism and Blackness also locate this on the level of the social and cultural signifier for racist discrimination. In particular these links can be seen in social psychological approaches, which concentrate on interpersonal and intergroup prejudice and discrimination. The work of Henry Tajfel will be examined more closely here, for it is both the most influential in Britain and that which has related most specifically to the question of Blackness.

Henry Tajfel (1965, 1978) considers the relations between social groups as determined both by

> the 'objective' conditions of their co-existence; that is, the economic, political, social and historical circumstances which have led to – and often still determine – the differences between the groups in their standards of living, access to opportunities . . . or the treatment they receive from those who wield

power . . . and the 'subjective' definitions, stereotypes and
belief systems (1978: 3)

with which these objective conditions are always associated. In his
work Tajfel has concentrated on the study of these 'subjective
definitions' while clearly recognizing the limitations of this
approach in actually explaining prejudice and discrimination. For
these one needs to look for more macro-social and specific historical factors. While social attitudes contribute to social conflicts
and should not be overlooked, they are not in themselves
sufficient explanation (1965: 128). It is within this self-confined
social psychological framework of analysis that Tajfel has
attempted to look at the question of colour as an independent
variable in racial prejudice. As a proof that such an independent
variable exists, he quotes the Political and Economic Planning
(PEP) survey on colonial students in Britain, published in 1955,
which reported that less than half of the light-skinned West Indian
students experienced prejudice as compared with 80 per cent of
dark-skinned West Indians.

Tajfel offers three complementary and very convincing explanations, or rather observations, for the specificity of Blackness in
racist prejudice beyond other forms of racist stereotyping. Firstly,

is the fact that, whatever may be the nature of scientific
evidence, racialism finds one of its manifold expressions in
the widespread tendency to 'explain' historical or social
phenomena in terms of mysterious and inherent differences
between human beings, causally attributed to 'race'. (1965:
130)

Colour of the skin as an inherited characteristic lends itself easily
to crude 'scientific' racist genetic theories.

Secondly, Blackness is visible. Once the powerful dynamic of
hostile stereotyping has been established, it is very resistant to
change; this is a result of the selective perception of prejudiced
people. Thus visibility reinforces racist classification as a salient
factor in every social interaction.

These two characteristics of Blackness are universal, in the sense
that they can be found in any anti-Black racist cultural or historical
context. In other racist historical or cultural contexts, however,
other inherited or visible characteristics can become the focus for
racist theorization or stereotyping: 'red-skin wild Indians', 'yellow

peril Japanese' or Jews with 'Jewish noses' are examples which easily come to mind. What is especially significant about visible inherited characteristics in comparison with visible non-inherited characteristics (such as accent or dress) which are used as signifiers within other specific racist social contexts, is the fact that it is not generational specific. The children have them as attributes just as the parents had. Also, assimilation is impossible as a coping strategy for the victims of such racism and their children, as long as the inherited characteristic continues to be used culturally as a signifier for racist discourse and practice.

However, another important factor to observe in that context emerges very clearly in the interviews which Tajfel quotes (as well as in other surveys of racial prejudice including that of Anthias, Cain, and Yuval-Davis 1988). While the category of Black skin signifies the category of people to denigrate and discriminate against, the specific contents of the racial stereotyping and the ethnic boundaries it draws are not necessarily fixed or consistent. Some people justified their racial prejudice against West Indians by contrasting them with the 'goody' Asians, while others thought West Indians were OK but it was the 'Pakis' who were 'ponces', smelly, etc. Moreover, the contents of the racist stereotype vary widely and specific racist images are attached to specific 'Black' ethnic minorities. Some are portrayed as violent and others as wimps, some as dumb and others as sneaky. Blackness, therefore, is not in itself a sufficient signifier for specific intersubjective racist stereotyping or practice, let alone other forms of racist ideologies and practices in specific historical contexts. So it is not racism but multi-racisms which can be triggered by the signifiers of Blackness, and Blackness in itself cannot explain specific racist ideologies and practices. Similarly, other visible, especially inherited characteristics, can act as signifiers in particular historical contexts, including what is grouped under the category of 'Black' itself (as we shall see later in the chapter).

What is common, however, to all multi-racist stereotyping, is its negative, potentially dangerous, characteristics. This links to the third observation Tajfel makes about the nature of racist attitude to Blacks: the attitude in western cultural tradition to the colour Black:

> 'Black' and 'White', which represent so crudely the differences
> in the shade of skin between groups of human beings – are used

to symbolize distinctions between vice and virtue, hell and heaven, devils and angels, contamination and purity. (1965: 130)

This is an expression of a historical cultural tradition which operates on deeper, sometimes unconscious, levels in western civilization, of demonological collective representation.

'Half-devil and half-child' are the 'sullen people' who are 'The White Man's Burden' during Victorian times, according to Rudyard Kipling. Winthrop D. Jordan (1974) looks at constructions of 'the Negroes' in Elizabethan times as the combined result of the adventurous and puritanical spirits of the time. He presents the example of George Best who, when he encountered Blacks in his travels in Africa, saw them as cursed people, the descendants of disobedient Cham, the son of Noah: 'English perceptions integrate sexuality with blackness, the devil and the judgement of God who had originally created man not only "Angel-like" but "white"' (1974: 23).

These demonological traditions preceded Elizabethan Europe. Although, the word 'Black' did not acquire its negative connotations until the late Middle Ages, Hunter has shown how the preconceptions of Englishmen were shaped by ideas transmitted through the medieval Church before there was any face-to-face contact with Blacks. Christian De la Campagne (1983) studied, from a different angle, earlier European demonologies in which Blackness played a part. A major step forward was taken by Daniel Siboni (1974) and following him by Phil Cohen (1988 and 1989a) who linked this demonology to unconscious racism. In the words of Phil Cohen:

> Unlike previous psychoanalytical theories, Siboni does not argue that racial prejudice is just another instance of certain very general defence mechanisms (splitting, projection, displacement) mobilized in certain social situations to denigrate and exclude certain groups. Instead he shows that the construction of The Other in racist discourses follows a route which is specific to its unconscious mode of functioning. Its surface structures of conscious reasoning are traced back to a phantasy system in which representations of sexuality and generation are organized in a peculiarly perverse way. Positions of racial superiority are associated with an ideal desexualized

image of the body – an 'immaculate conception' of origins, an eternally regenerated destiny; whilst racial inferiority is associated with a degenerate or monstrous body, in which the power of sexuality, repressed at the other pole, returns as a purely negative principle. (1989a: 8)

This ideology of split mind and body which equals superiority and inferiority has racist and sexist double standards underlying it. Siboni and Cohen claim it has been part of the unconscious history of reason in western civilization and has been made to function as an instrument of class and ethnic domination. This explains some of the deep-rooted resistance to 'reasoned' anti-racist strategies.

Unlike Jordan, however, Siboni and Cohen do not look at the racist construction of 'the other' as exclusively attached to Blackness. For example, Siboni has written a book which looks at the operation of the racist imagination in relation to 'the Jew' (1983).

There is, then, a specific European tradition which has associated Blackness with evil, monsters, and base sexuality, and which constitutes part of the Europeans' cultural resources and therefore ethnicity. As such, it is part of their *Weltanschauung* and operates on unconscious as well as conscious levels. And it is specific to racism against Black people.

It is specific to racism against Black people, but as we have seen, it is not the only tradition of demonology which has fed European racism. Parallel traditions, which have also become part of the unconscious construction of European ethnicities exist also, for instance, in relation to the Jews and Gypsies. In both cases they were perceived not only as outsiders but as a demonic threat: the Jews as Anti-Christ, as well as money and power grabbers, conspiring to take over the world, and the Gypsies as having magical powers in telling fortunes and preparing potions as well as being thieves, and dirty and lazy people.

Racism exists, however, not only in the unconscious minds of the racists, but also in those who have been the victims of racism. It was Franz Fanon, the Martinique psychiatrist, who explored the damaging effects of racism and colonialism on Black people's psyche, the condition of being constituted as the 'other' in their own, as well as in the hegemonic White psyche. 'The white man is sealed in his whiteness. The black man in his blackness' (1986: 11). He pointed out that the way to freedom for the Black man is to 'recapture the self and to scrutinize the self . . . Freedom requires the effort as disalienation' (p. 231).

Fanon located the alienated state of the Black man in the fact that 'the black is not a man' (1986: 10). The activists in the Black Power movement which arose in the 1960s in the USA and which, in its turn, has affected the British Black (and many other) radical movements, were very affected by Fanon's work and saw their task as reclaiming their manhood (in terms of the 'humanhood' of Blacks as well as with a touch of machismo).

'BLACKNESS' AS A POLITICAL CATEGORY IN CONTEMPORARY BRITAIN

Stuart Hall has pointed out that

'Black' could not be converted to 'black is beautiful' simply by wishing it so. It had to become part of an organized practice of struggles requiring the building up of black resistance as well as the development of new forms of black consciousness. (1982: 62)

The category of 'Black' as a category of organized struggle and of positive identification first arose during the 1960s in the USA in the Black Power movement. It replaced the label 'Negro' as a term of empowerment. In the words of Sivanandan,

"Black Power" is a political metaphor – comprehending, at once, the history, condition, manifesto and programme of the black people of America. Powerlessness, the antonym of power, has characterized their history and accounted for their present condition. To transform that condition it needed the power to determine their own lives and destiny – at all levels. The strategy, the programme to achieve such power entails their solidarity as a people. This in turn implies the concepts of self help, pride and indigenous culture. (1982: 57)

The Black Power movement had a tremendous effect on radical politics in the 1970s and 1980s, and not only in terms of the specific achievements (partial and yet fundamental) in the relative position and self-assertion of Black people. It gave Black people a voice and established the principle of self-empowerment, which became a model of political activism for other disempowered groupings, such as women, gays and lesbians, the disabled, etc

(Brah 1992). The other side of it was that it promoted and legitimized an alternative principle of organization for radical politics,
that is the principle of prioritizing an ascriptive membership in a
disadvantaged community, to the traditional 'leftist' principle of a
universalistic membership based on ideological solidarity. In the
words of Stokley Carmichael and Charles V. Hamilton,

> The concept of Black Power rests on a fundamental premise:
> before a group can enter the open society, it must first close its
> ranks. By this we mean that group solidarity is necessary before
> a group can operate effectively in a pluralistic society. (1968)

Without entering into a specific discussion on 'community
politics' here (see discussion in Chapter 6), it is important that we
note crucial differences in the definition of 'the Black community'
in the USA and in Britain. The boundaries of the category of
'Blacks' in the USA have been relatively clear and the members of
this category have had a relatively homogeneous origin and history,
as well as a particular location in the American social structure.
They were all descendants of Africans who were originally brought
to America as slaves. In the 1970s and 1980s, in a later stage of the
development of Black politics in the USA, when Jesse Jackson and
other major local Black candidates (for example, Mel King in
Boston and Harold Washington in Chicago) began promoting
themselves as the representatives of oppressed ethnic minorities
(as well as of all other disadvantaged groups) in American society,
the category of Black was not wide enough for this purpose. It did
not include, for example, Hispanic people who are the other
major disadvantaged ethnic minority in contemporary USA, and
therefore mobilization took place under the notion of people of
colour, or – with even wider boundaries – of the 'Rainbow
Coalition'. Moreover, the label 'African-Americans' is gradually
replacing 'Blacks' in the USA through the active promotion of
Jesse Jackson and others, in an attempt to 'normalize' American
Blacks into a minority equivalent to other ethnic minorities in the
USA, with their own country (or, in this case, continent) of origin
and a cultural heritage.

In Britain, the notion of the 'Black community' developed in
the 1960s, partly as a result of the influence of the American Black
Power movement, but also because of the specific history of British
anti-Black racism. The visits of Martin Luther King, and, according
to Sivanandan (1983: 16), even more so of Malcolm X in 1965, had

a major effect on anti-racist activity in Britain in general and on Black consciousness and militancy in particular.

The initial organization to promote the ideology of Black Power at its most extreme was RAAS (the Race Relations Adjustment Society), headed by Malcolm X. By 1969 more than fifty organizations combined to form the national body, the BPA (Black People Alliance), 'a militant front for Black Consciousness and against Racialism' (Bryan *et al.*. 1985). The overall character of Black militancy, however, as in the USA, was more that of a social movement than that of a co-ordinated national political organization. Struggles developed in various locations, within the work-place, the education system, and increasingly in the 1980s within the women's movement, local authorities, the Labour Party and the 'Race Relations Industry' itself (Sivanandan 1983, Bryan *et al.* 1985). Salman Rushdie (not incidentally in the pre-Rushdie affair time) (1982) claimed that 'Britain is now two entirely different worlds and the one you inherit is determined by the colour of your skin'.

In comparison with the American counterpart, however, the category of 'Black' in Britain has been ambiguous from its inception, and its boundaries have been fiercely contested both from inside and outside the anti-racist movement. Sometimes it has even led to the rupture of specific organizations (for example, OWAAD, the Organization of Women of African and Asian Descent (Bryan *et al.* 1985). There is no space here to give an account of the history of the various positions taken. It is important to note, however, that beyond the racist definition of skin colour, there have been two major criteria used for defining the boundaries of the category 'Black' in Britain. First there is the notion of Blacks as sharing a common origin and culture and all that this implies, and secondly, the notion of Blacks as sharing a common experience (destiny) of racism and all that this implies. In the USA these two criteria overlapped in the history of the African-Americans. In Britain they could impose different boundaries on the Black category. The first definition, when used in relation to Africa, could encompass Africans and African-Caribbeans, and the second could also include Asians from the Indian subcontinent and, according to some political definitions, Middle Eastern, oriental, Latino and other Third-World peoples. Origin, and sometimes even culture, however, could also be defined as coming from the British empire or from the Third World as a whole. The extent to which these definitions have been used as exclusionary boundaries has depended on the politics and interests of those who promoted them in specific contexts.

Black cultures in Britain, of course, cannot be reduced to instruments of political struggles, and definitely not just to anti-racist struggles (Gilroy 1987). First of all, the various immigrants brought with them cultural, linguistic and religious traditions which they continued to practise, reproduce and evolve under the different conditions of the British social structure. Among the second generation especially, new forms of culture have evolved which combine cultures of origin with influences of British, especially working-class British, popular cultures. It is interesting to note that, as Gilroy and Lawrence rightly claim (in Cohen and Bains 1988), contemporary British White working-class culture has been heavily influenced in its turn by Black youth culture. At the same time political struggles have also emerged, in particular by women who challenged some of the more reactionary, especially sexist, assumptions in the traditional immigrant cultures as they have affected the lives of those subjected to them (Southall Black Sisters 1990).

Nevertheless, culture has also been used as an explicit political anti-racist instrument by Black nationalists, who saw in the promotion, for instance, of the knowledge of African languages and culture among African-Caribbean youth (thereby linking up with lost 'roots') an organic connection with the Pan-African liberation movement and the establishment of positive identity and pride among Blacks. This attitude was very influential in promoting multi-cultural education as an anti-racist educational policy in the British educational system in the 1970s (see discussion in Chapter 6).

Among those with stronger socialist tendencies, African nationalism also constituted part of a wider coalition. This was constituted by those who defined the boundaries of the Black category in Britain as based on the common experience of all Blacks coming from communities which have been victims of and resisters to British colonialism. The coalition was to unite 'the (Asian) coolies', 'the (African) savages' and 'the (West Indian) slaves'. The experience of colonialism and the international anti-colonial solidarity movement was politically important in the militant Black movement in Britain, especially in the late 1960s and 1970s. In the 1980s, however, the parameters of the debate changed; more and more Blacks had been born in Britain, where their Black identity was constructed as a direct product of racism in Britain rather than in the colonies. Some continue to view origin from a NCWP (New Commonwealth Country and Pakistan) as the delineating principle in determining who is Black and who is not (for example the Black trade unions and Black women's conferences that took place in London in 1983 and 1984 did not allow the participation of other people from Third-World countries (North Africa, the Middle East, the Philipines, etc) and defined themselves as Black as a political category). Amina Mama expressed this exclusionary tendency most clearly in a complete rejection of attempts to include all Third-World people under the label of 'Black', a proposition she considered as 'historically inaccurate and politically foolish'. She claimed,

> In Britain it is clear that black refers to Africans (continental and of the Diaspora), and Asians (primarily of Indian sub-continent descent). All have a shared history of oppression by British colonialism and racism (1984: 22).

However, when she continues to discuss Blackness in her paper she exclusively relates it to African-related traditions of struggle. This ambiguity, according to Tariq Modood (1988) is typical of discourses about Blacks in Britain, in which Asians generally come out the losers. He quotes as a typical example a sentence from a booklet published in 1985 by the Labour Party, in which Asians are first mentioned as a separate category only to be subsumed later under the category of Black people:

> Too often when the party discusses the membership of black and Asian people it centres on the level of black public representativeness, magistrates and MPs, rather than on ways in which black people can play a role in the party without necessarily aspiring to hold office; this not to diminish the important point that many more black people should hold such offices. (Modood 1988: 400)

Modood's position is that there is a need to separate Asians out of the Black category. He argues that an all-inclusive definition of Blackness 'sells short the majority of the people it defines as "Black"' (1988: 399). Others (the Black section of the Labour Party, for instance) insist, on the other hand, that in spite of all internal differences, there is a need for unity and solidarity for all those who are subjected to racism in Britain because of their skin colour.

Another type of critique has been developed by Gita Sahgal (1992). Criticizing the way the notion of 'Blackness' has been used by some Black feminists, Sahgal argues that emphasizing the common experiences of racism does not allow women to relate to the specific social structures within which they are located. This would have made them critical of their own patriarchal cultures as well as the wider racist social structures. Given such consciousness, a critique of Black patriarchal cultures would not automatically be constructed as a racist 'pathologization' of minority cultures.

Recently, there has been a growing tendency to accept self-definition as a criterion for defining the boundaries as well as the specific meaning of the Black category. This is, for example, the definition which is used in the Black sections of the Labour Party. Indeed, given the racist origin and use of the term 'Black', self-determination as a form of Black pride can be the only viable alternative to being other-defined in a racist manner, according to colour of skin and facial features.

However, as Brah argues, it is very important to differentiate between the use of the term 'Black'

> as a term adopted by subordinate groups to symbolize resistance against oppression *and* the appropriation of the same term by some local authorities as a basis for formulating policies for the allocation of resources. (1991: 6)

This appropriation – the result of the different, but coinciding political strategies of the Tories, Left Labour as well as grass-roots Black activists – will be discussed in Chapter 6. However, it is important to note here that once this appropriation had taken place in the 1980s, Blackness stopped to be politically just a category of resistance, and became also a system of power brokery; it stopped being just a form of solidarity, and became also a divisive category in competing for and of holding on to funds and other resources. From a dichotomous category in a political struggle which constructed the social universe into Black/White, Blackness has become, at least to a certain extent, an ethnicized category, in which the 'Black community' exists next to, as well as in partial overlap of, the 'Asian community' and other 'ethnic minorities, migrants and refugees'.

Moreover, the legitimacy of the term 'Black' in its anti-racist form in official discourse, has blurred the fact that state agents are carrying out racial identifications in a racist manner. Institutions such as the Police (and the Social Services and the NHS) are conducting a so-called ethnic monitoring which is based not on the subjective perceptions of people regarding their own ethnicity, nor even on objective data of origin, but on visual assessment of 'racial' physical characteristics, such as colour of skin, type of hair and structure of the nose. The so-called 'Ident Code Key' of the police (as received by us from a Metropolitan Community Relations Officer in 1987) divides the people into:

1   White-skinned European types;
2   Dark-skinned European types;
3   Negroid types (can be light or White-skinned);
4   Indian or Pakistani types
5   Chinese or Japanese types;
6   Arabian Egyptian types.

They, however, know that 'Negroid types' are not necessarily identified as such, by the Black colour of their skin.

The multiple dimensions in which Blackness is being experienced and constructed in Britain and the conflicts around the boundaries of the category, have, therefore, brought out certain contradictions and paradoxes, not least in the arena of official statistics, which we examine next.

BLACKS AND OFFICIAL STATISTICS

The Commission for Racial Equality (CRE) Fact Sheet No. 1 aims, and rightly so, to expose the myth that most of the postwar immigrants to Britain have been Black. However, while doing so, it creates myths of its own. It says,

> The 1981 Census: Country of Birth, Great Britain, table 1, shows that nearly 3.4 million people in Britain were born overseas. Well over half of these (1.89 million) are *white*; over 607 thousand were born in Ireland, 153 thousand in the Old Commonwealth countries (Australia, New Zealand and Canada) and about 1.3 million in other countries including those in Western Europe. The remainder (1.41 million) are *black* or *brown*, having been born in the New Commonwealth countries and Pakistan (NCWP) which are as follows: Eastern Africa – Kenya, Malawi, Tanzania, Uganda, Zambia; Southern Africa – Botswana, Lesotho and Swaziland, Zimbabwe; Western

Africa – Gambia, Ghana, Nigeria, Sierra Leone; Caribbean – Barbados, Jamaica, Trinidad and Tobago, Antigua, St. Kitts-Nevis, Anguilla, Belize, Guyana; South Asia – Pakistan, Bangladesh, India, Sri-Lanka; South East Asia – Hong Kong, Malaysia, Singapore; Mediterranean – Cyprus, Gibraltar, Malta (including Gozo); Remainder – Mauritius, Seychelles, Falkland Islands, other islands and territories. About 100 thousand white people were born in the Indian sub-continent and East Africa while their parents were on overseas service. (1985a: 1)

We found it necessary to include this quotation as a whole, because it exemplifies the two-staged mystifying euphemisms which are so common in the British 'Race Relations Industry' and popular discourse. The first stage is the equivalence of country of birth with the colour of the skin, as if there are no countries which 'export' both Black and White people to Britain (such as USA, South Africa, Zimbabwe, etc). Moreover, the world is hardly composed of a dichotomy of colour of skin; are Chinese people considered White or Black/brown according to this categorization? The answer is that it depends on their country of origin; if they come from Hong Kong (even if they happen to be White businessmen) then they are considered to be Black or brown. If they come from China, then they are considered to be White. This is so, because the second stage of this mystification is that one is Black or brown only if one's country of origin has been part of the British empire (even if one comes from the Falkland Islands which do not have one Black person in sight . . . let alone Cypriots and Maltese). But if one has come from a country, such as Mozambique, Morocco, the Philippines or Latin America, which happened to be part of other western powers' empires, not Britain's, then one is often counted as part of the 'remainder' White immigrants to this country.

The collapse of 'NCWP origin' to 'Black' and of 'Blacks' to 'ethnic minorities' has been by no means specific to the CRE. The Population Statistics Division, OPCS, estimating the size of ethnic minority populations in the 1980s, advanced from the 1970s types of study; this included the 1981 census, which looked at ethnic minorities only on the basis of those who lived in households headed by people born in NCWP countries. Instead, the Labour Force Study looked at the ethnic minorities born in Britain as well as those born in any other foreign country. However, the first filter in the questionnaire was whether or not the person answering the questionnaire considered himself or herself to be White. Therefore, there was an equation of the concepts of ethnic minorities and of being 'non-White'. Gypsies, Irish, Jews – to mention just the main 'White' ethnic minorities subjected to some forms of racism in this country – were absent from this count as well.

The paradoxes and distortions which are inherent in these forms of representation are probably the product of the very entangled and unresolved ideological struggles in Britain which take place among racists, anti-racists and those who have been subjected to racism, about the ideological categories as well as about strategies of action, how to locate racism and how to tackle it.

The gradual (and partial) transition from categories of country of origin to categories of skin colour represents a certain shift in the predominant official conceptions of these issues and the 'ethnicization' of the colour Black. A particularly peculiar product of the ongoing struggle over these issues are the 'country of origin' and 'ethnic' questions for the 1991 census.

THE CENSUS

The government attempted to include an 'ethnic question' in the 1981 census. The debate on this question, however, had already started with the 1961 census. This attempt was abandoned after a failed pilot study in Haringey in London. The reason for this failure, according to Banton (1988: 5) was this:

> Whereas in surveys of this kind normally 70 per cent of people co-operate, in this instance only 14 per cent of West Indian and 34 per cent of Asian households completed their forms. There was resistance to the whole inquiry, partly because of suspicions about the government's intentions, but in some measure because of objections to the wording of the questions.

There was a considerable active struggle by Black activists (in addition to the passive resistance of not completing the form) against the inclusion of an ethnic question in the census. They argued that there is enough available information on racial discrimination in Britain and that the information gathered by the census would be used for purposes of surveillance of them rather than for their benefit.

However, ten years later, most Black activists are supporting and promoting the 'ethnic' census question, which although with a somewhat changed wording, is not very different from the one that was rejected then. They accepted the argument that gathering factual data is crucial in struggles for anti-racist social policies. The change in attitude to the census reflects a change in attitudes towards ethnic monitoring in general. The argument has been that data for purposes of surveillance are collected anyhow, while only public monitoring of the actual extent of discrimination could provide an effective base to counteract it. Black activists in local authorities and in the CRE have been particularly keen on ethnic monitoring, which has formed the basis for a more general anti-racist strategy of positive action (see discussion in Chapter 6).

In order to evaluate the anti-racist effectivity of ethnic monitoring, however, it is not enough to look at the strategy in the abstract. We also have to look at the specific information this monitoring would actually provide.

The categories of classification of the 1991 census question changed several times. Series of field tests were carried out in order to find 'reliable and publicly acceptable questions on these [ethnicity and related topics] which could be included in the [1991] census if that was the wish of the Government of the day' (OPCS press notice, 23 July 1987).

This definition of the aim of the field tests in the OPCS press notice on the subject does not include, as would be immediately obvious to any social scientist, any attempt to find questions which would be methodologically *valid* on the subject. The need for public acceptability easily overtakes the need for any analytical validity. Moreover, the final question differs from the one suggested in this press notice, not as a result of further 'scientific' tests, but as a result of further 'consultations' with the 'community', as was determined by the CRE recommendation.

Reviewing the wordings of the suggested 1981 question, the 1987 question and the final version approved by Parliament in December 1989 for the 1991 census, might illuminate the specific constructions of ethnicity which were found to be politically most viable at that time. By the time the census was actually carried out, things had somewhat changed again.

The proposed question for the 1981 census (quoted in Banton 1988: 6) was as follows:

A   1) Person's country of birth
      2) Person's father's country of birth
      3) Person's mother's country of birth

B   Racial or ethnic group to which the person belongs:
      1) English, Welsh, Scottish or Irish
      2) Other European
      3) West Indian or Guyanese
      4) African
      5) Indian
      6) Pakistani
      7) Bangladeshi
      8) Arab
      9) Chinese
     10) Any other racial or ethnic group or if of mixed racial or
         ethnic descent.

The suggested structure at the 1987 press notice was as follows:

   Race/Ethnic Group – Please tick the appropriate box:
   1) White
   2) Black
   3) Asian – please also tick one box below to show ethnic
      origin or descent:
      5) Indian
      6) Pakistani
      7) Bangladeshi
      8) Chinese
      9) Other Asian – please describe below
   4) Any other Race or Ethnic group (please describe below)

The structure of the final 1991 ethnic question is:

   Ethnic Group – please tick the appropriate box:
   0) White
   1) Black Caribbean
   2) Black African
      Black Other – please describe
   3) Indian
   4) Pakistani
   5) Bangladeshi
   6) Chinese
   Any other ethnic group – please describe.

If the person is descended from more than one ethnic or racial group, please tick the group to which the person considers he/she belongs, or tick the 'Any other ethnic group' box and describe the person's ancestry in the space provided.

A separate question in the census questions the person's country of birth:

Please tick the appropriate box:

1) England
2) Scotland
3) Wales
4) Northern Ireland
5) Irish Republic
   Elsewhere

If elsewhere, please write in the present name of the country.

Several interesting similarities as well as differences can be detected in these different versions of the question. Except for the category of 'Arab', all the specific categories of the planned 1981 census basically covered the same countries of origin as in the 1987 and the 1991 censuses. These are roughly the NCWP countries, with the exception of Cyprus and Malta, the 'White' countries in NCWP, which are absent. The major differences are that in the first question ethnic and racial groups are equated with countries of origin. In the second, the categories of 'Blacks' and 'Asians' (British produced categories) are introduced in order to group together some of the different minorities, as well as 'White' UK citizens and other 'Europeans'. The 'mixed race' category disappears, only to partially reappear in the 1991 census. There, the category of 'race' disappears altogether (except in the case of the mixed race category). Blackness is constructed as a form of ethnicity and is divided into Caribbean, African and a self-defined wider category. The 'Asian' category disappears altogether. Self-defined Asians can appear in the census either as members of specific Asian nationalities (unless they come from any Asian country which is not NCWP), or as 'Black-others' or as just 'others'. This compromise solution, between those who wanted to be defined as 'Asians' and those who wanted to be defined as 'Blacks' creates serious problems of reliability in addition to problems of validity when analysing the results of this census question, but the primary aim of its acceptability to consulted community leaders would be met.

The sensitivity of the categories used in the question is also very uneven. The people of Britain will be divided after the next census into six nationalities (English, Scots, Welsh, Northern Irish, Irish and Others) and nine ethnic categories (White, Black-Caribbean, Black-African, Black-Other, Indian, Pakistani, Bangladeshi, Chinese, and Other). There is no perceived interest in knowing the ethnicity of 'White' minorities (such as Gypsies or Jews; and 'White' NCWP immigrants such as the Cypriots have been omitted as well), the number and nationality of migrant workers from the EC countries, or, for that matter, of migrant workers or refugees from any Third-World countries which used not to be part of the British empire (the old NCWP category). It also does not provide information about the citizenship status of Black people, how many of them are actually settled in Britain, and for how many generations they have been in the UK. It completes the racialization of ethnicity in Britain by constructing 'Whiteness' as an 'ethnic' category.

While it is questionable whether these formulations reflect the needs of the most disadvantaged minority people in Britain today, these classifications fit most closely the arguments used for resources and power within the 'Race Relations Industry' during the period in which the census questions were formulated, and therefore met with the least resistance. Because of timing it does not take into account the racialization of Islam in Britain, after the 'Rushdie affair' and the Gulf War (see discussion in Chapter 2). We would not be surprised to find on the 2001 census, after the 'decade of evangelism', a census question on religion also.

The focus of the census, and of the British 'Race Relations Industry' on Blacks and Asians, should not divert our attention, however, from a certain fact. A growing number of people in Britain who call themselves 'Black', and even more so, who suffer from racism, are not African-Caribbean nor Asians from NCWP countries (or have come from them too late to benefit from the legal rights which the earlier immigrants have enjoyed). Migrant workers and refugees from Third-World countries in Britain have no settlement rights, are vulnerable to being declared illegal immigrants and being deported, and are therefore exploited economically and harassed in very similar ways to 'guest workers' in other European countries. The moves towards a Single European Act in 1992 and the removal of movement restrictions among the members of the European Community is going to intensify even more the process of polarization between those who are settled and have legal civil rights in Britain and therefore in Europe, and those who are going to continue to be under continuous threat of harassment and deportation. And the division between those two categories of people is not necessarily going to be a colour line. As Sivanandan has pointed out (1990), because of their lack of civil rights, the ability of these migrant workers and refugees to organize themselves in an anti-racist movement is much more limited than that of Black immigrants in earlier times.

While much of the day-to-day casework of British Race Relations organizations is engaged in attempts to help these people, they are peripheral to the professional Black power structure within these organizations. A small example would demonstrate the point. A booklet by the London Strategic Policy Unit (1987) described the work of LSPU as giving 'priority consideration to the development of a political awareness of how race, together with other variables of class and gender, underpin the community struggles for justice and freedom' (1987a: 11).

The interesting point is the use of the word 'race' in this context. The specific communities they work with are far from being homogeneously of one 'race'. They are described as 'Asian, African, Caribbean, Travellers, Irish, Cypriots, Migrants and Refugees' (p. 12). But still the booklet stresses, 'Race advisers [*who are supposed to deal with all racism against all ethnic minorities*] should become actively involved in black struggle and look upon *black* community as their power base' (p. 9, our emphasis).

It is possible that the definition 'Black' in this context is inclusive of all those who suffer from racial disadvantage. Another interpretation, however, which seems more plausible in this context, is that the categories of 'Black struggle' and 'anti-racist struggle' which have become subsumed into each other in the Black Power movement, have been used to monopolize positions of power within the 'Race Relations Industry'; and this has happened also when the victims of racism are not Black and certainly not settled NCWP Blacks. Only in those few places where there were other large settled ethnic minorities, like the Cypriots in Hackney and Haringey, have other ethnic minorities been involved in the relative shift of political power within the 'Race

Relations Industry' from the dominant majority to the minorities. The equation of 'Blacks' with 'victims of racism' has excluded other ethnic minorities from access to political power positions in the 'Race Relations Industry' even when such positions seemed to have become available, to a limited extent, in the last few years.

Nevertheless, overall, there is a process of heterogenization within the anti-racist movement, if not within the 'Race Relations Industry'. In addition to the growing visibility of migrant workers discussed above, who are starting to be organized on a European level, two other major issues have arisen during the late 1980s which are changing discourses about racism and are causing major divisions within the anti-racist movement as well as within the Left as a whole.

First is the racialization of the Muslim category in Britain. The catalyst was the Rushdie affair, but it reflects a much more general phenomenon which started to gain momentum after the Iranian revolution. Muslim fundamentalism has come to occupy, to a certain extent, the role of the demonic 'other' that the Soviet Union had occupied during the height of the Cold War. Within Britain, multi-cultural policies which emphasized essential cultural differences have created the space for new militant Muslim leadership to rise within the Muslim communities (see Sahgal and Yuval-Davis 1989). The Left has been divided on the issue. There are those who see any criticism of Muslim fundamentalists as racist, and therefore to be opposed. Others, like Women Against Fundamentalism, while fighting against the racialization of Islam, see as both racist and sexist the reification of Black communities as separate 'others' in whose internal conflicts and political struggles one should not take a stand.

The second issue which has arisen recently is that of anti-Semitism. Jews have been absent from the 'Race Relations Industry' partly because of the Jewish fear of visibility which would render them vulnerable to racist attacks. An exception are the Jewish Orthodox in Hackney who, as a result of their style of hair and clothing, are already visible and who have found it useful under 'positive action' policies to be registered as an ethnic minority in Hackney. Even after the publicity about desecration of Jewish graves in Britain and in France, and against the background of virulent anti-Semitism in Eastern Europe, there is a bitter debate within the Jewish Board of Deputies as to what extent public acknowledgement of anti-Semitism contributes to resistance to it or rather to its reinforcement.

However, another major reason for the absence of Jews from anti-racist organizations is that anti-Semitism does not fit with the construction of racism within them, which is concerned with Black people of ex-colonial origins. This construction is understandable, given the specific history of both the Black movement and the history of Race Relations in Britain. But this specific construction of racism should not be perceived as summing up what racism is – not in general, and not even in contemporary Britain.

CONCLUSION

This chapter argues that Blackness can signify membership of collectivities which are subjected to racist ideologies and practices, but that in itself, Blackness cannot explain the specific nature of these ideologies and practices. Moreover, racism can use all kinds of signifiers and markers for its projects.

Collapsing Blackness as a signifier into Blackness as a specific sign has caused a lot of confusion and ambiguity among those who are trying to fight racism in Britain, both in anti-racist organizations and in political movements.

This collapse is just one aspect of the confusion between analysing racism and analysing notions of race (see Chapter 1). Blackness can define boundaries of a socially constructed racial category, something which is always based on an immutable and inherited biological difference. Racism, or rather, racisms – for they vary depending on the specific historical contexts, the perpetrators as well as the targets of the specific racism – involve political, economic and ideological relations. These relations can be based on exploitation, with the ultimate logic of slavery, or on exclusion, with the ultimate logic of genocide, and are historically specific. They can be directed against any ethnic collectivity which undergoes a process of racialization. Therefore, it is not just physical appearance, but also language, religion, clothing or any other cultural project which can be used as racist signifiers, as long as they come to be perceived as the identification of a separate human stock with an immutable heritage. The dichotomous categories of 'Black' and 'White' homogenize the objects of racism, as well as its perpetrators, reducing racism to just what White people do to Black people because they are Black.

In postwar Britain, anti-Black racism has been the most important and socially significant racism. However, Blacks have not been a unitary category; different groupings of Blacks have suffered from different forms of racisms, and they are not the only victims of racism in Britain.

Common origin and common experience of racism in Britain should be seen more as a continuum than as a dichotomy in determining the boundaries of the British Black category, which are subject to shifting coalitions and emphases. Blackness has been a signifier of experiences of exclusion and harassment, of discrimination and suffering. It has also come to be, since the Black Power movement, a signifier of experiences of empowerment, albeit an empowerment that is locked into a category of disadvantage. In the 1980s, with changes which have taken place in the 'Race Relations Industry' and the equal opportunities policies, it has also become a signifier for allocated access to some resources and jobs as part of the Positive Action policy (see discussion in Chapter 6).

The 1980s have also seen the hesitant beginning of the construction of the category of the 'Black British'. Unlike other constructions of 'Blackness' in Britain, this category is inclusionary, rather than exclusionary. It signifies a place for the Blacks in the construction of the British national collectivity as a pluralistic, multi-racial society. Not incidentally, however, it has been, at least until now, mainly national sport and entertainment figures, such as Lenny Henry and Frank Bruno, who have popularly represented this category.

At the same time, as a result, among other factors, of the shifting nature of immigration to Britain, and the effect of the upcoming 1992 Single European Act (see discussion in Chapters 2 and 6), Blacks are losing their 'monopoly' in signifying the victims of racism in Britain. These days the popular phrase used in political forums is 'Blacks, ethnic minorities and refugees'. Others have replaced the race-related discourse altogether and express their resisting 'otherness' with a fundamentalist religious discourse. This tendency may get stronger in the atmosphere of the post-Gulf War 'new world order'.

The arena in which many of the struggles on the 'Black' question take place is the arena of the 'Race Relations Industry' – the specific laws, statutory and voluntary organizations which have been established with the specific project of fighting racism in Britain. In the next, and last, chapter we shall discuss this 'industry' as part of a more general critical evaluation of anti-racist strategies.

Chapter 6

Resisting racism

Multi-culturalism, equal opportunities and the politics of the 'community'

INTRODUCTION

A great deal of this book is devoted to showing different facets and different constructions of racism and their articulations with ethnic, class, gender and colour divisions; these take place both within the state realm as well as within civil society. Any strategy for effectively resisting racism, therefore, cannot be unitary – and probably not even unified.

Racism is far from being defeated. All of page 2 of the *Guardian* of 26 April 1991 was dedicated to the rise in incidents of racial harassments (including murders), as well as the general activity of extreme-right racist groups now active in Britain, part of the background of growing racism and fascism all over Europe. On the back page of the same newspaper was a major article on the various means the Home Office is using in order to avoid giving sanctuary to as many Kurdish refugees as possible 'for the sake of harmonious race relations'.

In this chapter we decode some of the assumptions about 'good race relations' underlying the formulation of major anti-racist policies in Britain. In particular we examine the ideology of the 'community' which underlies, in different ways, both the 'multiculturalist' and the 'anti-racist' schools of thought in the fields of education and of service provision. Although the specific constructions of both legislation and policies are British, similar solutions, often more consistent and radical, have been applied by countries such as the USA, Australia and Canada. In Europe, the British model of race relations legislation is unique and one of the major struggles which is taking place in the progression towards the unification of Europe is about the extent to which specific legislations and institutions such as in the British 'Race Relations Industry' should be established.

Of basic importance in understanding the specific constructions of the various ideologies we are examining in this chapter, is their location within Race Relations legislation. Specific Race Relations Acts were passed in 1965, 1968, and 1976. Inherent in them is the paradox that we have discussed throughout the book: the collapse of the discourse of racism into the discourse of race. The Acts have been calling for the elimination of various forms of racial discrimination while accepting the following assumptions: first, that the population is composed of people of different races, and second, that racism mostly, if not only, affects those races. The definition of those races, as we discussed earlier in the book, directly relates to Britain's imperial past, and until recent years dealt virtually exclusively with NCWP immigrants.

'MULTI-CULTURALISM' AND 'ANTI-RACISM'

'Multi-culturalism' and 'anti-racism' have been the two major ideological approaches within the British 'Race Relations Industry'. Both of them were a reaction to previous liberal approaches which assumed that racism is caused by the 'strangeness' of the immigrants, and that with the acculturation and eventual assimilation of the immigrants, or their children, the issue would disappear (see discussion in Chapter 1).

Multi-culturalism emerged as a result of the realization, originally in the USA, and then in Britain, that the 'melting-pot' doesn't melt, and that ethnic and racial divisions get reproduced from generation to generation (Glazer and Moynihan 1965, 1975; Wallman 1979; Watson 1977). Multi-culturalism constructs society as composed of a hegemonic homogeneous majority, and small unmeltable minorities with their own essentially different communities and cultures which have to be understood, accepted, and basically left alone – since their differences are compatible with the hegemonic culture – in order for the society to have harmonious relations. It is a model which particularly suited the first generation of British 'Race Relations Experts', who got their training in the colonial and missionary machine of the British empire; there they ruled through a stratum of local leaders and chieftains without too much intervention in the 'internal affairs' of those they ruled, unless they were in conflict with their interests in the area. Correspondingly, in the composition of the 'Community Relations' boards and councils, minority groupings were represented by leaders of the various religious and cultural organizations of NCWP immigrants.

The 'anti-racist' model was developed by grass-roots political movements, inspired both by Black Power movements in the USA and by anti-colonial movements in Britain's ex-empire, and it opposed both assimilationist and multi-culturalist approaches. As discussed in Chapter 5, they organized around the unifying notion of 'Blackness', and saw in multi-culturalism a divisive mechanism, a distraction from the focus on the differential power relations, discrimination and disadvantages of Black people. During the 1980s the anti-racist model has been adopted, at least partially, by the 'Race Relations Industry' also.

A lot of the debate between the 'multi-culturalists' and the 'anti-racists' has taken place within the educational field. It has been the convention to divide educational policies in this field into four major stages (see, for example, Swann Report 1985, Cohen and Cohen 1986): assimilation; integration; multi-culturalism; and anti-racism. The publication of the Macdonald Report (1989) probably heralds the beginning of another stage.

Assimilation policies were predominant up until the early 1960s and the first race riots in postwar Britain. It was assumed that the problems were temporary, related to culture shock and lack of knowledge of the language, and as long as immigrant children were spread, rather than concentrated in specific schools, no major special educational policies had to be promoted.

Integration policies were developed in the early 1960s when more and more educationalists believed that more detailed, planned programmes of educational and social support of immigrant children were required for integration into the general society to be effective.

Multi-culturalist educational policies emerged in the late 1960s and early 1970s. These were related to the emergence of the second generation of NCWP ethnic minority pupils. Unlike previous policies, multi-culturalist policy-makers saw in the immigrant minority cultures an integral part of British society. The specific construction of multi-culturalism, as well as construction of the limits of difference, are best expressed in the opening chapter of the Swann Report (1985), which investigated British education from the point of view of multi-culturalism:

We consider that a multi-racial society such as ours would in fact function most effectively and harmoniously on the basis of pluralism, which enables, expects and encourages members of all ethnic groups, both minority and majority, to participate fully in shaping the society as a whole within a framework of commonly-accepted values, practices and procedures, whilst also allowing, and where necessary assisting, the ethnic minority communities in maintaining their distinct ethnic identities within this common framework.

For this purpose, multi-cultural education put a lot of emphasis on developing curricula in which different ethnic cultures (or at least some schematic and selective version of them) were taught in school, for the children both to learn to be proud of 'their heritage', and to respect those of other ethnic minorities. Minority communities, then, are defined in this educational approach by their 'culture', which is increasingly being collapsed into matters of religious identity. This could be seen in the ways children in multi-cultural schools were taught about various religious holidays as one of the main ways of acquainting them with other cultures.

The fourth stage of anti-racist education was promoted by ILEA and other radical educational authorities in the mid- and late 1980s. Rather than cultural diversity, anti-racist education was preoccupied with questions of the discrimination against and disadvantage of Black people, both within and outside the educational field. Rather than just teaching pupils about their own culture and other pupils' cultures, anti-racist policies were concerned with employing more Black teachers and taking out racist ideological elements from majority curricula.

The 'moralistic tone' of anti-racism, as well as its simplistic perspective and its exclusion of Whites from its definition of the community, were severely criticized by the Macdonald Report (1989), which investigated the crisis over the murder of Ahmed Iqbal Ullah, in Burnage High School in Manchester.

Ali Rattansi has developed a systematic critique of both multi-culturalism and anti-racism in education, in which he points out the common weaknesses of these educational approaches, in spite of their diametrical differences over many concrete issues:

None of the anti-racist analyses . . . display an awareness of contradictions, inconsistencies and ambivalences . . . their conception of racist ideologies and racist subjects or individuals is no more sophisticated than that of multi-culturalists. (1992: 32)

Towards the end of the 1980s two very different educational approaches have been gaining more influence. On the one hand, the movement for separate Black and especially religious schools, which has existed all along, has been gaining power, especially among the Muslim community. Moreover, with the government educational reform and the encouragement for schools to 'opt out' from local educational authorities' control, there has been a growing support for separate religious schooling, a direction which has been causing grave concern to, among others, feminists of minority communities (Women Against Fundamentalism 1991, Sahgal and Yuval-Davis 1992).

A very different alternative educational approach has been developed by Phil Cohen (1988, 1989b). Inspired by the 'cultural studies' approach (originally developed in Birmingham by Stuart Hall and others), his research is not only concerned with the overall power relations within schooling, but primarily attempts to prevent racist cultures from becoming part of the 'culture of resistance' of working-class children. It aims at tackling racist 'common-sense' notions of the children about themselves and others, and is sensitive to the shifting boundaries of allegiances and groupings among children, in which complex notions and articulations of race, sex, ethnicity, age and other constructions play their part.

The shift from multi-culturalist to anti-racist policies, and the growing disillusion with both, has not been particular to the sphere of education. In the aftermath of the 1981 and 1984 riots, and during the rise of radical local authorities, such as the Greater London Council in the 1980s, the 'Race Relations Industry' has changed its character as well (Yuval-Davis 1985). It expanded considerably with the large amounts of funds which were directed to it by the government. Of special importance have been the growth of the voluntary sector as well as the establishment of race units and race advisors in various departments of local governments. With them grew anti-racist practices such as ethnic monitoring, positive action, contract compliance and outreach community work. More and more Blacks gained power positions within Race Relations organizations as well as generally within public sector employment. There has also been gradual growth in the number of Blacks with political positions, especially as councillors in local authorities.

All this has been a result of at least three different types of initiatives which have taken place roughly at the same time. Although very different in their political orientations they became intermeshed in actuality at least to some extent, although in the late 1980s the picture started to change. The first one was the government attempt to contain rebellion and protest and to incorporate potential opposition leadership among the minorities. The second type of initiative emerged from the GLC and other radical Labour Party segments which directed funds and positions to Black activitists as part of their 'popular planning' policies. Third, but probably most important, has been the crystallization of a new generation of Black militant intelligentsia who developed an 'entryst' strategy (a strategy to enter a party while continuing to hold another ideology or belong to another organization), which attempted simultanously to fight racism as well as to gain them political and professional positions via a new network of community organizations both in the public and the voluntary sector. As many of them had earlier been active in grass-roots movements, they brought with them the organizing principle of Blackness and incorporated it into the multi-culturalist model of the Race Relations organizations as they found them.

A common but problematic notion in both multi-culturalist and anti-racist approaches is that of the 'community', although the multi-culturalist notion of the 'community' is based on culture, and that of anti-racism on colour.

The 'community' has been widely used as a euphemism for civil society, whether one talks of the 'European Community' at large, or a specific 'community' in a housing estate in east London. At the same time, those who do not belong to the hegemonic ethnic groupings have been constructed as deviant within this community (for example, the definition of Commonwealth immigrants in Section 11 of the Local Government Act is as those with the 'special needs the rest of the community do not have'. To the extent that government bodies, from local authorities to central government, are expected to 'represent the community', the construction of the boundaries of the 'community' is therefore extremely important.

In addition, during the 1980s, representations based on political parties and trade union membership have come to be seen – in Britain especially, but in other parts of the world as well – as less and less satisfactory, reflecting imbalances of power and access which exist within the civil society itself as well as in the state. To a certain extent this development has been due to a developing critique of the above. Women and ethnic minorities have been the primal foci of attempts to create new selection mechanisms which will be more just in their representative and distributive power. The notion of autonomous 'community organizations' as the basis of an alternative mechanism of representation to the more traditional ones has been promoted for that purpose (Gortz 1982).

Certain analytical problems arise with these formulations. The notion of the 'community' assumes an organic wholeness. The community is a 'natural' social unit. It is 'out there' and one can either belong to it or not. Any notion of internal difference within the 'community', therefore, is subsumed to this organic construction. It can be either a functional difference which contributes to the smooth and efficient working of 'the community', or it is an anomaly, a pathological deviation. Moreover, the 'naturalness' of the 'community' assumes given boundaries; it allows for internal growth and probably differentiation, but not for ideological reconstructions. It assumes a given collectivity. This 'natural community' does not allow for an ideological and material construction, whose boundaries, structures and norms are the result of constant struggles and negotiations, or more general social developments (Yuval-Davis 1991b).

In the following section, we examine the constructions of the 'Community' within the 'Race Relations Industry' and 'Equal Opportunities' policies towards the disadvantaged, and explore some of the problems which have arisen from the application of the 'anti-racist', 'equal opportunities community' in its work. The examples used have mostly been collected during observations of various statutory and voluntary organizations which were carried out by us in a south-east borough in London during the late 1980s. (Anthias, Cain and Yuval-Davis 1988). In spite of the very real, if partial, gains that have been achieved, we believe that a critical examination of what happened is of crucial importance for future struggles. Some of the internal contradictions and vulnerabilities of these policies have opened the doors for a backlash from the Right – both within the White majority and within the minorities themselves – and the notion of the 'community' has played a central role in this.

THE 'COMMUNITY' IN THE BRITISH 'RACE RELATIONS INDUSTRY'

When the British 'Race Relations Industry' started to emerge in the 1960s, it was informed by two separate ideologies of 'the community', in which 'community' had virtually opposing meanings. On the one hand, when urban poverty was being rediscovered within British social policy of the 1960s, 'community' was very much tied up with the geographical concept of locality, in particular working-class areas. This appeared, for instance, in rationales for slum clearances. In this sense, the term could have been collapsed into meaning 'the working class while not at work', a working class that was seen then as homogeneous, White and British, if not actually English (Wilmot and Young).

On the other hand, the American experience of race riots in the early 1960s brought Black civil rights on to the political agenda there. Policies were developed which were targeted at predominantly Black and other poor ethnic minorities in the American inner cities (Katznelson 1973). The multi-cultural and anti-discrimination approach to the immigrant problem, which was adopted with haste in Britain after its own race riots in Nottingham and Notting Hill, was greatly influenced by America's Community Action Policy. In the American context, the term 'community' has meant 'ethnic community' or 'Black community'; the WASPs (White Anglo-Saxon Protestants) were not referred to in terms of the 'community' at all. The British 'Race Relations Industry' has adopted unproblematically both meanings – the British and the American, and therefore good race relations were promoted, as the first Race Relations Act states, for 'the sake of harmony in the community' – encompassing the whole of the national population, while specifically it dealt with the 'immigrant or ethnic minority communities'.

With the development of racial divisions, both as a reality and as a perceived problem in Britain of the late 1960s and early 1970s, the British government adopted a two-pronged strategy. On the one hand, a series of measures to restrict immigration was introduced, and on the other, a substratum of semi-statutory institutions were created. These included the Community Relations Committee (CRC) under the Race Relations Acts, and compensatory policies, such as Section 11 of the 1966 Local Government Act, and Urban Aid which began directing funds to inner-city areas. The peripheral, random and unco-ordinated nature of these initiatives reflected not only a contradictory approach towards issues of 'race' and 'community' but also an overwhelming requirement to channel limited resources into specific areas of need. During the 1960s and 1970s crisis management ruled the day, as conflicting interests and political objectives became fused in various notions of 'communities', all of which, however, implied the presence of an underlying pathology. 'Community centres' were set up in working-class areas and often had links with the churches. Special 'community relations councils' were established to deal with 'immigrants' and were run, at that time, mostly by concerned Whites. The social and political organizations that the immigrants themselves set up at this period tended to be informal and unrecognized, and usually had names linking them with country of origin.

The formalization of the Community Relations Councils in the 1968 Race Relations Act is the major historical reference to the specific term 'community' in the 'Race Industry'. Just after the Second World War, a spontaneous movement grew up, involving the churches, welfare groups and notable individuals, who founded local voluntary liaison committees to oversee the welfare of immigrants from the New Commonwealth countries. These appeared to materialize because of the absence of any other sort of organized provision by the state. They were White organizations of a philanthropic nature, which were concerned with promoting peaceful integration, and they did not receive government funding until the 1960s.

The first Race Relations Act (1965), contained no reference to 'community'. Rather, it established a national committee for what were still called Commonwealth immigrants. However, under the 1968 Race Relations Act this body was renamed the 'Community Relations Committee', a title which had much more than an integrationist ring to it. At no point in the Act is the community defined, but the duty of the CRC was to secure and encourage 'harmonious community relations'; 'to establish services for giving advice on community relations to local authorities', 'collecting information with respect to community relations'; and 'to provide courses in training in connection with community relations'. This was to be operated through the network of local Community Relations Councils, the whole structure having an intermediary role. It would seem clear from the context that for 'community relations' we should read 'problems caused by Black immigrants', concentrated as they were in a few major industrial centres. In 1975 the Association of County Councils, in evidence to the House of Commons Select Committee on Race and Immigration, was talking about 'community relations problems'. However, after the 1975 Act, the CRC was renamed the Commission for Racial Equality (CRE) to show its commitments to racial equality.

It should be noted, however, that in spite of earlier criticisms of the mission towards 'harmony' at that time (Katznelson 1973), which were effective enough to direct changes in the law, the notion of 'community' itself was never questioned and in fact became an increasingly central theme in race relations rhetoric, as the ethos of multi-culturalism solidified.

The change in the Race Relations Act towards emphasizing racial equality reflected progress made in other areas of anti-discrimination struggle (the 1975 Sex Discrimination Act and Equal Pay Act). This made the term 'equality' a bit more accessible to Blacks, and the use of the term 'community' shifted from the majority communities into the minorities.

The local CRCs remained voluntary under the new legislation and were dually funded by both the CRE and local authorities. Their main areas of involvement became: casework; 'community development' ('the community' is again not defined but this time the connotation implied is of the ethnic minorities' communities); campaigning; public education; and attempting to influence policy and practice, thus constituting 'a broad forum for the discussion of matters of concern to the minority "communities"' (CRE 1988).

The undertone of 'pathology' often remained. Cheetham *et al.* (1986) mention a fund, established by the CRC for West Indians who were 'considered to be beyond the reach of the normal special services'. It was intended to help build bridges back into society for young Blacks who were becoming estranged, using the principles of self-help and being based on religious or cultural organizations:

> Because of the nature of such projects, often [the projects] are likely to be unorthodox in their style. This is unavoidable and is generally of positive value in that it might enable them to have better contact with their alienated and at risk clients, who might be put off by a more conventional style. (1986: 189)

The 'unconventional' nature of such projects might in practice have been little more than the fact they tended to be staffed by

Blacks themselves, thus the implications of a pathological nature are linked directly to colour. Worse still, the term 'Black youth', the target group of many of these projects, has tended to embrace Black men of any age.

Generally, during the growing economic crisis of the 1970s, the ideology and use of the 'community' continued to broaden. With the rise of the 'anti-racist' opposition to 'multi-culturalism', the attachment of the 'community' to the notions of poverty or disadvantage continued to intensify. 'Community development projects' were established in ten specified areas of urban decline (and then phased out when their recommendations were too unpalatable); 'community policing' was developed but as a rule only in the most run-down and racially mixed neighbourhoods, such as Brixton, Toxteth and Hackney. Blacks, especially West Indian young males, were constructed as those who were breaking down law and order. The notion of the disadvantaged young in general developed a particular association with the ideology of the community. For instance, in the 1970s, the Youth Services were renamed the Youth and Community Service.

But it wasn't until the 1980s that the use of the 'community' became completely universalized. As well as the poor, the Blacks, the young, women now began to be perceived as an under-represented and disadvantaged group. They could conveniently, if not simplistically, be slotted into 'minority communities' – even more so if they happened to be Black. In addition, translation services became an industry in their own right as an awareness of peoples' different mother tongues finally dawned. The Swann Report of 1985 drew attention to negative attitudes (termed 'linguistic prejudice') towards the speakers of minority 'community' languages. In practice translators were drawn from the largest ethnic groups, for example, the Turkish and the Indian. However, the CRE report on ethnic minority languages (CRE 1982) had already pointed out that community languages of the UK were not foreign languages but rather 'speech communities', thus broadening the concept of 'community' to include anyone whose mother tongue was not English.

The celebration of the 'community', as well as the confusion about it reached its peak during the 'popular planning' strategy of the GLC under Ken Livingston during the early and mid-1980s. By describing its strategy as 'working for the community', the GLC aimed at intensifying popular participation in policy-making in

London, and including elements in the population that never had a voice before: gays and lesbians, Blacks, women, disabled people, old people, the unemployed, etc. Many cultural events and open conferences were held genuinely to encourage 'community participation'. However, they added to the conflation of the categories of 'equal opportunities' policies and the 'community'.

In the face of severe cuts, local authorities in London and in other big cities utilized Section 11 resources to employ 'special' Black workers to both reflect and serve the 'community' where they had been absent previously. Such workers were often employed singly and in a vacuum, and whether African-Caribbean or Asian, African or Irish, were often expected to serve either all 'minority communities' or just their own 'minority community', both of which categories remained undefined. Inevitably this source of funding was often used as a top-up mechanism, especially in education, as local governments came under increasing pressure to tighten their belts; at the same time local authorities' credibility demanded new or extended Race Units, Community Relations Departments and Community Ethnic Advisers.

Coincidental with this development and in some ways outlasting it, has been the growth of the voluntary sector. The organizations in the voluntary sector, unlike CRCs, for instance, are not statutory bodies, nor are they private. They include so-called community groups which have played an increasingly important role in terms of advocacy and service provision both locally and nationally. The role of their management committees is crucial, as they exist to liaise with the relevant statutory and funding bodies, and they also represent the local population which the groups were established to serve. One of the main problems with these committees is that their members remain unpaid, and therefore the level of management skills and motivation is not necessarily what it would be with remuneration. Because of the tightening of the funding process in the mid-1980s, which was encouraged by central government, a new tier of professionals appeared in the voluntary sector, whose role and function became more and more related to fund-raising, grant applications and financial management. It is worth noting that this tier had an ample recruiting ground in the wake of unemployment and cuts in local government, especially after metropolitan authorities, including the GLC, were abolished and the funds of other local authorities were severely cut.

Funding for the local projects has been available from the local authorities, the Rate Support Grant, via Sections 11 and 137 of the 1966 Local Government Act, the Department of Industry's Task Forces Areas, Urban Aid, the Department of Education, the European Social Fund, charities and other sources in the private sector. All these channels make great use of the term 'community' and thus, in the 'post-GLC period' up to the time of the community charge – the poll tax which brought down Margaret Thatcher (together with her stand on the European 'Community') – 'community organizations' to a large extent retained their positions. However, their nature has changed. While cultural, especially religious organizations, have retained, and perhaps increased their power, political organizations, and by now many secondary service organizations, have collapsed. The community enterprises receiving finance in the early 1990s tend to be those training unemployed youth, especially Black youth. There has been a shift in emphasis from collectivism to individual rights and self-help in social policy under the umbrella notion of 'equal opportunities'.

This shift has been partly a result of the growing hegemony of Thatcherite ideology within social policy – which might expect some erosion under a Major government, however. Although the motivation, efforts and major achievements of the popular planning strategy of the GLC and other radical local authorities should not be undervalued, it must be seen that this change is also due to the fact that many of the struggles against structural disadvantage falter on the current ambivalence between 'equality', 'community rights' and 'individual rights' inherent in them. Having to be categorized as underprivileged and to become slotted into a hierarchy of rival disadvantages in order to compete equally in a climate of 'materialistic individualism' could be interpreted as a contradiction, and this catch 22 often causes turmoil in the overall objectives of many minority groups.

'Popular planning' has been promoted as both popular and radical. Although there was the possibility that the two things were contradictory (as we shall discuss later on in the chapter), it was premised on the existence and development of a collective democratic tradition, as well as a commitment to anti-racism and anti-sexism. Many organizations set up along these lines, tended, by default, to fall back on the only tradition they knew, one which was hierarchical and inflexible. This did not necessarily negate some of their achievements but did add to the myriad contradictions and stresses often apparent in the operation of these organizations.

We shall now turn to look more closely at some of the issues which have arisen for anti-racist struggles in relation to the 'community'. We shall discuss issues of representation and access to power, individual and collective, in the 'community' and in the 'Race Relations Industry', and the role that funding has played in relation to these issues. Finally we raise some general questions about the significance of the constructs of 'community', 'culture', 'colour' and 'identity' in resisting racism.

THE 'EQUAL OPPORTUNITIES COMMUNITY'

There can be no doubt that great strides were made by the GLC (the existence of which now sounds like a pipe dream) and those working in the 'Race Relations Industry'. However, we are moved with an overwhelming sense that the gains that have been made have been invariably in the context of marginalization, especially as the mere struggle for individual survival has become more brutal. We believe that the confusion about the boundaries of the 'community' is central in understanding some of the issues which have bogged down and have created obstructions, divisions and frustrations in anti-racist struggles.

Does the 'community' include everybody who lives in a certain area, does it refer to a particular grouping conscious of itself as a grouping, or is the 'community', paradoxically, all those who have been excluded from feeling part of it in the specific sphere of the 'Race Relations Industry' and in the urban politics of Britain of the 1980s? We would argue that in the specific sphere of the 'Race Relations Industry' and in the urban politics of Britain of the 1980s, the hegemonic answer to the question of who is the 'community' has made three conceptual jumps and the following conflations:

First: from focusing the attention on disadvantaged sections of the population, motivated by populist and democratic aspirations, the 'community' in actuality has become, to a large extent, reduced to the categories of 'equal opportunities' – those previously excluded to a large extent from definitions of the 'community'.

Second: from focusing on the 'equal opportunities' disadvantaged sections of the population, the politics of the community have become reduced to the voluntary sector and local government-sponsored organizations which aspire to represent and serve them.

3 Third: from focusing on the disadvantaged section of the population, the 'community' has become reduced, to a large extent, to the professional 'community activists'.

We shall now turn to look at some of the ways these conflations have occurred.

Social policy conceptions of the 'community' have often ignored marginal sections in the population. The intimate, close and rooted image of the community implied a homogeneity of family, neighbourhood and parish, all of whom conformed to a hegemonic culture, often English and usually working class. It was against this mould that the 'popular planning' approach, heralded by the GLC and other radical local authorities, was developed in the late 1970s and early 1980s. They struggled to include in this vision of the community all those previously excluded, who, at least in some areas of the inner city, constitute a major part of the local population. This might include single parents, gays, Blacks, refugees, etc, all of whom share common objectives. This approach, however, brought new contradictions in its wake, as the various groupings viewed themselves in very different and autonomous terms, thus creating frequent conflict and competition as a result of the ways the social planners constructed them.

Metropolitan Labour authorities showed their commitment to equal opportunities either by setting up serialized units, or by placing representatives in local government departments to ensure the implementation of equal opportunities, in terms of their own specialities, for example, race, gender, sexuality or disability. Committee structures were reorganized along the same lines and grants became distributed on the basis of what was to become known as 'positive action'. Formally as well as practically, the 'equal opportunity' categories and the 'community' were often referred to interchangeably.

In 1983 a Community Affairs Department was established in the local council of the south-east London borough where we worked. Its official aim was, as it was publicized in the local press, to be 'a powerful new people's committee . . . with the objectives of trying to reach a situation where the council is and is seen to be accessible and acceptable to all'. In practice, like many other similar units which flourished in the 1980s, the Community Affairs Department incorporated specialist workers in the areas of race, gender, disability, welfare rights, police liaison and grants to local projects.

A similar approach was adopted in the establishment during this period of an 'alternative community training centre' by a consortium of local statutory and voluntary organizations. This centre had input, over a period of time, from both the GLC and GLTB (Greater London Training Board) and the local council, who to all intents and purposes shared the same aims and political philosophy. In one of the centre's original policy documents its objectives were outlined as follows: 'It was necessary to be clear and sensitive to race, disability, sex and class difference, an image which would hopefully be reflected by centre staff. '

Given the shortage of training places in an area where unemployment was abundant, places on the courses were actually only offered to people who could prove that in addition to class disadvantage they also were in at least one other 'Equal Ops' category, for example, were Black, lesbian, a single parent or disabled. In other words, people who would have had greater difficulty in gaining access to more traditional training.

We shall discuss later on the implications this method of recruitment has had on the trainees. What is relevant here, however, is that 'community' was restructured exclusively as the groups which are marginal and relatively small in number in the more traditional spatial definition of the 'community' in the borough. It was one of the reasons this strategy and such projects were so vulnerable to public resentment and right-wing backlash. What is more, it assumed a unity of interests and constructed 'a community' among people whose only commonality had been disadvantage. The training centre was built round the principles of equal opportunities and popular planning, and the assumption was that given funding, the 'true' objectives of Blacks, women, the disabled and gays, would not only be the same, but would result in a joint platform. However, these groups were arbitrarily defined, and any commonality of interests was just an assumption.

Moreover, the criteria with which these groups were being defined were not mutually exclusive. This created much competition, bitterness and in-fighting among the groups. For instance, a fierce conflict broke out in the local council as to who could lay most claim to a Black woman worker (who was to be funded using Section 11) – the Race Unit or the Women's Unit.

Ultimately, they were forced to bid against each other, and consequently the bitterness continued.

Sometimes struggles developed in several organizations we observed, between Black caucuses and women's caucuses. In addition, spokespersons from the African-Caribbean groups often resented Asian religious groups getting funds from the council; they felt at a disadvantage in speaking on behalf of their own smaller and less cohesive group. They considered Asians to be getting more of the available resources precisely because they had so many different religious and cultural practices. As a result of this debate the Asians and African-Caribbeans became even more entrenched in their own exclusivity.

The dynamics of these struggles are necessarily very complex. What is fundamental here, however, is that having to compete within the hierarchy of oppression for one's bread and butter does little to ease the tensions. This is especially so when the underlying ideological assumption within the overall political strategy within which the dynamics of the struggles developed, is of unity, if not oneness.

Hilary Wainwright's description of an amalgam of peripherals (1985) betrays perhaps more about the GLC's definition of the 'community' than the nature of mass participation: 'The GLC Jobs for a Change Festival . . . [attracted] over 80,000 punks, skins, unemployed Blacks and other dispossessed Londoners [who] crowded into the County Hall'. Margaret Thatcher may, more aptly, have chosen to call them the average person in the street. Nevertheless, while the main protagonists at the GLC were genuinely committed to creating a new political culture, such public-relations jamborees may only have served to create a 'false consensus' as Ben Tovim *et al.* (1985) have argued. A possible result is that real contradictions are missed and false conclusions are drawn which result in a gap between policy and practice.

A reason that such a consensus would be false, or at least fragile and temporary, has been suggested by Saunders (1981). He argues that urban politics have their own specificity, with no necessary relation to class politics and suggests that local struggles inevitably develop around issues of social consumption. As a result they are isolated from broader movements, thus becoming insular and limited in their objectives. The tendency then is to become competitive, with any possible alliance being flimsy and opportunistic.

A backlash could be seen to be inevitable, as the whole working class, as a category, is noticeably absent from the equal opportunities policies. This is because what is at issue is endemic structural disadvantage rather than discrimination, and that does not fall under the rubric of equal opportunities (although issues of race and gender may exacerbate it). There is an assumption within equal opportunities strategy that it is discriminatory practices that produce disadvantage and discriminatory practices alone. So it is that the Tories have been able to develop a more popular and universalistic approach by 'repacking meanings' and unifying people in their common self-interest. One example was their election slogan 'Labour calls him Black, we call him British', another their response to parents' demands to choose the schools of their children. Within such a context, the superficial appearance of minority groups as exclusively furthering their own interests could appear as unfair, and contrary to the whole ethos of equality.

The other side of the coin is that the category of 'needs' or 'minority groups' can be used by the existing power structure to undermine equality. There are many examples of this. One is the employment of Black people in jobs for which they are considerably over qualified. And the converse occurs when a totally inept person is placed out of his or her depth in a problematic position in order, as it were, to take the flak. Where either of these situations occur, we may conclude that individuals are employed, not for their capacity, but as a statistic, and this is one of the negative consequences of positive action. Particular resentment has also been engendered when an individual is presented as representing more than one factor in the 'hierarchy of oppression', such as the 'Black superwoman' phenomenon. In this context, it has been argued that Black women are more likely to be employed in the public sector than Black men.

'REPRESENTATION' OF THE 'COMMUNITY'

Under the leadership of the GLC, when 'community' became a rallying cry, the tendency was to assume that politically funded projects reflected the aspirations of the public at large, or at least the public which they represented. However, although the GLC made genuine attempts at opening its doors to the public, many of the 'community representatives' in the local borough who sat on management committees were already employed by local groups, the council or the CRE, and the few candidates that were co-opted on to committees were in fact interchangeable and part of a network. This became particularly apparent in our research, as the only way to find out about or to become involved in anything of consequence was to become accepted as a member of the network, and this often proved difficult.

The 'community representatives' who sat on management committees may be divided into two types. Firstly, there were gender and ethnic positions within the council, where, for instance, a race advisor would be required to represent all 'Black' or ethnic minority people to the particular council department. And secondly, lower down in the hierarchy, there were the 'community representatives' from the grant-aided organizations. Needless to say, neither of these would have been elected in a democratic fashion by the 'community' which they were assumed to represent; indeed, such an election would have faced very practical difficulties. However, if consultation took place only with people of those groups which were recognized or funded by the council, then a closed shop would inevitably develop. Thus one finds that the participation of the 'community' beyond such 'representatives', was often negligible. For instance, in the local borough where we worked, a 'Race Day' was organized by the local Race Unit. Few among those who came for the day were not active participants or workers in one or more of the organizations which participated in organizing the day.

Lees and Mayo (1984) articulate the stance of the GLC when they describe the new vision of the Labour Party's future as complying with and emerging from the work of the very 'community' activists who are involved in local participation. But the problem remains that they may only be representative in terms of being advocates.

Moreover, their 'representativeness' assumes a unified and consensual 'community' with its own multi-culturalist specific character, which might affect the criteria by which certain people are picked up as the leaders of their community; the more 'different' they are, the more 'authentic' they would be perceived to be (Sahgal and Yuval-Davis 1989).

When the 'community organizations' are not primarily cultural but relate to training and youth the gap between the leaders and the led take another form. In his critique of Black self-help projects, Gus John accuses the CRE of encouraging projects in which there is no real power sharing with the Black community, except with a handful of those who are seen as their 'community' leaders:

> Young people themselves (and, as we observed, some are as old as 30), are seldom party to the negotiations being made with the Local Authority, or anyone else, on their behalf . . . A project is started and a worker appointed on account of a specific group of people identified by police, social services, career services and the CRC as a serious problem both to law and order and community relations. In time that project will increase its staff, set itself completely different objectives and seek to exclude those 'disruptive' young people in response to whose 'needs' it came into being in the first place. (Gus John in Cheetam *et al.* 1986: 193)

Peter Newsome, the CRE director himself, stated that 'the role of the "community leader", a creature of bureaucracy, and highly unrepresentative of community views, must be reviewed' (CRE 1986a). In a manner similar to others, he questions the concept of 'community leader' but, interestingly enough, not the assumed, organic existence of 'community' or 'community views'. And which 'community' in particular he is referring to remains undefined.

People who become active in local politics are not necessarily in touch with the feelings and aspirations of those they profess to represent. In the borough in question, many 'community spokespersons' both in local government and in the voluntary sector lived outside the borough. Their very positions, not to mention their class positions, tended to isolate them from their client group, since they necessarily had to operate more and more like (and with) local government officials.

In the south-east London area in question, because of a lack of representation of Black women, co-options into sub-committees were suggested. This approach was felt to be ideally suited to situations where a small number of organizations represented a larger proportion of the population, that is, the women directly affected by the committee's activities. But to pick a handful of Black co-opted members, who were, in this case, all workers in the voluntary sector, is problematic, not to mention unrepresentative. In fact, there were so few Black women working in this area that the same faces appeared and reappeared. One possible way of escaping from this impasse was to make spokespersons for local projects accountable to and representative of a larger, but undefined group.

Even if we accept the role of 'community representatives' as being advocates rather than representatives, their task is far from being simple. Much of the Race Unit's work necessarily involves looking after the interests of Black employees in the statutory and voluntary sector, in the face of resistance and criticisms from racist Whites and trade unions, and the reality is that there is little else they can influence. At the same time, the nature of their work also brings them up against other equal opportunities categories, like women's units, which may or may not be racist in their assumptions. Moreover, because employment in the 'community' sector is relatively accessible to Black people, the very same workers are often seen as the instigators of confusing and contradictory policies which are inherent in 'community politics'.

Thus, Black 'community representatives' are often on the front line for criticism from both racists and non-racists alike. A White backlash is inevitable. A young White lesbian feminist told us of one organization she had been encouraged to join:

> It was as if I was tolerated, as if the White people down there are tolerated. They [White people] are there because they [Black people] wouldn't get away with it if there weren't. It's the same everywhere these days – you just can't employ 20 White people any more. It's this sort of attitude which is wrong.

In the transition from policy to common sense, descriptive and analytical categories become confused and reinforced by racism.

'COMMUNITY' AND ACCESS TO POWER

In the previous section we considered some of the inter-relationships between the 'community' and its representatives. We concluded that at best, these are more advocates than representatives. Here we want to look at some of the implications of this state of affairs, which concerns the access to power that both the communities and their advocates have gained as a result. After all, as Hilary Wainwright has said, 'The aim of popular planning is to change power relations. It involves both sharing power with the community and workplace organizations and helping to build their power' (1985).

We shall therefore look firstly at the process of consultation – the primary mechanisms used by the GLC and other radical local authorities to 'share their power', and secondly at the process of power – the major way in which the 'community' was helped to build its power. We shall end this section by looking at some of the effects this strategy has had on participants in community organizations.

The CRE (1982) considered the encouragement of consultative committees to be one of Lord Scarman's most important recommendations in the aftermath of the 1981 riots. This became a cornerstone of the popular planning of the GLC. Popular planning policy papers pointed out that specialist workers, despite special efforts being made to recruit them from the relevant groupings, were not representative of the minority ethnic communities. The ethnic communities themselves should determine their own responses to GLC policies. Consultation, therefore, occupied a central place in the equal opportunities policy as outlined by Herman Ousley, the ex-race relations adviser for the GLC. He laid out the aims and objectives for local authorities and other organizations concerned to tackle racism as follows:

> Adopting an Equal Ops policy statement and implementing it with positive action programmes and targeting; establishing a race committee of elected members and appointing race or ethnic advisors; agreeing codes of practice covering personnel matters and running anti-racist training for staff; introducing race dimensions into policy making procedures and consulting local ethnic groups; monitoring ethnicity in employment and reviewing service take-up for Blacks. And finally, supporting Black self-initiatives through grant aid, promotion and publicity of race issues and contract compliance. (Boddy and Fudge 1984)

Because of the difficulties of consultation, the GLC opted for a series of meetings which took place in 1982/3 and which focused on specific issues, for example the arts, the Irish, women, health, Travellers, etc, all of which were well attended owing to the large publicity machine of the GLC. The last meeting in the series was a huge conference, 'Challenging Racism in London'. It is an open question, however, how many of those who participated in such consultations were not 'professional' activists, to what extent these consultations could be described as 'consulting the community', and most importantly, to what extent these consultations, in addition to being published by the GLC, have actually affected the practical policies of the GLC and of other local authorities. For instance, Avtar Brah and others have observed that local authorities were increasingly appointing race advisers as their sole response to 'community demands'.

When the borough produced its five-year 'popular' local plan, there was a flurry of inefficient publicity, advertising consultation with the 'local community'. It contained special sections on ethnic minorities and women, and people were invited to attend meetings at various centres around the borough. Very few people turned up, sometimes none at all, and the document under consideration was so complex, apart for a good measure of equal opportunities and 'community' rhetoric, as to be incomprehensible to anyone but a town planner.

Even when the bureaucratic process is a bit more efficient, some people observed (and so did we) that such methods served to emphasize inequalities between consultors and consulted, and that the participants' recommendations are often ignored or opposed. A great favourite is one-off or *ad hoc* meetings, which similarly do not give participants access into the maze of decision-making structures. Worse still, community groups often find themselves locked into a more or less rigid relationship of patronage with their sponsor. As Holmes (1985) has observed,

The co-incidence of perception and intentions of . . . community groups . . . with those of the GLC ruling Labour groups (even assuming total coherence between different political aims and the strategies of implementation) could not be assumed. Any tendency for a community organization seeking GLC support to propose or take actions contrary to GLC policy aims, causes tension in terms of the response made by the GLC. The stated commitment to a 'participatory' form of government and to giving the voluntary sector 'a full partnership role' precludes an authoritarian response. Inevitably, unless the GLC withdraws public support from the community organization, there will be a tendency for key members and officials of the GLC to attempt to influence the direction being taken by the organization.

Where real participation is attempted, for instance in the election of management committees, power is often exercised by confining the scope of decision making to non-controversial issues. Debates are often squashed before they become public and it is often difficult to find out who decides what the agenda should be.

Sometimes, however, the effects can be even more paradoxical, as in the case of an Asian Women's refuge, where the local authority insisted that some fundamentalist leaders should be included in the management committee as 'representatives of the community', thus destroying the whole project of the refuge as a safe haven (Sahgal and Yuval-Davis 1989, Sahgal 1992).

Because the 'needs of the community' may be ill defined, but still assumed to be homogeneous, local projects can become accountable to more than one set of interests. It then becomes especially difficult for them to function while they are held accountable to local or national government guidelines, when at the same time they aim to be sensitive to the 'needs and preferences of the local community', needs and preferences which should be autonomously defined by the community and not interfered with. These aims will invariably conflict.

Many have questioned whether the GLC and similar Labour boroughs have actually extended democracy or rather further emphasized inequalities between consultors and consulted. In a provocative paper, the Beresfords (1978) have suggested that the advocacy agencies promoted leave the clients passive in a way which reinforces helplessness. And while pressure groups can work for public participation, their very existence may be an obstacle to participation where it matters. Thus, they say, their importance in the present methods of participation is perhaps one of the major measures of the inadequacy of commitment to participation. This is not the fault of pressure groups, but rather of their environment and the lack of other means of representation.

THE ROLE OF FUNDING

The process of funding can be seen as playing a major role in terms of how, why and which organizations and groups receive financial backing. For this reason it will be necessary to look at the extent to which the bureaucratic sponsorship process, along with policy guidelines, has a formative part to play in directing the course of grant-aided projects, and in many cases their very survival. Targeting public funds has played a role in breaking the monopoly of more privileged and mainstream interest groups, and has given a voice to sections of the population who were hitherto silent. However, the consequences of the development of a 'project mentality' – to use Herman Housley's expression – and among marginalized and fragmented groupings, have far-reaching implications. Related to this is also the fraught question of financial accountability mentioned earlier.

After the 1981 riots the urban aid programme was stepped up and even more funds were channelled into self-help for locally specific groups, particularly African-Caribbean ones, as they were seen as the main protagonists in social unrest. However, second and third generation migrants from the NCWP built up the momentum of campaigns over issues such as deportations, education and policing, which were articulated in terms of demanding both political rights and service provision. As funding became increasingly available in the mid-1980s, those organizations with an emphasis on political rights fared less well, while those that focused predominantly on better services seemed to flourish. Their very existence and definition as 'community' projects reflected, however, their marginality on the one hand and the growing use of 'community' as a euphemism for Blacks and ethnic minorities on the other hand. It is through the funding process that central government was able to pass the dilemma of drawing up a clear policy on handling racial tension on to the local authorities, who were then able to pass it on to whoever was prepared to take it on in the local population by way of setting up grant-aided projects. As an opportune way of assuaging local dissatisfaction, such measures provided an easy option for local authorities, who were able to claim 75 per cent of funding for such initiatives back from central government. Local projects may provide a focus for common problems and demands, and do allow some space for homing in on specific race-related issues, but because they are peripheral and issue specific, there is a limit to what effect they can have on institutional racism and state provision. On the other hand, the channelling of so much energy into fund raising has drained considerable political energy from political activists. Once local projects were dependent on state funds, the effect of the cutting off of these funds (as happened to so many groups during the late 1980s, after the abolition of the GLC and the growing pressure on local authorities), was quite devastating.

Since the early 1970s it seems that the groups receiving such funds which survived changing policies were those concerned with cultural or ethnic differences. Asian religious groups or a scheme set up to promote, for example, African drumming, would have a stronger chance of survival than, say, a group concerned with the treatment of young West Indians in police detention. This has proved to be true, whether the primary use of funding as a means of empowering the 'community' was done with primarily multi-cultural or with anti-racist views of the community. A notorious case, which was brought to light by the Channel 4 television programme *Bandung File*, was the financing of two fascist Hindu organizations by the GLC as part of its 'empowering communities' strategy (Sahgal 1992).

It seems that the use of funding in this area has not often had clearly defined goals. Certainly, with one of the major 'community' organizations we looked at, the intervention of the GLC appeared to be a reactive strategy. The proposals and applications for funding arose primarily as a response to closure, rather than as a planned development. In our research at this particular organization, it was very difficult to find any policy documents outlining modes of operation, except for vaguely rhetorical, but necessary, statements about equal opportunities, with no details of how these could be implemented. A worker of another, similar 'community' group funded by the council wrote in one of his reports,

> In their scramble for council funds, some groups are sewn up overnight, with very little thought behind their objectives, others wheel in professional funding advocates from outside the borough to present their case to the council. (Webber 1985)

The funding process has also played a major role in the categorization or naming of groups, and the criteria for designing groups in terms of race, colour, oppression, deprived, not only are imposed from the outside, but are both opportunistic and contradictory. A grouping would have to emphasize its members' deprivation and marginality in order to claim funding. This then leads to ghettoization of 'needs groups'. It is in this way that minorities indirectly become defined and constructed by the state and their 'empowerment' can be of a very limited and specific nature.

The development of special funding has enabled statutory and voluntary agencies to lump together many issues which are supported by workers, officers and politicians alike on a localized level. However, expectations were made greater than what, for instance, local authorities could ever hope to provide. Saunders (1981) has said that local government agencies and the voluntary sector, by their very nature, are more easily accessible to pressure. It is for that reason that the Left has found it easy to gain control on the local level, although it may face insurmountable problems when it comes to delivering the goods. Increasingly central government holds a tighter reign on social investment policies, whereas social consumption is left more and more to the influence of market forces. As central government holds a grip on the purse strings, the scramble for resources has engendered rivalry, not because of class, but because of specific interest groups, often claiming to represent the 'community'. This has had a devastating effect, at least for a time, on those political organizations and traditions based on solidarity. It is noticeable that once funding from local government started to dwindle, Black groups and local grant aided projects in many urban areas increasingly turned to the Department of Employment/Training for survival and have thus changed their role. Whereas the resourcing process previously narrowed them into service provision, they have now become narrowed even further into mainly providing training. This subsidizes private industry as well as being the government's panacea for unemployment, especially young Black unemployment. However, it would seem that those in the voluntary sector, the organizations, who are able to make the transition from local funds to Department of Employment funds, would not be under threat.

In the shrinking local authority realm itself, all councils have had to cut 'community' funds severely, and in many cases they have closed down specialized units such as race and especially women's units. Instead of 'community' units, 'equality' units are emerging. According to Herman Ousley (1991), such units have the potential to tackle issues of disadvantage in ways which might correct some of the endemic problems of the 'community' approach. However, at the time of his paper delivery (spring 1991) it had been used mostly to shift responsibility of the cuts from councillors to managers, and to continue to deliver a watered-down version of the policies from an earlier phase.

IDENTITY AND THE 'EQUAL OPPORTUNITIES COMMUNITY'

Equal opportunities grew out of the multi-culturalist approach, and at its simplest, focuses on the cultural diversity of life-styles, with a view to cultural pluralism. This allows room for ethnic groupings to retain their cultural identity and secure compensatory resources, but may lead to a struggle between different groups to prioritize their cultural differences. Given the racist culture within which this operates, an alternative strategy could be to play down culture, and rather prioritize experiences of racism.

The dilemma between the approach of cultural empowerment and anti-racist struggle can be seen to be played out over and over again. When, for instance, a local authority race unit we observed decided to take a radical stance, and proposed withdrawing funding from the myriad small local Asian community groups which defined themselves according to specific religious practices, as irrelevant to the struggle against racism, there was an immediate outcry; the various groups' entire social lives were cemented by functions that were organized around the temples. But it went deeper than that – withdrawing financial support from these organizations could be interpreted as a racist rejection of non-western, non-Christian cultures in which the local Asians have constructed their identity, and therefore is in itself racist. Interestingly enough, Black churches have not usually been financed by the 'Race Relations Industry', in spite of the major role they play in the lives of Black people. This withdrawal of funds could happen within an anti-racist perspective which identifies the maintenance of cultural difference and identity as a precondition, if not the actual goal, for anti-racist struggle. Such an approach would, of course, lead to problems of essentialism and ahistoricism around the notion of 'culture' and 'cultural difference', in addition to the fact that it homogenizes all the members of the specific minority, without taking into consideration differences of class, gender, age etc. It thereby reinforces existing power relations within that 'community' by adding the political and financial resources of the state to support them.

The critiques of multi-culturalism are to a large extent applicable to equal opportunities policies, in the sense that the focus on life-styles and cultural diversity will inevitably become problematic. An example of the aberration such an orientation can bring about is the attempt at a local community training centre to politicize, or sensitize, its users to Blackness, by promoting images and discussions on Rastafarian culture. Presenting a video on the subject at the beginning of the carpentry course raised vehement objections on a number of grounds. Firstly, the Black users were indignant that their trainers assumed that they should automatically identify with the culture, while inappropriateness and irrelevance was expressed by African-Caribbeans, Asians, White, gay, lesbian, young and old. Part of the explanation for this is most certainly that they felt the issue was divisive in a racially mixed training unit, and that their very involvement would implicitly bring them up against issues of racism.

Secondly, attempting to deal with racism, in all its complexity, by homing in on what has become a stereotype of Black culture was viewed as a gross oversimplification. Putting Rastafarianism into context, both from a historical point of view and in varying settings where it takes its meaning today, is not only complex but contentious. Not withstanding Paul Gilroy's analysis (in CCCS 1982) of the historical roots of 'Ethiopianism' and its role as a culture of resistance, the tendency is to romanticize and idealize a movement which takes on different connotations in different settings, and which can by no means sum up the cultural identity of most Blacks in Britain. Although 'Blackness', 'woolly hair' and African roots are images that most of the Black population have identified with on some level in a positive sense, there are limits to organizing around culture, particularly in Britain, where new and negative meanings have been superimposed on what is often termed a 'sub-culture'; these negative meanings are rarely, if ever, explicitly alluded to in such films.

Many groups and organizations are involved in and represent a whole variety of interests and activities within the Black population, all of which are supposed to represent the interests of the 'community'. Ignoring these opposing and contradictory messages risks paving the way for an individualistic backlash, which Thatcherism has capitalized on. If the fundamental principles or approaches are inconsistent, contradictions will soon surface, only to become more confused in the minds of those on behalf of whom the group claims to speak. For example, in the community training centre, it became apparent that the reasons women took up non-traditional training were all different. Most White, African-Caribbean and young women were interested in pursuing a trade and enhancing their career prospects, while Asian and older women viewed it as useful for the purpose of self-sufficiency. However, all were unified in their enthusiasm for carpentry, and none were publicly interested in pursuing the broader objectives of challenging racism and sexism. Had these issues been dealt with in a way which was relevant to their lives or to carpentry, there may have been some interest. However, they all remained adamant that these issues were irrelevant and divisive in this particular setting. Additionally, of course, everything they observed around them in their training centre: the tension between workers, antagonism, secrecy, authoritarianism and power struggles, things often verbalized in terms of either gender or race issues, proved to them that it was indeed a hopeless cause. The training centre, they thought, should just get on and do training.

The use of equal opportunities categories as access categories for positions (as trainees or staff) can guarantee that those people who tend to be rejected in traditional settings would have access. However, becoming involved in this may not only be confusing for the individuals concerned, but also open them up to abuse. For example, on one of the management committee meetings we attended, the Chair announced, without having consulted anyone, and to the horror of other committee members and staff, that she had personally appointed a White male personnel officer, within what was seen as predominantly Black organization. To quell the uproar, she calmly pointed out that the person in question was disabled. At this point everyone was silenced and later fell into bitter dispute as to whether their objection was that he was White, or male, or unqualified to do the job. What was discussed least was the fact that a unilateral decision had been made, in contempt of the stated democratic principles of the organization, and that such a move undermined equal opportunities policies in that more than one applicant had not been considered. The person appointed was then subjected to personal snubs, and his position was generally undermined. He may well have been the best person for the job, but was unable to prove it, as the formal bureaucratic channels had not been adhered to. This is a common scenario which has caused much personal suffering. When those involved are unable to stand back and unpack the complexities of such situations, the animosity created often degenerates into a racialized issue, and the fundamental point is missed entirely. In this case the Chair was Black, but for the purpose of this particular debate she was subsequently labelled as 'White'.

We found many instances where equal opportunities rationales were taken up in such a way as to perpetuate in-fighting between sectional groupings, which often serves the interests of those whose power remains unquestioned. For example, we observed that where a leader of an organization was White, any conflict tended to be seen as a management against worker conflict. However, if the leader was Black, differences became racialized, with White liberals choosing not to throw their weight behind public criticisms, but rather resorting to more subtle methods of tackling the problems behind the scenes. Black workers, on the other hand, tended to become defensive, fearing the common criticisms that Black people are not able to run their own affairs. Therefore most Black workers were not able to challenge decisions on either count. If the manager was White, their voices were not heard and where a manager was Black, they deferred in the cause of Black unity.

As we have seen, popular planning is vulnerable both to pressures of conventional politics and bureaucracy, and to the need to involve more than a few key activists who have the relevant knowledge and contacts. We do not mean to imply that local projects do not provide a service, or are riddled with corruption. However, we found that where they do work well, they tend to be cohesive, not because of their professed democratic, collective principles, but rather because they have a charismatic leader with whom the project could be identified. In such instances, cohesiveness and sense of purpose would be at a high personal cost to, and because of strong commitment by, a particular individual. The people in such roles are usually aware that the issues involved in fighting racism or other forms of discrimination and disadvantage are far larger and often very different from the immediate focus of the particular project. But through dealing with specific needs, they try to demonstrate more widely the possibility of challenging or subverting the existing state channels. Yet their very personal commitment militates against this generalizing possibility.

There is a limit to what can be gained if success or failure is dependent on a few committed individuals. Major decisions at points of crisis are usually made by key protagonists who take it upon themselves to keep the whole show going. They are invariably well intentioned, and because they get results, it is never questioned how they get their power and to whom they are accountable. If the leaders who take on this role happen to be White or male (which they often are, given that as such they have more access to resources, in the broadest sense of the word), not only are they subject to much criticism, but they also go through pangs of guilt, experiencing a dilemma between genuine commitment and awareness of their privileged position.

Being categorized, or being forced to squeeze oneself in one of the equal opportunities categories in order to get employment or to compete, also has consequences for the individual and on an interpersonal level, although little attention has been paid to this. When interviewing a user of one 'community' organization about her experience, it became clear that the need to resist to being defined as disadvantaged was paramount to her:

> I felt there really is a lot of patronizing going on, like we was all little poor things from the community that was so deprived. None of us see ourselves as underprivileged or massively oppressed. We are all oppressed, I agree with that, but none of us majorly so, except perhaps X.

It would seem that several things are being said here at the same time: a vehement resistance against an imposed category, a simultaneous acceptance of equal opportunities rhetoric and finally a projection outwards; 'not me, but perhaps somebody else'. This must seem all the more contradictory, when those imposing such definitions are themselves Black, or lesbian, disabled, etc. And the power imbalance which becomes disguised in this process takes on its own dynamics and has contradictory effects on individual empowerment.

The effect of trying to read off individuals from abstract social categories is invariably divisive. Everyday experience does not fit into such divisions and even if it did, it is unlikely that people would conceive of themselves within such strictly defined parameters as a matter of course.

In the highly fraught environment in which most groups tend to operate, a retreat into personalized issues often becomes an outlet for frustration and powerlessness. The lack of clarity about the needs of diverse interest groups tends to take fragmentation further, because in situations of tension it becomes difficult to discern all the issues at hand at any one time. In this situation we found that only superficial issues were taken up as a vehicle for frustration, as it is easier to do this than push for real change from a powerless position. Precisely because equal opportunities stereotypes are the common currency in such organizations, any stereotype which comes to hand is used to rationalize the conflict and issues become overloaded. Minor differences between individuals become articulated in 'equal opportunities' terminology.

Racism will continue to creep through the back door, as in the following situation which struck us as a common scenario. When a Black worker was found to be working against the interest of a Black subordinate, White colleagues expressed verbally their shock and horror. This could be interpreted as a racist reaction in the sense that Black people are perceived as a unified category with exactly the same interests – not divided, for instance, by class or gender. In such situations of conflict, it tends not to be the issue in hand which is taken up, that is, management against worker conflict, as it would throw the various categories into disarray. Rather, minor issues become overloaded with race or gender meanings and people align themselves accordingly. The categorizing of people becomes a useful vehicle by which to grind individual axes, which often perpetuates racism, homophobia, sexism, etc. Similarly we found that where a woman was in conflict with her female colleagues, often the rational for the onslaught would be in terms of not belonging to the right category. Mixed race women have been especially subject to such pressures, being included or excluded from the category 'Black' by other Black people according to sides taken in particular. A hidden agenda then becomes blown into mammoth proportions around which others can unwittingly be rallied, and in such situations people often assume honorary positions. One Black woman may call another 'White', a feminist may call another 'separatist' or 'racist', a heterosexual woman may choose to call herself a 'political lesbian'. Consequently individuals become perceived or accepted as representing a category, which gives them or denies them empowerment in specific conflict situations (as well as in access to resources). For example, one Black trainee criticized another in these words: 'She is not Black. Black is a universal name for so many things. You can have a Black skin and be a Bounty. '

Meanwhile genuine instances of sexism, racism, homophobia, etc., can often pass totally unnoticed, and on the odd occasions that they were taken up, we found they proved to be so divisive as to be dropped immediately.

'COMMUNITY' AND 'IDENTITY POLITICS'

A number of authors (for example Gilroy 1987, H.K. Bhahba in GLC 1984) have in the past suggested that the concepts of culture and community need to be redefined, since they have been shown to be ethnocentric and conservative. For example, the appeal to a 'common culture' obscures the divisions and exclusions within it. Even the socialist appropriation of these terms, according to Bhahba (GLC 1984) often strengthens an ideology of 'English-ness' which is unquestionably racist, culturally discriminatory and invariably sexist. A new definition and interpretation of the areas of culture and community is, from this point of view, necessary, in order to transform them into sites of positive resistance. However, although this is necessary, the task is daunting and the end result by no means clear.

No doubt, those who have been actively involved in construc-ting 'community politics' in terms of 'equal opportunities' and 'popular planning' already perceive themselves as being engaged in such a task. After all, their categories of 'Black', 'woman', 'gay' and 'disabled' are not cultural in the traditional sense. Yet they have created a politics of fragmentation and divisiveness which has incorporated, rather than transcended the older traditions of multi-culturalism in the 'Race Relations Industry', which were based on the more conservative tradition. The new uses of the term 'community' have succeeded in breaking with the old monopoly of an essentialist cultural category constructed around country of origin, but in the process have constructed new essentialist categories of difference (be it 'Black', 'Asian', 'woman', 'gay', or 'disabled'), to the extent that individuals continue to be reduced to an all-encompassing category both in terms of their treatment as well as their identity and empowerment. This raises many difficulties.

It has to be stressed, however, that these difficulties by no means cancel the important fact that 'equal opportunities' policies have given access to power and employment to people who were denied it previously.

'IDENTITY POLITICS' AND THE 'NEW ETHNICITIES'

Kobena Mercer (in Rutherford 1990: 57) recites 'the postmodern riddle of political subjectivity':

> What do a trade unionist, a Tory, a racist, a Christian, a wife-beater and a consumer have in common? *They can all be the same person.*

So can be all the equal opportunities community categories; the same person can be a Black, a woman, a gay person and disabled. 'The return to the subject' as a political act, on which Stuart Hall is talking (1980), runs into problems if 'the subject' is constructed in reified (if not essentialist) identity categories, and where there is an unproblematic collapse of collective identity categories into personal ones. In other words, the different discourses and practices of culture, ethnicity and identity have been collapsed together. This collapse can be traced back to the tradition of consciousness-raising, and when practising the political slogan of 'the personal is the political' (Yuval-Davis 1984, Sivanandan 1990).

Consciousness-raising is a powerful tool which has been used for several positive and important purposes within the feminist and other ethnic and leftist movements since the late 1960s. It can empower people, bond them together in a sense of solidarity which is emotional as well as intellectual or political. It can also problematize arenas of life and social norms which tend to be 'naturalized' within hegemonic cultures and which were formerly considered to be outside the arena of normal politics (such as 'the politics of the bedroom').

On the other hand, consciousness-raising techniques assume as a basis for political action a reality that has to be discovered and then changed, rather than a reality which is being created and re-created when practised and discussed. Moreover, this reality is assumed to be shared by all members of the social category within which the consciousness-raising movement operates who are perceived to constitute a basically homogeneous social grouping sharing the same interests. Internal differences, rather than being acknowledged, have been interpreted by those holding the hegemonic power within the movement as mainly reflections of different stages of raised consciousness. While to a large extent this has been acknowledged by the women's movement in recent years, the solution has often been to develop essentialist notions of internal difference within the former categories, such as, for example, between Black and White women, or between Black women and men, or between Blacks and Asians. And within each of these prototypes, the previous assumptions about discovered homogeneous reality usually continue to operate.

As Rosalind Brunt so correctly states (but does not pursue) in her paper 'The politics of identity', the issue of 'representation' is the starting point of any politics of identity. There are, she points out, two separate questions which need to be asked in relation to the issue of representation. The first is 'how our identities are represented in and through the culture and assigned particular categories'; the second is 'who or what politically represents us, speaks and acts on our behalf' (Brunt 1989: 152).

Referring to the second question first, the politics of the 'equal opportunities community' have confused representation with advocacy, as discussed earlier in this chapter. Moreover, as a result of scarce resources, one 'representative' may often represent people of different categories. In other words, this politics of community representation assumes that the interests of women, Blacks, and disabled people, for instance, are inherently non-conflicting and intrinsically the same, because they are all categories of disadvantage. In actuality, the politics of identity often devalues the actual separate, and often conflicting experiences of the people it attempts to represent.

This is the situation not only in relation to different identity categories, but also within them, especially in regard to racial and ethnic categories. What does it actually mean to be, for instance, 'Black'? Are only people of African descent included, or also those of Asian origin? And if Asians are a separate category, what are the implications of somebody of Hindu (or Sikh or Muslim) origin, for instance, representing 'the Asians'; a Pakistani rather than an Indian (let alone Vietnamese); a person born in India, rather than a person born in Britain, a man rather than a woman, etc., etc. In other words, the form of political representation which has grown out of identity politics and equal opportunitites and which has attempted to represent social difference more genuinely, has created an impossible mission for itself.

This said, the 'popular planning' approach, unlike the structure of earlier periods in the British 'Race Relations Industry', for instance, attempted to be sensitive to internal differentiations within these categories. Projects which catered to specific, often oppositional groups within these communities were funded, such as 'alternative' youth centres and Black women's organizations. However, in general, anti-racist and community politics incorporated rather than replaced the old structures. The traditional organizations continued to be financed together with the new, and when funding was reduced, once again it was the religious and cultural organizations which proved to be the most resistant, probably because of the constructs of cultural difference they evoked. These assume cultures to be static, ahistoric and in their 'essence' to be mutually exclusive, especially of the host society. Moreover, as we discussed above, 'culture' in the multiculturalist discourse often collapses to 'religion', with religious holidays becoming the signifiers of cultural difference within school curricula.

Fundamentalist leaders have benefited from the adoption of multi-culturalist norms (Sahgal and Yuval-Davis 1989, 1992). Within the multi-culturalist logic, their presumptions about being the keepers of the 'true' religious way of life, are unanswerable. External dissent is labelled as racist and internal dissent as deviance (if not sheer pathology, as in the case of 'self-hating Jews'). In the politics of identity and representation they are perceived as the most authentic 'Others'. At the same time, fundamentalists are also perceived as a threat, and their 'difference' as a basis for racist discourse. Unlike older versions of multiculturalism, fundamentalist activists refuse to respect the limits of multi-culturalism, which would confine ethnic cultures to the private domain or to some limited cultural community spheres. Fundamentalists aim to use modern state and media powers in order to impose their version of reality on all those whom they perceive as their constituency (Sahgal and Yuval-Davis 1989, 1992, Yuval-Davis 1991). However, they also vehemently refute any notion of internal pluralism which has been the basis of leftist 'popular planning' feminist identity politics in recent years.

This has proved to be very confusing for the Left, and impossible to grapple with within the paradigm of multi-culturalism based on identity politics. The ILEA document (1977) promoted multi-culturalism as a policy 'which will ensure that, within a society which is cohesive though not uniform, cultures are respected, differences recognized and individual identities are ensured'. While the contents of the ideology promoted by religious fundamentalist activists are often anathema to all the Left believe in, in terms of women's equality, individual freedom etc. , they are committed to 'respect different cultures and ensure different identities'. The ideology of autonomous self-determination and empowerment, which is at the base of identity politics and multi-culturalism, forbids 'intervention in the internal affairs of the community' as being Eurocentric and racist, part of a tradition of cultural imperialism which must be rejected.

As Val Moghadam pointed out, the Left has been caught in what can be seen as an insoluble dilemma: 'Does a critique of Orientalism and of Eurocentrism mean a hands-off attitude towards the cultural artifacts of non-Western and/or Islamic countries?' (1989: 96).

Val Moghadam's argument, with which we agree, is that this dilemma, in its present dichotomous construction, is misleading, because, as Sami Zubaida has claimed,

> The world of thought was and remains universal in the sense of generating forms of knowledge, thought and argumentation which were drawn upon by intellectuals from different cultures and religions to formulate problems and solutions relevant to their particular contexts. (Zubaida 1989: 28–9)

Constructing a discourse of cultural difference which is based on mutually exclusive categories of 'equal opportunities' and 'identity politics' denies the possibility of such a universality. However, such a discourse can serve other purposes. As Trin T. Minh-ha claims, 'Differences that cause separation and suspicion therefore do not threaten, for they can always be dealt with as fragments' (1989: 90).

Such differences become part of a hegemonic ideology of multi-culturalism. They are also part of the hegemonic culture; according to her, accepting this model of thinking about 'differences made between entities comprehended as absolute presences – hence the notions of pure origin and true self – are an outgrowth of a dualistic system of thought peculiar to the Occident' (Minh-ha 1989: 40).

Thus, establishing a system of identity politics as a form of resistance to Eurocentrism, orientalism and racism, fails exactly because its basic assumptions have been formed within the discourse of difference it most wants to attack.

CONCLUDING CONSIDERATIONS: POLITICAL ACTION, 'IDENTITY POLITICS' AND THE 'COMMUNITY'

What are the implications of the above for forms of political action and organizing? Two recent major positions which relate directly to 'identity politics' but which differ thoroughly in their attitudes to it, are those of Jenny Bourne (1987) and Rosalind Brunt (1989). Not incidentally, the former published her paper in *Race and Class*, edited by A. Sivanandan, while the latter appears in *New Times*, a volume co-edited by Stuart Hall. These two articles demonstrate very well the general ideological and political differences between the two approaches, which were summed up by Sivanandan (1990).

Jenny Bourne vehemently objects to identity politics. She claims that identity politics has come to replace political struggles which aim at 'social change' and 'the transformation of society', goals which were articulated as the primary purpose of the first British Women's Liberation conference. For her, 'identity politics' are

> separatist, individualistic and inward looking. The organic relationship we tried to forge between the personal and the political has been so degraded that now the only area of politics deemed to be legitimate is the personal. (Bourne 1987: 2)

According to Bourne, a major pitfall in the politics of identity is that it tends to reify cultural resources as signifiers of identity and thus overlooks, or even reverses, the 'difference between asserting who we are and trying to recreate who we no longer are' (Attar 1985).

'What we do', claims Bourne, 'is who we are.' Moreover, 'we do not need to seek out our identity for its own sake, but only to discover in the process "the universality inherent in the human condition"' (Bourne 1987: 22).

Rosalind Brunt, on the other hand, sees identity politics as indispensable. Partly for reasons which would also seem legitimate to Bourne, she argues that if political activitists recognized their own identities as the basis of their social positioning and of their difference from each other, rather than repressing all parts of their identities except for their identification as political activists, the polarization between the 'vanguard' and the 'masses', and the self-righteousness leading to politics in which the ends justifies the means, could disappear. Brunt argues that

unless the question of identity is at the heart of any trans-
formatory project, then not only will the political agenda be
inadequately 'rethought', but more to the point, our politics
aren't going to make much headway beyond the Left's own
circles. (Brunt 1989: 150)

Brunt, however, who sees herself operating within the tradition of
Gramsci as well as Foucault, perceives the political arena as more
complex and contradictory. Reflecting upon one's separate
identities, the 'return to the subjective', does not imply, for her (or
for Stuart Hall), withdrawal from politics, but rather the opposite.
It means, for her, locating grids of power and resistance which are
horizontal and not just vertical, while keeping political frameworks
of action heterogeneous and floating. She rejects the logic of
'broad democratic alliances' and 'rainbow coalitions' which
emanates from Bourne's argument, because, she argues, political
action should be based on 'unity in diversity', which should be
founded not on common denominators but on

> a whole variety of heterogeneous, possibly antagonistic, maybe
> magnificently diverse, identities and circumstances . . . the
> politics of identity recognizes that there will be many struggles,
> and perhaps a few celebrations, and writes into all of them a
> welcome to contradiction and complexity. (1989: 158)

As a positive example for this type of political struggle Brunt points
to the support activities which surrounded the miners' strike in
1984–5. This is, however, an unfortunate example, because this
strike ended up in such a crushing defeat, not only of the miners
and the trade union movement, but of the anti-Thatcherite
movement as whole.

Real politics aside, Brunt's model of politics seems very seduc-
tive: it incorporates theoretical insights of highly sophisticated
social analysis, is flexible, dynamic and is totally inclusive.
However, it is in this last point that the danger lies. What ultimately
lies behind Brunt's approach is a naive populist assumption that in
spite of contradictions and conflicts, in the last instance all popular
struggles are inherently progressive. She shares with multi-
culturalists the belief about the compatible boundaries of
difference, which has been precisely the source of the space that
has encouraged the rise of fundamentalist leaderships.

It is beyond the scope of our book to recommend specific

modes of political action in general, and against racism in particular. Moreover, this task is senseless outside specific and concrete historical situations, and would have to relate in different ways to the 'multi-racisms' which exist in different levels of society, that is, racial harassments, discrimination and disadvantage in employment and education, marginalizations and exclusions. Moreover, political action would be needed to tackle in different ways both systemic and ideological racisms which are constructed differently against different racial, ethnic, class and gender groupings in society.

The general principle, however, should be not so much Brunt's 'unity in diversity' but rather 'universal diversity'. Political struggle does not have to be uniform, nor does it have to be united. Differences of interest and of foci of struggles should be recognized, otherwise any notion of solidarity would be inherently racist, sexist and classist. However, the boundaries of solidarity and co-operation should also be very clear within specific historical contexts, and they should be based upon the shared universal dialogue discussed above.

And within such 'universal dialogue', 'real politics' cannot be forgotten. One of the strongest arguments of Sivanandan in his attack on the 'New Times' approach is that,

> The GLC might have succeeded in constructing all sorts of social blocs and movements (the pride and joy of the new Marxists) to challenge Tory hegemony, but all that Mrs. Thatcher had to do was abolish it. (1990: 18)

Indeed, what prevented the abolition of the Race Unit in the council of the south-east London borough where we worked, in contrast to other similar boroughs after the abolition of the GLC, and despite the growing pressures on the borough for financial cuts, was the election there of eleven Black councillors in the previous local elections. (Symbolically enough, with the cuts which did take place, the Community Development Unit was moved into the Race Unit.)

We agree with Sivanandan that the state, as a separate arena from the civil society, with the intentionality of control, has to be regarded as the prime arena for political struggles.

But not the only one. All the questions which we have raised concerning the 'politics of the community' remain valid, once the continued existence of the Race Unit has been assured. Who and what do these Black councillors represent; in what ways can their election and the survival of the Race Unit promote anti-racist struggles, and of what kinds; who are included and who are excluded in their coalition; and what other forms of counter-narratives concerning race, ethnicity, gender and class, both in the society at large and within their 'communities', would be permitted a voice?

Only by contextualizing race within ethnic processes, by considering how the racialization of ethnic boundaries takes place and by examining gender and class differences and exclusions, can the more concrete issues of fighting the attributions and practices of exclusion and subordination be more effectively undertaken. Only in this way will we avoid the futility and marginality of being locked into tunnel vision resistance to racism.

Bibliography

Abercrombie, N. and Turner, B. S. (1980) *The Dominant Ideology Thesis*, Allen & Unwin, London.

Alibhai, Y. (1988) 'Tribal Dance', *New Statesman & Society*, 22 July.

Allen, S. and Wolkowitz, C. (1987) *Homeworking*, Macmillan, London.

Allen, S., Anthias, F. and Yuval-Davis, N. (1991a) 'Diversity and commonality-theory and politics', *International Review of Sociology*, New Series, No.2, April.

Allen, S., Anthias, F. and Yuval-Davis, N. (eds) (1991b) Monographic Section, 'Gender, race and class', *International Review of Sociology*, New Series, No. 2, April.

Althusser, L. (1969) *For Marx*, Allen Lane, London.

Althusser, L. (1971) *Lenin and Philosophy and Other Essays*, New Left Books, London.

Amin, S. (1978) *The Arab Nation*, Zed Books, London.

Amos, V. and Parmar, P. (1984) 'Challenging imperial feminism', *Feminist Review*, No. 17.

Amos, V., Gilroy, P. and Lawrence, E. (1982) 'White sociology, black struggle', in D. Robbins *et al.* (eds) *Rethinking Social Inequality*, Gower, Aldershot.

Anderson, B. (1983) *Imagined Communities*, Verso, London.

Anthias, F. (1978) 'Does femininity keep the family going?', in *International Socialism Journal*, Ser. 2, No. 2, Autumn.

Anthias, F. (1980) 'Women and the reserve army of labour', *Capital and Class*, No. 10.

Anthias, F. (1982) 'Ethnicity and Class among Greek Cypriot migrants – a study in the conceptualisation of ethnicity', Ph.D. thesis, University of London.

Anthias, F. (1983) 'Sexual divisions and ethnic adaptation', in A. Phizacklea (ed.) *One Way Ticket*, Routledge & Kegan Paul, London.

Anthias, F. (1986) 'The case of Cyprus', in C. Clarke and T. Payne (eds) *Security and Development in Small States*, Allen & Unwin, London.

Anthias, F. (1989) 'Women and nationalism in Cyprus', in N. Yuval-Davis and F. Anthias (eds) *Woman–Nation–State*, Macmillan, London.

Anthias, F. (1990) 'Race and class revisited – conceptualising race and racisms', *Sociological Review*, Vol. xxxviii, No. 1, February.

Anthias, F. (1991) 'Parameters of difference and identity and the problem of connections', *International Review of Sociology*, New Series, No. 2, April.

Anthias, F. (1992) *Ethnicity, Class and Migration – Greek Cypriots in Britain*, Gower, Aldershot.

Anthias, F. and Ayres, R. (1983) 'Ethnicity and class in Cyprus', *Race and Class*, Vol. xxv, No. 1, Summer.

Anthias, F. and Yuval-Davis, N. (1983) 'Contextualising feminism: ethnic gender and class divisions', *Feminist Review*, No. 15.

Anthias, F. and Yuval-Davis, N. (1989) 'Introduction', in N. Yuval-Davis and F. Anthias (eds) *Woman–Nation–State*, Macmillan, London.

Anthias, F., Cain, H. and Yuval-Davis, N. (1988) Report on the Ethnic and Gender Divisions Project, unpublished paper.

Ardill, N. and Cross, N. (1987) *Undocumented Lives: Britain's Unauthorized Migrant Workers*, Runnymeade Trust, London.

Armstrong, J. (1982) *Nations before Nationalism*, University of North Carolina Press, Chapel Hill.

Attar, D. (1985) 'Why I am not a Jewish feminist', *Shifra*, No. 2.

Attar, D. (1990) 'The portable cage', *Trouble and Strife*, No. 19.

Balibar, E. (1988) 'Propositions on citizenship', *Ethics*, Vol. 98, No. 4, July.

Balibar, E. (1989) 'Y-a-t-il un "neo-racisme"?', in E. Balibar and I. Wallerstein (eds) *Race, classe, nation: les identités ambigués*, Editions la Decouverte, Paris.

Ballard, R. and Ballard, C. (1977) 'The Sikhw: the development of South in Britain', in J. L. Watson (ed.) *Between Two Cultures*, Blackwell, Oxford.

Banton, M. (1977) *The Idea of Race*, Tavistock, London.

Banton, M. (1987) *Racial Theories*, Cambridge University Press, Cambridge.

Banton, M. (1988) *Racial Consciousness*, Longman, London.

Barker, M. (1981) *The New Racism*, Junction Books, London.

Barrett, M. (1982) *Women's Oppression Today*, Verso, London.

Barrett, M. and Mackintosh, M. (1980) 'The family wage: some problems for socialists and feminists', *Capital and Class*, No. 11.

Barrett, M. and Mackintosh, M. (1985) 'Ethnocentrism in socialist feminist theory', *Feminist Review*, No. 20.

Barron, R. and Norris, G. (1976) 'Sexual divisions and the dual labour market', in D. Barker and S. Allen (eds) *Dependence and Exploitation in Work and Marriage*, Longman, London.

Barth, F. (1969) *Ethnic Groups and Boundaries*, Allen & Unwin, London.

Barton, L. and Walker, S. (1983) *Race, Class and Education*, Croom Helm, London.

Baucock, R. (1991) 'Immigration and the boundaries of citizenship', paper presented at the conference *Transitions*, Science Centre for Social Research, May 13–14, Berlin.

Bauer, O. (1940) *The National Question* (Hebrew), Hakibutz Haartzi, Rehavia.

Bauman, Z. (1988) 'Britain's exit from politics', *New Statesman & Society*, 29 July.

Bauman, Z. (1991) *Modernity and the Holocaust*, Polity Press, Oxford.

Beechey, V. (1977) 'Some notes on female wage labour', *Capital and Class*, No. 3.

Beechey, V. (1978) 'Women and production: a critical analysis of some sociological theories of women's work', in A. Kuhn and A. M. Wolpe (eds) *Feminism and Materialism*, Routledge & Kegan Paul.

Beechey, V. (1986) *Unequal Work*, Pluto Press, London.

Ben Tovim, G., Gabriel, J. Law, I. and Stedder, K. (1985) 'A political analysis of local struggles for racial equality', in D. Mason and J. Rex (eds) *Theories of Race and Ethnic Relations*, Cambridge University Press, Cambridge.

Ben Tovim, G., Gabriel, J., Law, I. and Stedder, K. (1986) *The Local Politics of Race*, Macmillan, London.

Benedict, R. (1968) *Race and Racism*, Routledge & Kegan Paul, London.

Benyon, M. (ed.) (1984) *Scarman and After*, Pergamon Press, Oxford.

Benyon, J. (1986) 'A tale of failure: race and policing', *Policy Papers in Ethnic Relations*, No. 3.

Beresford, P. and Beresford, S. (1978) 'A way in the future', in *Planning, Participation and Meeting Social Needs*, Battersea Community Action, London.

Beresford, P. and Croft, S. (1981) *Community Control of Social Services Departments*, Battersea Community Action, London.

Beresford, P. and Croft, S. (1983) *Making our own Plans: Going Local or Popular Planning*, Chartist, London.

Beresford, P. and Croft, S. (1988) 'The new paternalism', *Social Work Today*, Vol. 19, No. 51.

Beveridge, W. (1942) *Report on Social Insurance and Allied Services*, HMSO, London.

Bhabha, H. K. (1989) 'The other question', *Oxford Literary Review*.

Bhabha, H. K. (ed.) (1990) *Nation and Narration*, Routledge, London.

Bhachu, P. (1988) 'Apni Marzi Kardhi. Home and work: Sikh women in Britain', in S. Westwood and P. Bhachu (eds) *Enterprising Women*, Routledge, London.

Billig, M. (1978) *Fascists: A Social Psychological View of the National Front*, Academic Press, London.

Blackburn, R. and Mann, M. (1979) *The Working Class in the Labour Market*, Macmillan, London.

Blauner, R. (1969) 'Internal colonialism and ghetto revolt', *Social Problems*, Vol. 16, No. 4.

Boddy, M. and Fudge, C. (eds) (1984) *Local Socialism*, Macmillan, London.

Bottomley, G. and de Lepervanche, M. (1984) *Ethnicity, Class and Gender in Australia*, Allen & Unwin, Sydney.

Bourne, J. (1983) 'Towards an anti-racist feminism', *Race and Class*, Vol. 25, No. 1.

Bourne, J. (1985) *Racism and Jewish Feminism*, Institute of Race Relations, London.

Bourne, J. (1987) *Homelands of the Mind: Jewish Feminism and Identity Politics*, Race and Class pamphlet, No. 11.

Bourne, J. (with Sivanandan, A.) (1980) 'Cheerleaders and ombudsmen: the sociology of race relations in Britain', *Race and Class*, Vol. 21, No. 4.

Brah, A. (1991) 'Difference, diversity, differentiation', in S. Allen, F. Anthias, and N. Yuval-Davis, (eds) special edition of *Revue Internationale de Sociologie*, New Series, No. 2, April.

Brittan, A. and Maynard, M. (1984) *Sexism, Racism and Oppression*, Basil Blackwell, Oxford.

Brook, S. (1989) *The Club – The Jews of Modern Britain*, Constable, London.

Brown, C. (1984) *Black and White Britain*, Policy Studies Institute Survey, Heinemann, London.

Bruegel, I. (1978) 'What keeps the family going?', *International Socialism Journal*, Ser. 2, No. 1, Summer.

Bruegel, I. (1979) 'Women as a reserve army of labour', *Feminist Review*, No. 3.

Bruegel, I. (1989) 'Black women in the labour market', *Feminist Review*, No. 32.

Brunt, R. (1989) 'The politics of identity', in S. Hall and M. Jacques (eds) *New Times*, Lawrence & Wishart, London.

Bryan, B., Dadzie, S. and Scafe, S. (1985) *The Heart of the Race: Black Women's Lives in Britain*, Virago, London.

Bryson, L. and Mowbray, M. (1981) 'Community: the spray-on solution', *Australian Journal of Social Issues*, Vol. 16, No. 4.

Bulmer, M. (1978) *Social Policy Research*, Macmillan, London.

Bulmer, M. (1986) *Neighbours, the Work of Philip Abrams*, Cambridge University Press, Cambridge.

Burney, E. (1988) *Steps to Social Equality: Positive Action in a Negative Climate*, Runnymead Trust, London.

Cain, H. and Yuval-Davis, N. (1990) '"The Equal Opportunities Community" and the anti-racist struggle', *Critical Social Policy*, Autumn.

Cambridge, A. X. and Feuchtwang, S. (1990) *Anti-racist Strategies*, Gower, Aldershot.

Carby, H. (1982) 'White women listen! Black feminism and the boundaries of sisterhood', in Centre for Contemporary Cultural Studies, *The Empire Strikes Back*, Hutchinson, London.

Carmichael, S. and Hamilton, C. V. (1968) *Black Power: The Political Liberation in America*, Cape, Boston.

Casey, J. (1982) 'One nation: the politics of race', *Salisbury Review*, Autumn.

Cashmore, E. (1989) *United Kingdom? Class, Race and Gender since the War*, Unwin Hyman, London.

Cashmore, E. E. and Troyna, B. (1983) *Introduction to Race Relations*, Routledge & Kegan Paul, London.

Castells, M. (1975) 'Immigrant workers and class struggle in advanced capitalism', in *Politics and Society*, Vol. 5, No. 1.

Castles, S. (1984) *Here for Good: Western Europe's New Ethnic Minorities*, Pluto Press, London.

Castles, S. and Kosack, G. (1973) *Immigrant Workers in the Class Structure in Western Europe*, Oxford University Press, Oxford.

Castles, S., Booth, H. and Wallace, T. (1984) *Here for Good: Western Europe's New Ethnic Minorities*, Pluto Press, London.

Cavendish, R. (1982) *Women on the Line*, Routledge & Kegan Paul, London.

Centre for Contemporary Cultural Studies (CCCS) (1982) *The Empire Strikes Back*, Hutchinson, London.

Cheetham, J., James, W., Loney, M., Mayor, B. and D. Prescott (eds) (1986) *Social and Community Work in a Multi-Racial Society*, Harper & Row, London.

Cleaver, E. (1968) *Soul on Ice*, Dell Publishing, New York.

Cockburn, C. (1983) *Brothers*, Pluto Press, London.

Cohen, A. (ed.) (1974) *Urban Ethnicity*, Tavistock, London.

Cohen, G., Bosanquet, N., Ryan, A., Parekh, B., Keegan, W. and Gress, F. (1986) *The New Right, Image and Reality*, Runnymeade Trust, London.

Cohen, L. and Cohen, A. (1986) *Multi-cultural Education*, Harper & Row, London.

Cohen, P. (1987) 'Racism and popular culture: a cultural studies approach', Working Paper No. 9, Centre for Multi-cultural Education, Institute of Education, University of London.

Cohen, P. (1988) 'The perversions of inheritance', in P. Cohen and H. S. Bains (eds) *Multi-racist Britain*, Macmillan, London.

Cohen, P. (1989a) 'Lessons in and out of school', introductory essay to *Second Year Report of the Research Project on Multicultural Education*, Institute of Education, London.

Cohen, P. (1989b) 'On the wrong side of the tracks', *Contemporary Issues in Geographical Education*, Vol. 4, No. 1.

Cohen, P. and Bains, H. S. (1988) *Multi-racist Britain*, Macmillan Education, London.

Cohen, R. (1987) *The new Helots: Migrants in the international division of labour*, Avebury, Farnborough.

Cohen, S. (1988) *From the Jews to the Tamils, Britain's Mistreatment of Refugees*, South Manchester Law Centre, Manchester.

Commission for Racial Equality (CRE) (1982) *Ethnic Minority Community Languages – A Statement.*

Commission for Racial Equality (1985a) *Fact Sheet*, No. 1.

Commission for Racial Equality (1985b) *Looking for Work, Black and White School Leavers in Lewisham.*

Commission for Racial Equality (1985c) *Racial Equality and Social Policies in London.*

Commission for Racial Equality (1986a) *Annual Report.*

Commission for Racial Equality (1986b) *Black Business Development*, a strategy paper.

Commission for Racial Equality (1986c) *Ethnic Minorities in Britain: Statistical Information on the Pattern of Settlement.*

Commission for Racial Equality (1986d) *Positive Discrimination on Local Authority Employment.*

Commission for Racial Equality (1987) *Principles of Practice for Contract Compliance.*

Commission for Racial Equality (1988) *Medical School Admission, A Report of a Formal Investigation into St. George's Hospital Medical School.*

Cook and Watts (1987) 'Racism, women, and poverty', in C. Glendinning and J. Millar (eds) *Women and Poverty in Britain*, Wheatsheaf, Brighton.

Cox, O. (1970) *Castle, Class and Race: A Study in Social Dynamics*, Modern Reader Paperbacks, New York.

Crompton, R. (1988) 'Class theory and gender', *British Journal of Sociology*, Winter.

Cupitt, D. (1991) 'Back to basics', *Marxism Today*, April.

Curtis, L. (1984) *Ireland: The Propaganda War*, Pluto Press, London.

d'Orey, S. (1984) *Immigration Prisoners – A Forgotten Minority*, Runneymead Trust, London.

Dabydeen, D. (1986) *Hogarth's Blacks*, Manchester University Press, Manchester.

Dahya, B. (1974) 'The nature of Pakistani ethnicity in industrial cities in Britain', A. Cohen (ed.) *Urban Ethnicity*, Tavistock, London.

Darcy de Oliveira, R. and Darcy de Oliveira, M. (1975) *Scientific Research and Political Power*, IDAC, Geneva.

Davis, H. B. (1978) *Towards a Marxist Theory of Nationalism*, Monthly Review Press, New York.

Davis, A. (1982) *Sex, Race and Class*, Women's Press, London.

De la Campagne, C. (1983) *L'invention du racisms – antique et moyen age*, University of Paris Press, Paris.

de Lepervanche, M. (1980) 'From race to ethnicity', *Australian and New Zealand Journal of Sociology*, Vol. 16, No. 1.

de Lepervanche, M. (1989) 'Women, nation and the state in Australia', in N. Yuval-Davis and F. Anthias (eds) *Women–Nation–State*, Macmillan, London.

de Lepervanche, M. (1992) 'Holding it all together: multiculturalism, nationalism, women and the state in Australia', in S. Allen, F. Anthias, and N. Yuval-Davis, *Gender, Race and Difference*, special issue of the *International Review of Sociology*, Winter.

Delphy, C. (1977) *The Main Enemy*, Women's Research and Resource Centre, London.

Department of Employment (1981, 1984, 1986) *Labour force surveys.*

Department of Employment (1991) *Employment Gazette*, February and April.

Deutch, K. W. (1966) *Nationalism and Social Communications: An Inquiry into the Foundations of Nationality*, MIT Press, Cambridge, Mass.

Dex, S. (1987) *Women's Occupational Mobility*, Macmillan, London.

Doeringer, P. B. and Piore, M. J. (1971) *Internal Labour Markets and Manpower Analysis*, D. C. Heath & Co., Lexington, Mass.

Downing, J. (1980) *The Media Machine*, Pluto Press, London.

Durkheim, E. (1933) *The Division of Labour in Society*, Collier-Macmillan, Canada.

Edwards, R. C., Reich, M. and Gordon, D. (eds) (1975) *Labour Market Segmentation*, D. C. Heath & Co., Lexington, Mass.

Eggleston, J., Dunne, D., and Anjali, M. (1986) *Education for Some*, Trentham Books, Stoke-on-Trent.

Eisenstein, Z. (ed.) (1979) *Capitalist Patriarchy and the Case for Socialist Feminism*, Monthly Review Press, New York.

Eisenstein, Z. (1984) *Feminism and Sexual Equality: A Crisis in Liberal America*, Monthly Review Press, New York.

Elster, J. (1985) *Making Sense of Marx*, Cambridge University Press, Cambridge.

Engels, F. (1968) 'The origins of the family, private property and the state', in *Marx and Engels, Selected Works*, Lawrence & Wishart, London.

Enloe, C. (1990) 'Womenandchildren: making feminist sense of the Persian Gulf Crisis', *The Village Voice*, 25 September.

Essien-Udom, E. U. (1962) *Black Nationalism: A Search for Identity in America*, Dell Publishing, New York.

Ethnic and Gender Divisions Research Project (1987) 'Local attitudes towards anti-racist politics', unpublished survey, Sociology Division, Thames Polytechnic.

Fanon, R. (1986) [1952] *Black Skin, White Masks*, Pluto Press, London.

Fevre, R. (1984) *Cheap Labour and Racial Discrimination*, Gower, London.

Field, S. (1987) 'The changing nature of racial disadvantage', *New Community*, Vol. 14, No. 1/2, Autumn.

Firestone, S. (1971) *The Dialectic of Sex*, Cape, London.

Fitzgerald, M. (1987) *Black People and Party Politics in Britain*, Runnymeade Trust, London.

Foreman, A. (1977) *Femininity as Alienation*, Pluto Press, London.

Fryer, P. (1984) *Staying Power: The History of Black People in Britain*, Pluto Press, London.

Fuller, M. (1983) 'Qualified criticism, critical qualifications', in L. Barton and S. Walker (eds) *Race, Class and Education*, Croom Helm, London.

Gabriel, J. and Ben Tovim, G. (1978) 'Marxism and the concept of racism', *Economy and Society*, Vol. 7, No. 2, May.

Gaitskell, D. and Unterhalter, E. (1989) 'Mothers of the nation: a comparative analysis of nation, race and motherhood in Afrikaner nationalism and the African National Congress', in N. Yuval-Davis and F. Anthias (eds) *Women–Nation–State*, Macmillan, London.

Gans, H. J. (1979) 'Symbolic Ethnicity: the future of ethnic groups and cultures in America', *Ethnic and Racial Studies*, Vol. 2, No. 2.

Garrison, L. (1979) *Black Youth, Rastafarianism and the Identity Crisis in Britain*, Acer, London.

Gay, P. (1988) *Community Relations Councils, Roles and Objectives*, Commission of Racial Equality, London.

Geertz, C. (ed.) (1963) *Old Societies and New States*, Free Press, New York.

Gellner, E. (1983) *Nations and Nationalism*, Basil Blackwell, Oxford.

Gellner, E. (1987) *Culture, Identity and Politics*, Cambridge University Press, Cambridge.

Gender and Race Project (1983–1986) Thames Polytechnic, School of Social Sciences.

Genovese, E. D. (1968) *In Red and Black*, Vintage Books, New York.

Gilroy, P. (1987) *There Ain't No Black in the Union Jack*, Hutchinson, London.

Gilroy, P. (1988) *Problems in Anti-Racist Strategy*, Runnymeade Trust, London.

Gilroy, P. and Lawrence, E. (1988) 'Two-tone Britain: white and black youth and the politics of anti-racism', in P. Cohen and S. B. Harwant, *Multi-Racist Britain*, Macmillan, London.

Glazer, N. and Moynihan, D. P. (1965) *Beyond the Melting Pot*, MIT Press, Cambridge, Mass.

Glazer, N. and Moynihan, D. P. (1975) *Ethnicity, Theory, and Experience*, Harvard University Press, Cambridge, Mass., and London.

Gordon, P. (1983) *White Law*, Pluto Press, London.

Gordon, P. (1986) *Racial Violence and Harassment*, Runnymeade Trust, London.

Gordon, P. (1989) *Fortress Europe? The Meaning of 1992*, Runneymead Trust, London.

Gordon, P. and Newnham, A. (1985) *Passport to Benefits? Racism in Social Security*, Child Poverty Group, London.

Gordon, P. and Newnham, A. (1986) *Different Worlds*, Runneymead Trust, London.

Gortz, A. (1982) *Farewell to the Working Class*, Pluto Press, London.

Greater London Council (1984) *Section 11 of the Local Government Act 1966: Take-up by London Local Authorities for Non-Educational Uses*, London.

Greater London Council (1984) *Ethnic Minorities and the National Health Service in London*, London.

Greater London Council (1984) *Challenging Racism in London*, Report of the conference held on 12 March 1983, London.

Grewal, S. (1989) *The Role of Immigration Law on Asian Marriages*, research project for Asian Resources Centre, Greenwich.

Guillaumin, C. (1988) 'Race and nature: the system of marks', *Feminist Issues*, Autumn.

Hadley, R. (1981) 'Social Services Department and the community', in E. Goldberg and S. Hatch (eds) *A New Look at the Personal Social Services*, Policy Studies Institute, London.

Hall, J. W. (1927) *The Revolt of Asia*, New York and London.

Hall, S. (1980) 'Race, articulation and societies structured in dominance in UNESCO', *Sociological Theories: Race and Colonialism*, UNESCO, Paris.

Hall, S. (1982) 'The rediscovery of ideology: return of the repressed in media studies', in M. Gurevitch, J. Curran and S. Woolacott (eds) *Culture, Society and the Media*, Methuen, London.

Hall, S. (1988) 'New Ethnicities', in *Black film/British cinema*, ICA Document 7, London.

Hall, S., Critcher, C., Jefferson, T., Clarke, J. and Roberts, B. (1978) *Policing the Crisis: Mugging, the State and Law and Order*, Macmillan, London.

Hall, S. and Held, D. (1989) 'Citizens and citizenship', in Stuart Hall and Martin Jacques (eds) *New Times*, Lawrence & Wishart, London.

Hall, S. and Jacques, M. (1989) *New Times: the Changing Face of Politics in the 1990s*, Lawrence & Wishart, London.

Harding, S. (1986) *The Science Question in Feminism*, Open University Press, Milton Keynes.

Haringey Employment Project (1980) *The Clothing Industry in the Cypriot Community*, Borough of Haringey, London.

Harrison, J. (1973) 'The political economy of housework', *Bulletin of the CSE*, Winter.

Hartmann, H. (1979) 'Marxism and feminism: towards a more progressive union', *Capital and Class*, No. 8.

Hartmann, H. (1981) 'The unhappy marriage of Marxism and feminism: towards a more progressive union', in L. Sargent (ed.) *Women and Revolution: The Unhappy Marriage of Marxism and Feminism*, Pluto Press, London.

Hayes, C. J. H. (1948) *The Historical Evolution of Modern Nationalism*, Macmillan Inc., New York.

Hechter, M. (1975) *Internal Colonialism: the Celtic Fringe in British National Development*, Routledge & Kegan Paul, London.

Hechter, M. (1987) 'Nationalism as group solidarity', *Ethnic and Racial Studies*, Vol. 10, No. 4.

Hickman, M. (1985) 'The invisible Irish: racism, education and the Irish in Britain', in *Irish Dimensions in British Education Report*, Soar Valley College.

Hobsbawm, E. (1975) *The Age of Capital*, Weidenfeld & Nicolson, London.

Hobsbawm, E. (1990) *Nations and Nationalism since 1780*, Cambridge University Press, Cambridge.

Hobsbawm, E. (1991) 'Dangerous exit from a stormy world', in *New Statesman and Society*, 8 Nov.

Hoel, B. (1982) 'Contemporary clothing sweatshops, Asian female labour and collective organisation', in I. J. West (ed.) *Work, Women and the Labour Market*, Routledge & Kegan Paul, London.

Holmes, L. (1985) *Chronology of Events in C.T.C.*, unpublished paper, Polytechnic of South Bank, London.

Home Office (1986) *Immigration and Nationality Department Report*, HMSO, London.

Home Office (1987) *Control of Immigration Statistics*, HMSO, London.

Hooks, B. (1981) *Ain't I a Woman: Black Women and Feminism*, South End Press, London.

Hooks, B. (1991) *Yearning: Race, Gender and Cultural Politics*, Turnaround, London.

Husbands, C. (1982) *'Race' in Britain: Continuity and Change*, Hutchinson, London.

Inner London Education Authority (1983) *Race, Sex and Class*, ILEA, London.

Institute for Race Relations (1987) *Policing Against Black People*, IRR, London.

Irvine, J., Miles, I. and Evans, J. (1979) *Demystifying Social Statistics*, Pluto Press, London.

James, A. and Jeffcoate, R. (eds) *The School in the Multicultural Society*, Harper & Row, London.

Jayasuriya, L. (1990) 'Multiculturalism, citizenship and welfare: new directions for the 1990s', a paper presented at the 50th Anniversary Lecture Series, Dept of Social Work and Social Policy, University of Sydney.

Jeffery, P. (1976) *Migrants and Refugees: Muslim and Christian Pakistani Families in Bristol*, Cambridge University Press, Cambridge.

Jenkins, D. (1975) *The British, Their Identity and Their Religion*, SCS Press, London.

Jones, C. (1977) *Immigration and Social Policy in Britain*, Tavistock, London.

Jones, T., Maclean, B. and Young, J. (1986) *The Islington Crime Survey*, Gower, Aldershot.

Jordan, W. D. (1974) *The White Man's Burden: Historical Origins of Racism in the United States*, Oxford University Press, Oxford.

Kahn, J. (1981) 'Explaining ethnicity', in *Critique of Anthropology*, No. 16, Vol. 4.

Kamenka, E. (ed.) (1973) *Nationalism – The Nature and Evolution of an Idea*, Edward Arnold, London.

Kandiyoti, D. (1988) 'Bargaining with patriarchy', *Gender and Society*, Sept, Vol. 2, No. 3.

Katznelson, I. (1973) *Black Men, White Cities*, Oxford University Press, Oxford.

Kedourie, E. (1960) *Nationalism*, Hutchinson, London.

Kitching, G. (1985) 'Nationalism: the instrumental passion', *Capital and Class*, No. 25.

Klug, F. (1989) 'Oh to be in England', in N. Yuval-Davies and F. Anthias, *Woman–Nation–State*, Macmillan, London.

Knowles, C. and Mercer, S. (1991) 'Feminism and anti-racism', in R. Cambridge and S. Feuchtwang (eds) *Anti-Racist Strategies*, Avebury, Farnborough.

Kohn, H. (1967) [1944] *The Idea of Nationalism*, Collier-Macmillan, New York.

Kuhn, A. and Wolpe, A. M. (1978) *Feminism and Materialism*, Routledge & Kegan Paul, London.

Labour Force Surveys, 1981, 1984, 1985, 1986, 1987, Department of Employment, London.

Laclau, E. (1977) *Politics and Ideology in Marxist Theory*, New Left Books, London.

Laclau, E. and Mouffe, C. (1985) *Hegemony and Socialist Democracy*, Verso New York.

Laclau, E. and Mouffe, C. (1986) *Hegemony and Socialist Democracy*, Verso, London.

Land, H. (1978) 'Sex stereotyping in the social security and income tax systems', in J. Chetwynd and O. Hartnett (eds) *The Sex Role System*, Routledge & Kegan Paul, London.

Larragy, M. and Rossiter, A. (forthcoming) *Beyond the Pale? The Irish Question and British Feminism*, Women's Press, London.

Layton-Henry, Z. and Rich, P. B. (1986) *Race, Government and Politics in Britain*, Macmillan, London.

Lee, G. and Wrench, J. (1988) *Skill Seekers, National Youth Bureau*, London.

Lees, R. and Mayo, M. (1984) *Community Action for Change*, Routledge & Kegan Paul, London.

Lenin, V. I. (1972) *Collected Works*, Vol. XX, Dec. 1913–Aug. 1914, Lawrence & Wishart, London.

Lever-Tracey, C. and Quinlan, M. (1988) *A Divided Working Class–Ethnic Segmentation and Industrial Conflict in Australia*, Routledge & Kegan Paul, London.

Little, A. and Robbins, D. (1982) *Loading the Law*, Commission for Racial Equality, London.

London Borough of Greenwich (1985) *A Community Based Local Plan for the London Borough of Greenwich – Draft for Consultation*, London Borough of Greenwich, London.

London Strategic Policy Unit (1987a) *Racism Awareness Training: A Critique*, GLC, London.

London Strategic Policy Unit (1987b) *The London Irish*, GLC, London.

London, L. and Yuval-Davis, N. (1984) 'Women as national reproducers: the Nationality Act 1981', in *Formations on Nations and People*, Routledge & Kegan Paul, London.

Loveridge, R. and Mok, A. (1979) *Theories of Labour Market Segmentation*, Martinus Nijhoff, The Hague.

Lowy, M. (1976) 'Marxism and the national question', *New Left Review*, No. 96.

Luckman, T. (1967) *The Invisible Religion*, Macmillan, London.

Lukes, S. (1974) *Power: A Radical View*, Macmillan, London.

Luthra, M. S. and Bajwa, M. S. (1988) *Minority Ethnic Economy and Asian Retailers in London Borough of Greenwich*, The Indian Workers' Association of Great Britain, London.

Macdonald Report (1989) *Murder in the Playground*, Longsight Press, London.

MacDougall, H. A. (1982) *Racist Myth and English History*, Harvest House, Montreal.

Mama, A. (1984) 'Black women, the economic crisis and the British state', in *Feminist Review*, No. 17.

Mann, M. (1987) 'Ruling class strategies and citizenship', *Sociology*, Vol. 21, No. 3.

Mantle, A. (1985) *Popular Planning Not in Practice: Confessions of a Community Worker*, Greenwich Employment Resources Unit, London.

Marris, P. (1982) *Community Planning and Conceptions of Change*, Routledge & Kegan Paul, London.

Marshall, T. H. (1950) *Citizenship and Social Class*, Cambridge University Press, Cambridge.

Marshall, T. H. (1975) [1965] *Social Policy in the Twentieth Century*, London, Hutchinson.

Marshall, T. H. (1981) *The Right To Welfare and Other Essays*, Heinemann Educational Books, London.

Marx, K. (1975) 'On the Jewish Question', in *Early Writings*, Penguin, Harmondsworth.

Mercer, K. (1990) 'Welcome to the jungle: identity and diversity in postmodern politics', in J. Rutherford (ed.) *Identity, Community, Culture, Difference*, Lawrence & Wishart, London.

Miles, R. (1980) 'Class, race and ethnicity: a critique of Cox's theory', *Ethnic and Racial Studies*, Vol. 3, No. 2.

Miles, R. (1982a) *Racism and Migrant Labour*, Routledge & Kegan Paul, London.

Miles, R. (1982b) 'Racism and nationalism in Britain', in C. Husbands (ed.) *Race in Britain, Continuity and Change*, Hutchinson, London.

Miles, R. (1984) 'Marxism versus the sociology of race relations', *Ethnic and Racial Studies*, Vol. 7, No. 2.

Miles, R. (1985) 'Recent Marxist theories of nationalism and the problem of racism', a paper presented at the conference, *Marxist Perspectives on Ethnicity and Nationalism*, International Sociological Association, Belgrade.

Miles, R. (1989) *Racism*, Routledge, London.

Miles, R. and Rathzel, N. (1991) 'Migration and the homogeneity of the nation-state', in S. Bolaria (ed.) *World Capitalism and the International Migration of Labour*, Garamond Press, Toronto.

Millet, K. (1971) *Sexual Politics*, Hart-Davis, London.

Minority Rights Groups (1986) *The Gypsies in Britain*, Minority Rights Groups, London.

Mitter, S. (1986) *Common Fate, Common Bond*, Pluto Press, London.

Modood, T. (1988) '"Black", racial equality and Asian identity', *New Community*, Vol. 14, No. 3.

Modood, T. (1990) 'British Asian Muslims and the Rushdie Affair', *Political Quarterly*, Vol. 61, No. 2.

Moghadam, V. (1989) 'Against Eurocentrism and nativism: a review essay on Samir Amin's *Eurocentrism* and other texts', *Socialism and Democracy*, Fall–Winter.

Molyneaux, M. (1979) 'Beyond the housework debate', *New Left Review*, No. 116.

Montagu, A. (1974) *Man's Most Dangerous Myth: The Fallacy of Race*, Oxford University Press, Oxford.

Moroksovic, M. (1991) 'Transitions', opening paper given to conference, *Transitions*, Science Centre for Social Research, Berlin May 13–14.

Mowbray, M. (1983) 'Localism and austerity: the political economy of community welfare services', *Community Development Journal*, Vol. 18, No. 3.

Mullard, C. (1980) *Racism in Society and Schools*, Institute of Education, London.

Mullard, C. (1984) *Anti-Racist Education*, National Association for Multi-Racial Education, London.

Murphy, L. and Livingstone, J. (1985) 'Racism and the limits of radical feminism', *Race and Class*, Vol. 26, No. 4.

Murray, R. (1988) 'Life after Henry (Ford)', *Marxism Today*, October.

Nairn, T. (1977) *The Break-up of Britain*, New Left Books, London.

Newnham, A. (1986) *Employment and Black People*, Runneymead Trust, London.

Nikolinakos, M. (1975) 'Notes towards a general theory of migration in late capitalism', *Race and Class*, Vol. 17, No. 1.

Nimni, E. (1991) *Marxism and Nationalism*, Pluto Press, London.

Oakley, A. and Oakley, R. (1979) 'Sexism in official stats', in J. Irvine *et al.*, *Demystifying Social Statistics*, Pluto Press, London.

Omi, M. and Winant, H. (1986) *Racial Formation in the United States*, Routledge, London.

Office of Population Census Surveys Monitor (1986) *Labour Force Survey 1985: Ethnic Group and Country of Birth*, Government Statistical Service, London.

OPCS, press notice, 23 July 1987.

Ousley, H. (1987) Paper presented at the *Conference on Anti-Racist Education*, Institute of Education, London.

Ousley, H. (1991) 'Resisting institutional change', in W. Ball and J. Solomos, *Race and Local Politics*, Macmillan Education Ltd, Basingstoke.

Parekh, B. (1986) *The New Right: Image and Reality*, Runnymead Trust, London.

Parekh, B. (1990) 'The Rushdie affair and the British press: some salutary lessons', in *Free Speech*, a report of a seminar by the Commission for Racial Equality, London.

Parker, F. (1979) *Marxism and Class Theory*, Macmillan, London.

Parkin, F. (1979) *Marxism and Class Theory: A Bourgeois Critique*, Tavistock, London.

Parmar, P. (1982) 'Gender, race and class: Asian women in resistance', in CCCS, *The Empire Strikes Back*, Hutchinson, London.

Parmar, P. (1988) 'Gender, race and power', in P. Cohen and H. S. Bains (eds) *Multi-racist Britain*, Macmillan, London.

Pateman, C. (1988) *The Sexual Contract*, Polity Press, Cambridge.

Peach, C. (1968) *West Indian Migration to Britain*, Oxford University Press, Oxford.

Phillips, A. (1987) *Divided Loyalties: Dilemmas of Sex and Class*, Virago, London.

Phillips, A. and Taylor, B. (1980) 'Sex and skill: notes towards a feminist economics', *Feminist Review*, No. 6.

Phizacklea, A. (1983) *One Way Ticket*, Routledge & Kegan Paul, London.

Phizacklea, A. (1990) *Unpacking the Fashion Industry*, Routledge, London.

Phizacklea, A. and Miles, R. (1980) *Labour and Racism*, Routledge & Kegan Paul, London.

Phoenix, A. (1989) 'Theories of gender and black families', in T. Lovell (ed.) *British Feminist Thought*, Blackwell, Oxford.

Piore, M. J. (1975) 'Notes for a theory of labour market stratification', in R. C. Edwards, M. Reich and D. Gordon (eds) *Labour Market Segmentation*, D. C. Heath & Co., Lexington, Mass.

Poulantzas, N. (1973) *Political Power and Social Classes*, New Left Books, London.

Prasjar, Y. and Nocholar, S. (1986) *Routes or Roadblocks? Consulting Minority Communities in London Boroughs*, Runnymeade Trust, London.

Ramazanoglu, C. (1989) *Feminism and the Contradictions of Oppression*, Routledge, London.

Rathzel, N. (1991) 'The politics towards migration in West Germany', *Race and Class*, Jan.–March, Vol. 32, No. 3.

Rattansi, A. (1992) 'Changing the subject? Racism, culture and education', in A. Rattansi and K. Reedar (eds) *Radicalism in Education*, Lawrence & Wishart, London.

Reeves, F. and Ward, R. (1984) 'West Indian business in Britain', in F. Ward and R. Jenkins (eds) *Ethnic Communities in Business*, Cambridge University Press, Cambridge.

Renan, E. (1882) *Qu'est-ce qu'une nation?*, Paris.

Rex, J. (1970) *Race Relations in Sociological Theory*, Weidenfeld and Nicolson, London.

Rex, J. (1973) *Race, Colonialism and the City*, Weidenfeld & Nicolson, London.

Rex, J. (1981) 'A working paradigm for race relations research', *Ethnic and Racial Studies*, Vol. 4, No. 1.

Rex, J. and Moore, R. (1967) *Race, Community and Conflict*, Oxford University Press, Oxford.

Rex, J. and Tomlinson, S. (1979) *Colonial Immigrants in a British City*, Routledge & Kegan Paul, London.

Robinson, C. J. (1983) *Black Marxism*, Zed Books, London.

Rose, E. J. B. (1969) *Colour and Citizenship*, Institute for Race Relations, London and Oxford University Press, Oxford.

Rose, S., Kamin, L. J. and Lewontin, R. C. (1984) *Not in Our Genes: Biology, Ideology and Human Nature*, Penguin, Harmondsworth.

Rossiter, A. and Larragy, M. (eds) (forthcoming) *Beyond the Pale? The Irish Question and British Feminism*, Women's Press, London.

Rowthorn, B. and Wayne, N. (1988) *Northern Ireland: the Political Economy of a Conflict*, Polity Press, Oxford.

Rubery, J. (1978) 'Structured labour markets, worker organisations and low pay', *Cambridge Journal of Economics*, Vol. 2.

Rushdie, S. (1982) 'The new empire within Britain', *New Society*, 9 December.

Rutherford, J. (ed.) (1990) *Identity, Community, Culture, Difference*, Lawrence & Wishart, London.

Sahgal, G. (1992) 'Secular spaces: the experience of Asian women organizing', in C. Sahgal and N. Yuval-Davis (eds) *Refusing Holy Orders: Women and Fundamentalism in Britain*, Virago, London.

Sahgal, G. and Yuval-Davis, N. (1989) 'Refusing holy orders', *Marxism Today*, March.

Sahgal, G. and Yuval-Davis, N. (eds) (1992) *Refusing Holy Orders: Women and Fundamentalism in Britain*, Virago, London.

Saunders, P. (1981) *Social Theory and the Urban Question*, Hutchinson, London.

Scarman, Lord (1977) Lecture to Minority Rights Group.

Scarman, Lord (1981) *The Brixton Disorders 10–12 April 1981*, Special report, HMSO, London.

Schlesinger, P. (1987) 'On national identity: some conceptions and misconceptions criticized', *Social Science Information*, Sage, Vol. 26, No. 2.

Shanin, T. (1986) 'Soviet concepts of ethnicity: the case of a missing term', *New Left Review*, No. 158.

Shils, E. (1957) 'Primordial, personal, sacred and civil ties', *British Journal of Sociology*, No. 7.

Shils, E. (1960) 'The intellectuals in the political development of the new states, *World Politics*, No. 12.

Showstack Sassoon, A. (ed.) (1987) *Women and the State*, Hutchinson, London.

Showstack Sassoon, A. (forthcoming) 'Equality and difference: the emergence of a new concept of citizenship', in David McLellan and S. Sayers (eds) *Democracy and Socialism*, Macmillan, London.

Siboni, D. (1974) *Le Nome et le Corps*, University of Paris Press, Paris.

Siboni, D. (1983) *La Juive – uni transmission inconscient*, University of Paris Press, Paris.

Sivanandan, A. (1973) 'Race, class and power: an outline for study', *Race*, Vol. 14, No. 4.

Sivanandan, A. (1976) 'Race, class and the state – in black experience in Britain', *Race and Class*, Vol. 25, No. 2.

Sivanandan, A. (1982) *A Different Hunger*, Pluto Press, London.

Sivanandan, A. (1983) 'Challenging racism: the strategies for the 80s', *Race and Class*, Vol. 25, No. 2.

Sivanandan, A. (1985) 'Race and the degradation of black struggle', *Race and Class*, Vol. 26, No. 4.

Sivanandan, A. (1988a) 'Left, right and Burange', *Race and Class*, Vol. 30, No. 1.

Sivanandan, A. (1988b) 'The new racism', *New Statesman & Society*, Vol. 1, No. 22.

Sivanandan, A. (1990) 'All that melts into air is solid: the hokum of New Times', *Race and Class*, Vol. 31, No. 3.

Smith, A. D. (1971) *Theories of Nationalism*, Duckworth, London.

Smith, A. D. (1975) *Nationalism in the Twentieth Century*, Martin Robertson, Oxford.

Smith, A. D. (1986) *The Ethnic Origins of Nations*, Basil Blackwell, Oxford.

Smith, D. J. (1977) *Racial Disadvantage and Ethnic Minorities*, Policy Studies Institute, London.

Smith, D. J. (1981) *Unemployment and Ethnic Minorities*, Policy Studies Institute, London.

Snyder, L. L. (1968) *The New Nationalism*, Cornell University Press, Ithaca, New York.

Solomos, J. (1985) 'The social and political context of black youth unemployment: a decade of policy developments and the limits of reform', in L. Barton and S. Walker (eds) *Youth, Unemployment and Schooling*, Open University Press, Milton Keynes.

Solomos, J. (1986) 'Varieties of Marxist conceptions of race, class and the state: a critical analysis', in J. Rex and D. Mason (eds) *Theories of Race and Ethnic Relations*, Cambridge University Press, Cambridge.

Solomos, J. (1989) *Race and Racism in Britain*, Macmillan, London.

Southall Black Sisters (1990) *Against the Grain*, Southall Black Sisters, London.

Spearman, D. (1968) 'Enoch Powell's postbag', *New Society Race and Immigration Reader*, IPC Magazines.

Spelman, E. (1988) *Inessential Woman*, Women's Press, London.

Spence, M. (1990) 'Will the revolution be televised?', *Catalyst*, March–May.

Stalin, J. C. (1929, 1976) *The National Question and Leninism*, Mass Publications, Calcutta.

Stasiulis, D. and Yuval-Davis, N. (eds) (forthcoming) *Articulations of*

Gender, Race, Ethnicity and Class: The Social Formation of Settler Societies, Sage, London.

Stolke, V. (1981) 'The naturalization of social inequality and women's subordination', in K. Young, C. Walkowitz and R. McCullugh, *On Marriage and the Market*, Conference of Socialist Economists Books, London.

Stolke, V. (1987) 'The nature of nationality', a paper presented at the conference *Women and the State*, at the Wissenschafts Institute, Berlin, April.

Swann Report (1985) *Education for All*, report of committee of enquiry into education of children from ethnic minority groups, HMSO, London.

Tajfel, H. (1965) 'Some psychological aspects of the colour problem', in R. Hooper (ed.) *Colour in Britain*, BBC Publications, London.

Tajfel, H. (1978) *Differentiation Between Social Groups: Studies in the Social Psychology of Intergroup Relations*, Academic Press, London.

Thomas, D. (1983) *The Making of Community Work*, Allen & Unwin, London.

Tierney, J. (1982) *Race, Migration and Schooling*, Holt Education, London.

Tonnies, F. C. (1957) *Community and Society*, Harper & Row, New York.

Turner, B. (1990) 'Outline of a theory of citizenship', *Sociology*, Vol. 24, No. 2.

Urry, J. (1981) *The Anatomy of Capitalist Societies*, Macmillan, London.

Van den Berghe, P. (1967) *Race and Racism*, Wiley, New York.

Van den Berghe, P. (1979) *The Ethnic Phenomenon*, Elsevier, New York.

Vogel, U. (1989) 'Is citizenship gender specific?', paper presented at Political Sciences Association Conference, April.

Vogel, C. (1990) 'Segregation, sexism and labour supply', *Economic and Social Resources Committee Working Paper 21*, ESRC, London.

Wainwright, H. (1985) *Labour, A Tale of Two Parties*, Hogarth Press, London.

Walby, S. (1990) *Theorizing Patriarchy*, Blackwell, Oxford.

Walby, S. 'Woman and nation', unpublished paper, London School of Economics.

Walby, S. (1991) 'Citizenship, gender and universalism', unpublished paper, London School of Economics.

Wallace, P.A. (1982) *Black Women in the Labour Force*, MIT Press, Cambridge, Mass. and London.

Wallerstein, I. (1974) *The Modern World System*, Academic Press, New York.

Wallman, S. (1979) *Ethnicity at Work*, Macmillan, London.

Waterman, S. and Kosmin, B. (1986) *British Jewry in the 80s*, Jewish Board of Deputies, London.

Watson, J. (1977) *Between Two Cultures*, Blackwell, Oxford.

Webber, H. (1985) 'Homelessness among black youths in Greenwich and their needs', unpublished paper.

Weber, M. (1969) *Economy and Society*, Vol. 1, Bedminster Press, New York.

Weldon, F. (1990) *Sacred Cows*, Chatto, London.

Westwood, S. (1984) *All Day, Every Day*, Pluto Press, London.

Westwood, S. (1990) 'Racism, black masculinity and the politics of space', in J. Hearn and D. Morgan (eds) *Men, Masculinities and Social Theory*, Unwin Hyman, London.

Westwood, S. and Bhachu, P. (1988) *Enterprising Women*, Routledge, London.

Wilson, E. (1977) *Women and the Welfare State*, Tavistock, London.

Wilson, E. (1982) 'Women, the community and the family', in A. Walker (ed.) *Community Care: the Family, The State and Social Policy*, Blackwell, Oxford.

Wilson, P. and Stanworth, J. (1988) 'Growth strategies in small Asian and Caribbean businesses', *Employment Gazette*, January 1988, HMSO, London.

Wirth, L. (1956) *The Ghetto*, Chicago University Press, Chicago.

Women Against Fundamentalism (1991) Newsletter, No. 1.

Women, Immigration and Nationality Group (WING) (1985) *Worlds Apart, Women Under Immigration and Nationality Law*, Pluto Press, London.

Worsley, P. (1964) *The Third World*, Weidenfeld & Nicolson, London.

Wright, E. O. (1976) 'Class boundaries in advanced capitalist societies', *New Left Review*, No. 98.

Wright, P. (1985) *On Living in an Old Country: the National Past in Contemporary Britain*, Verso, London.

Yuval-Davis, N. (1980) 'The bearers of the collective: women and religious legislation in Israel', *Feminist Review*, No. 4.

Yuval-Davis, N. (1984) 'Anti-Semitism, anti-Zionism and the struggle against racism', *Spare Rib*, April.

Yuval-Davis, N. (1986a) 'Ethnic/racial divisions and the nation in Britain and Australia', *Capital and Class*, Spring.

Yuval-Davis, N. (1986b) 'Front and rear: sexual division of labour in the Israeli Military', in H. Afshar (ed.) *Women, State and Ideology*, Macmillan, London.

Yuval-Davis, N. (1987a) 'Marxism and Jewish nationalism', *History Workshop Journal*, No. 24, Autumn.

Yuval-Davis, N. (1987b) 'The Jewish collectivity and national reproduction in Israel', *Women in the Middle East*, Khamsin, London.

Yuval-Davis, N. (1989) 'National reproduction and the demographic race in Israel', in N. Yuval-Davis and F. Anthias (eds) *Women–Nation–State*, Macmillan, London.

Yuval-Davis, N. (1991a) 'Anglomorphism and the construction of ethnic/racial divisions in Britain and Australia' in R. Nile (ed.) *Multi-culturalism in Britain and Australia*, Commonwealth Institute, London.

Yuval-Davis, N. (1991b) 'The citizenship debate; women, the state and ethnic processes', *Feminist Review*, Autumn.

Yuval-Davis, N. (1991c) 'The gendered Gulf War: women's citizenship and modern warfare', in H. Bresheeth and N. Yuval-Davis (eds) *The Gulf War: Another Perspective*, Zed Books, London.

Yuval-Davis, N. (1992a) 'Fundamentalism, multi-culturalism and women', in J. Donald and A. Rattansi (eds) *Education and Racism*, Open University Press, Milton Keynes.

Yuval-Davis, N. (1992b) 'Identity politics and women's ethnicity', in V. Moghadam (ed.) *Women and Identity Politics*, Clarendon Press, Oxford.

Yuval-Davis, N. (1992c) 'Jewish fundamentalism and women's empowerment', in G. Sahgal and N. Yuval-Davis (eds) *Refusing Holy Orders: Women and Fundamentalism in Britain*, Virago, London.

Yuval-Davis, N. (forthcoming) *Gender and Nation*, Sage, London.

Yuval-Davis, N. and Anthias, F. (eds) (1989) *Woman–Nation–State*, Macmillan, London.

Zubaida, S. (1978) 'Theories of nationalism', in G. Littlejohn, B. Smart, J. Wakeford and N. Yuval-Davis (eds) *Power and the State*, Croom Helm, London.

Zubaida, S. (1988) 'Islam, cultural nationalism and the Left', *Review of Middle East Studies*, No. 4.

Zubaida, S. (1989) 'Nations: old and new', a paper presented at the *Anthropology Seminar Series*, University College, London.

Name index

Subject index